The
Rehabilitation
Planning
Game:

A Study
in the
Diversity of
Neighborhood

The MIT Press
Massachusetts
Institute of
Technology
Cambridge,
Massachusetts,
and London,
England

The
Rehabilitation
Planning
Game:

A Study
in the
Diversity of
Neighborhood

Langley
Carleton
Keyes, Jr.

Set in Linotype Baskerville,
printed and bound by
The Colonial Press Inc.
in the United States
of America.

Second printing, February 1973

ISBN 0–262–11027–x (hardcover)
ISBN 0–262–61012–4 (paperback)

Library of Congress catalog
card number: 69–10837

To Nancy

Preface

Because this study is one which relies upon personal interviews for much of its information, I am particularly indebted to the dozens of citizens and officials who have given generously of their time and knowledge to explain to me the complexities of renewal planning in the city of Boston. In particular I want to thank Dick Green and Frank Del Vecchio for their continued willingness to discuss big and little issues drawn from their experience in neighborhood planning with the Boston Redevelopment Authority (BRA). Richard Bolan was an enormously valuable source of information about BRA activities in the early years of planning in Washington Park, the South End, and Charlestown. I am deeply grateful to him for sharing his knowledge and critical abilities.

In each community I studied, there were numerous people without whose help and kindness I would have been lost. To Muriel Snowden in Washington Park, Gene Hennessey in Charlestown, and Royal Cloyd in the South End I owe a special debt of gratitude.

I also want to thank J. Clarence Davies, III and Edward J. Logue for reviewing my manuscript and giving me many valuable suggestions.

I am deeply indebted to several colleagues in the M.I.T. Department of City and Regional Planning: Bernard Frieden, for his continued encouragement and advice; John Howard, the department head, for minimizing academic and financial constraints during my graduate life; Lloyd Rodwin, for his aid in securing my research appointment at the Joint Center for Urban Studies of M.I.T. and Harvard University.

Finally, I thank the Joint Center for providing financial assistance and a stimulating climate in which to spin out this study.

Langley Carleton Keyes, Jr.
Cambridge, Massachusetts
April 1968

Contents

The
Rehabilitation
Planning
Game:

A Study
in the
Diversity of
Neighborhood

1
The
Rehabilitation
Planning
Game

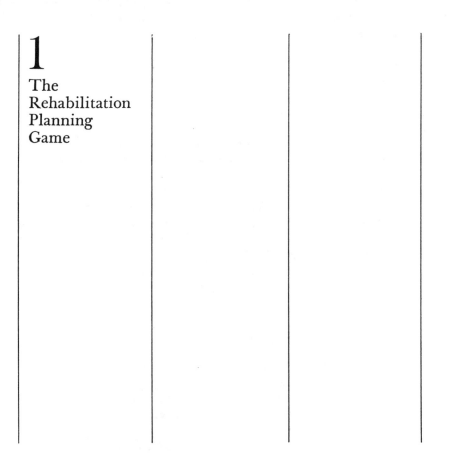

THE EVOLUTION OF URBAN RENEWAL:
FROM SLUM CLEARANCE TO RESIDENTIAL REHABILITATION

No public enterprise in the United States, with the possible exception of the War on Poverty, is monitored today by a more vociferous band of advocates and critics than the federal urban renewal program. Launched in 1949 with the blessings of Democrats and Republicans, liberals and conservatives, big labor and big business,[1] the program is today attacked from the political left as legalized exploitation of the poor for the benefit of the middle classes[2] and from the political right as an unconstitutional application of the government's prerogative to seize private property for public use.[3]

Renewal's supporters, like Charles Abrams,[4] chasten critics for "highlight-

[1] James Q. Wilson, "Planning and Politics: Citizen Participation in Urban Renewal," *Journal of the American Institute of Planners*, Vol. XXIX, No. 4 (November 1963), p. 242.
[2] Nathan Glazer, "The Renewal of Cities," *Scientific American*, Vol. 213, No. 3 (September 1965), p. 200.
[3] Martin Anderson, *The Federal Bulldozer* (Cambridge: The M.I.T. Press, 1964), p. 192.
[4] Charles Abrams, *The City is the Frontier* (New York: Harper and Row, 1965), p. x.

ing its faults more often than its virtues" and for ignoring its "contributions and potentials."

Some critics, such as Martin Anderson, recommend doing away with urban renewal entirely.[5] For James Wilson, "the housing problem . . . is . . . a fiction or very nearly so [while] the benefits of urban renewal . . . are for the most part symbolic, intangible, and deferred."[6] Others, who are more restrained, advocate, with Herbert Gans, a transformation of renewal "from a program of slum clearance and rehabilitation into a program of urban rehousing."[7]

While it is true, as Scott Greer says, that urban renewal "is so widespread, so varied, and so complex that few people have more than a skewed random image of it,"[8] those few that do have made their opinions resound in political science, sociological, economic, and physical planning circles.[9] Urban renewal is a process that neatly cuts across many formal lines of academic discipline to pose what has been rightly called the "Dilemma of Democratic Intervention."[10]

The program that has provided fuel for white-hot public debate and grist for a variety of academic mills emerged in the 1949 Housing Act, a comprehensive bill that not only established the national housing policy of "a decent home and suitable living environment for every American family,"[11] but also initiated a program that allows a Local Public Agency (LPA) to take privately owned urban land by right of eminent domain, clear it of structures, and sell it to private developers for construction of new residential buildings.

Emerging as it did out of the public housing–slum clearance movement, urban redevelopment as expressed in the 1949 Act was aimed at providing

---

[5] Anderson, *op. cit.*, p. 230.

[6] James Q. Wilson, "Urban Renewal Does Not Always Renew," *Harvard Today*, January 1965, pp. 2, 5.

[7] Herbert Gans, "The Failure of Urban Renewal," *Commentary*, Vol. 39, No. 4 (April 1965), reprint, p. 4.

[8] Scott Greer, *Urban Renewal and American Cities* (New York: Bobbs-Merrill, 1965), p. 3.

[9] For example, Martin Anderson, while lashing out at renewal from every possible point of view, concentrates on the economics of the process in *The Federal Bulldozer*. Herbert Gans, in *The Urban Villagers* (New York: The Free Press of Glencoe, 1962), combines sociology and city planning to immortalize renewal's nadir, the demolition of Boston's West End. As is evident from the titles, Harold Kaplan, in *Urban Renewal Politics* (New York: Columbia University Press, 1963), and Peter Rossi and Robert Dentler, in *The Politics of Urban Renewal* (New York: The Free Press of Glencoe, 1961), are concerned with the political process by which renewal projects are put into operation. Jane Jacobs, in *The Death and Life of Great American Cities* (New York: Random House, 1961), takes on the entire city planning profession and its approach to urban redevelopment.

[10] Greer, *op. cit.*, subtitle of the book.

[11] The Housing Act of 1949 as amended through June 1961 (Public Law 171, 81st Congress), Sec. 2.

more and better housing through the spot removal of residential slums.[12] Yet unlike the slum clearance formula which replaced each demolished structure with a new low-cost unit, there was no necessary link in the redevelopment program between the dwellings torn down and the units that went up in their place. Indeed, this dichotomy was sufficient to enable one congressman to say of the Housing Act of 1949, "I am in favor of the slum elimination section. I am opposed to the public housing section."[13] To calm those bothered by the absence of connection, the classic and much criticized theory of the filtering process was put forward, a theory which enables its supporters to argue that "for each good new home built one less family will have to live herded into an overcrowded slum tenement,"[14] because with each new occupied unit an old unit is vacated, thus setting off a residential upgrading process. With this general upward movement within the housing stock, it is not necessary, so the theory holds, that homes built on cleared sites be occupied by former residents of those sites.[15]

Whatever its debatable relationship to low-rent housing, the redevelopment program itself was not a success, as Charles Abrams makes clear:

Up to 1954 urban renewal lay in the dumps. Some 211 localities were interested, but only 60 had reached the land acquisition stage. . . . The passage of five years with almost nothing to show for all the fanfare was hardly progress.[16]

The few cities that did take advantage of the redevelopment program were criticized for displacing the poor without providing them with alternative residential locations. Experience demonstrated that clearance was not a sufficient mechanism for dealing with the complexities of central city housing.

In response to the deficiencies of the 1949 Act, amendments were offered in 1954 which transformed the program from one aimed at bulldozing residential slums to one concerned with conserving and rehabilitating the existing stock of housing within the broad framework of the Workable Program.[17]

---

[12] The evolution of the urban renewal program from the Housing Act of 1949 to the present is described in detail in the following: Greer, *op. cit.*; Abrams, *op. cit.*; Robert Weaver, *The Urban Complex: Human Values in Urban Life* (New York: Doubleday, 1964); William Slayton, "The Operation and Achievements of the Urban Renewal Program," in James Q. Wilson (ed.), *Urban Renewal: The Record and the Controversy*, (Cambridge, Mass.: The M.I.T. Press, 1966), pp. 189–229; "Citizen Participation in Urban Renewal," *Columbia Law Review*, Vol. 66 (March 1966), pp. 485–607.

[13] Greer, *op. cit.*, p. 17.

[14] Weaver, *op. cit.*, p. 51.

[15] See William Grigsby, *Housing Markets and Public Policy* (Philadelphia: University of Pennsylvania Press, 1963), for a definitive statement on the complexities of the filtering process.

[16] Abrams, *op. cit.*, p. 86.

[17] The Workable Program of the 1954 Act states that, in order to receive federal renewal funds, the local community must demonstrate it has developed the following: (1) appropriate building and housing codes; (2) a comprehensive plan for the community's development; (3) neighborhood analyses to determine problem areas; (4) an administrative

"Urban redevelopment" became "urban renewal."[18] Since 1954 the urban renewal program has branched out in two directions: one aimed at revitalization of Downtown,[19] the other at upgrading the city's residential districts.[20]

RESIDENTIAL REHABILITATION

Renewal began as an effort to replace the worst slums with standard residential units while relocating the slum dwellers into public housing or private stock made available through the filtering generated by the newly erected units. The residential side of the renewal program has gradually evolved into an approach in which "the maintenance and improvement of *existing* housing stock is a basic aim. . . . And since substandard houses tend to cluster by area, substandard *areas* are the focus of efforts at rehabilitation and conservation."[21] From the project-planning basis of the 1949 Housing Act to the Workable Program of 1954 to the General Neighborhood Renewal Plan of 1956 to the Community Renewal Program of 1959, the trend has been to expand the geographic scope of the renewal project from a plot of land chosen for its re-use value after clearance[22] to a total neighborhood in which preservation of that area's physical fabric is the basic concern.

The assumption underlying the area rehabilitation program is that the

organization capable of carrying out renewal activity; (5) financial resources to support the locality's share of the renewal program; (6) local citizen participation in developing and executing the urban renewal program; (7) housing resources for those displaced by the renewal process. Housing and Home Finance Agency, *Policies and Procedure of the Administrator #1–2–1* (O.A. [Office of the Administrator] Series).

18 The terms redevelopment and renewal are technically widely separated. Redevelopment means total clearance of an area and refers to treatment made possible by the 1949 Housing Act. The phrase "urban renewal," with its emphasis on revitalization of the existing physical plant, emerged with the 1954 bill. Today the two expressions have become hopelessly blurred in usage and will be employed here interchangeably.

19 Site clearance for nonresidential re-use constitutes the side of the program aimed at the revitalization of Downtown, a design which Scott Greer has called the "tall towers and green malls" (Greer, *op. cit.*, p. 34) approach to urban renewal. While I do not propose to discuss the use of renewal funds for purposes other than those directly related to housing, it is important to point out that nonresidential renewal constitutes a large and increasingly significant aspect of today's urban renewal program.

20 In December 1966 there were 1,812 approved renewal projects in 846 communities in 48 states, Puerto Rico, the Virgin Islands, and the District of Columbia. ("Progress Report on Federal Housing Programs," Subcommittee on Housing and Urban Affairs, U.S. Senate, May 9, 1967, p. 90.) As of June 30, 1966, 230 urban renewal projects were classified as predominantly residential, i.e., the rehabilitation section represented 50 percent or more of the total project area. In 187 of these projects the majority of buildings retained for rehabilitation were in residential use. (Letter to author from Renewal Projects Administration, Acting Deputy Assistant, August 23, 1966.)

21 Greer, *op. cit.*, p. 25.

22 Harold Kaplan's study of the politics of urban renewal in Newark, New Jersey, is a classic exposition of a "successful" program in which success "is used synonymously with high levels of clearance activity." (Kaplan, *op. cit.*, p. 2.) Priority areas for demolition were evaluated in terms of their potential appeal to the private developer rather than in terms of the impact of such bulldozing on the surrounding neighborhood.

old residential neighborhoods of the central city can be successfully revitalized by a combination of public and private investment, the one to root out the worst housing and to provide new public facilities, and the other to shore up aged dwellings and to build new housing, shopping facilities, and similar institutions.

In an area rehabilitation program the percentage of residential buildings cleared varies with each neighborhood. However, according to a June 1966 survey of the 187 predominantly residential urban renewal projects in the United States, "the average clearance section represents 19.5 per cent of the total gross project area."[23]

THE REHABILITATION PLANNING GAME

The significance of citizen participation in the renewal process has emerged as a direct result of the increased emphasis on rehabilitation and the expansion of the size of the area considered optimum for renewal treatment. While point six of the 1954 Workable Program does require a "citizens advisory committee to examine constructively the workable program goals,"[24] the committee, a city-wide organization, was seen by some as serving "only a limited role in satisfying the basic need to involve people in government"[25] and by others as an effective means of legitimatizing the redevelopment process at the total city level but having no impact on involvement at the neighborhood level.[26] So long as demolition in spot projects was the basis of urban renewal, there was probably universal truth to Kaplan's comment on the Newark program that "limited participation and low visibility seem to be necessary to the system's survival."[27] The strategy for successful demolition in Boston and New York included keeping the inhabitants of the proposed clearance area in the dark as long as possible in order to minimize their certain opposition to a program that was committed to tearing down their homes and their neighborhoods.[28]

However, as soon as one starts talking about rehabilitation and revitalization of the total neighborhood, the active support and involvement of local residents in determining the shape of physical plans for their area become a necessity. Since rehabilitation requires that local owners bring their property up to the standard imposed by the renewal program, those owners must

[23] Letter to author from Renewal Projects Administration, Acting Deputy Assistant, August 23, 1966.
[24] "Citizen Participation in Urban Renewal," *op. cit.*, pp. 491–492.
[25] *Ibid.*, p. 524.
[26] Robert A. Dahl, *Who Governs?* (New Haven: Yale University Press, 1961), pp. 133–137.
[27] Kaplan, *op. cit.*, p. 164.
[28] See J. Clarence Davies, *Neighborhood Groups and Urban Renewal* (New York: Columbia University Press, 1966) pp. 30–71, for an examination of clearance in New York, and Gans, *The Urban Villagers, op. cit.*, for Boston's experience with total clearance.

have confidence in the plan proposed for their area. Without the participation of such people and their commitment to the restoration of their neighborhood, rehabilitation has little future. Moreover, the fact that each residential renewal program contains a significant amount of clearance means that some citizens will be as directly threatened by the program as are residents of total clearance areas. Thus, the extent and location of clearance must be negotiated to secure at least the acquiescence of the majority of those in the neighborhood. While some opposition from groups and individuals is inevitable, there must be majority support.

The area chosen for residential rehabilitation generally includes institutions of the urban neighborhood—small stores, large businesses, churches, hospitals, settlement houses, and so on. These interests, like the resident owners and renters, are being asked to commit themselves to a revitalized community. The extent to which they become involved is determined by how they see residential renewal—as a threat to or as an enhancement of their position in the neighborhood. Furthermore, the leadership capacity of spokesmen for many of these institutions makes them potentially influential supporters or critics of a renewal effort.

In his seminal article "The Local Community as an Ecology of Games," Norton Long makes the point that

The structured group activities that coexist in a particular territorial system can be looked at as games. These games provide the players with a set of goals that give them a sense of success or failure. They provide them determinate roles and calculable strategies and tactics. In addition they provide the players with an elite and general public that is in varying degrees able to tell the score.[29]

The evolution of renewal from a real estate operation in cleared land, which did little to benefit anyone living in the area before demolition, to a program emphasizing the significance of existing neighborhoods changes the rules of what one might call "the urban renewal game." In the clearance approach "successful" playing on the part of the LPA calls for strategy which excludes the residents of the project area from knowledge of the planning process and emphasizes negotiation with prospective developers of vacant land.[30]

The rehabilitation game introduces neighborhood people as the players with whom the redevelopment authority must negotiate. A successful rehabilitation project requires the involvement of enough residents to ensure that public investment in the renewal area will be matched by significant investment from the local community. Moreover, the federal requirement that a public hearing be held by the LPA to enable citizens to express their views on the merits of the proposed renewal plan dictates that there be

29 Norton Long, *The Polity* (Chicago: Rand McNally, 1962), p. 141.
30 Once again Kaplan, *op. cit.*, provides the most vivid and structured account of the rules and regulations governing the players in the renewal clearance game.

people in the neighborhood sufficiently sold on the plan to stand up and support it at that hearing. The ritualistic and highly manipulated public hearings that were possible in the early days of urban redevelopment have become politically infeasible in the 1960's as both neighborhood citizens and public officials have become increasingly sophisticated about the implications of the urban renewal program.[31] While federal rules do not go beyond the requirement to hold the hearing, a negative response from the majority of neighborhood residents would clearly be an inauspicious start for a program dependent on local concern and involvement for its ultimate success. At bare minimum, a neighborhood rehabilitation program presupposes the involvement and approval of the majority of those elements in the local community who are the greatest potential source of support and, conversely, of opposition—were they to go into opposition.

Viewed as a game, neighborhood rehabilitation pits residents and institutions of the local community against the LPA. In simplified terms the game is one in which the LPA guarantees certain forms of public expenditure— schools, community facilities, new roads, easily accessible improvement loans and mortgages—in exchange for private investment in rehabilitation of residences, businesses, and institutions, and for support of clearance and willingness to express that support at a public hearing. The game presupposes that each side—the local community and the LPA—has or can obtain the resources to carry out its end of the bargain. The extent to which this mutual expectation is realized will not be evident until a renewal plan is actually put into operation.

The neighborhood rehabilitation planning game is basically a political one[32] in which the LPA bargains with the project area citizens over the nature of the proposal to be developed for their neighborhood.[33] Yet the structure of the game says nothing about the ease or roughness with which it will be played.[34] One can envisage situations in which local interests and individuals—churches, settlement houses, and so forth—are enthusiastic about the rehabilitation of their area. In such a case renewal negotiation

31 See Davies, op. cit., for a detailed portrait of the growing capacity of New York City residents to influence the direction and form of renewal planning between 1953 and 1963.
32 "Politics" is here used as defined by Martin Meyerson and Edward C. Banfield in Politics, Planning, and the Public Interest (New York: The Free Press of Glencoe, 1955), p. 304: "Politics is the activity (negotiation, argument, discussion, application of force, persuasion, etc.) by which an issue is agitated or settled." In our case political negotiation is the activity that takes place in the renewal-rehabilitation game. The members of the LPA and the local residents are parties to the issue of devising an acceptable renewal plan for the area under consideration.
33 One might argue that the boundaries of the project area might themselves be an issue to negotiate. Here we are assuming that, for the most part, the boundaries of the area are determined before the game begins. Whether they should be or not is another question.
34 Rossi and Dentler, op. cit., p. 287, maintain that "the maximum role to be played by a citizen-participation movement in urban renewal is primarily a passive one."

may be nothing more than an amicable discussion. One can also picture residents less than pleased at having to rehabilitate their homes, tenants fearful of rising rents, and institutions hostile to what they see as a threat to them and their clientele. To win majority support the LPA will then have to sell its program by hard bargaining and perhaps by promising additional public expenditures.

The renewal planning process is currently structured so that the comprehensive plan for neighborhood improvement has to be accepted or rejected in its entirety at the public hearing. There is no provision for approving part of the plan and sending the rest back for further discussion. The "either-or" quality of the process places great pressure on both teams, while providing each with powerful leverage. Because of the enormous investment in time, money, and labor involved in the process of delineating rehabilitation areas, acquiring survey and planning funds, and negotiating the plan at the neighborhood level, there is little likelihood that the LPA will permit a situation to arise in which a negative vote at a public hearing dissuades it entirely from its mission. Furthermore, if the LPA has prepared carefully, by the time of the public hearing opposition has been neutralized; the hearing becomes a democratic ritual expressing the results of negotiation in the community rather than a spontaneous outburst of neighborhood sentiment.

LOCAL PARTICIPATION IN
THE REHABILITATION PLANNING GAME

Since residential rehabilitation necessitates communication between renewal authority and local community, the characteristics of the interest groups who do or do not participate on the local team must be considered. Observers have suggested that, in general, "middle class persons who are beneficiaries of rehabilitation will be planned with; lower class persons who are disadvantaged by renewal will be planned without."[35]

The middle-class orientation of the rehabilitation game is argued in both sociopolitical and economic terms. The economic view points out that low-income home-owners will be hard hit by spot demolition in a neighborhood rehabilitation project because their property will be in poor condition, given their inability to finance repairs. Furthermore, the costs of rehabilitating to code standard make impossible demands on low-income owners, whose mortgage payments will increase, and on low-income tenants, whose rents will rise. As Staughton Lynd tersely says:

When Urban Renewal means merely kicking out the poor little by little rather than all at once, it brings dim consolation to the low-income site tenants.[36]

[35] Wilson, "Planning and Politics: Citizen Participation in Urban Renewal," op. cit., p. 247. See also Glazer, op. cit., p. 200, and Weaver, op. cit., p. 98.
[36] See Staughton Lynd, "Urban Renewal—For Whom?" in Shostak and Gomberg (eds.), New Perspectives on Poverty (Englewood Cliffs, N.J.: Prentice-Hall, 1965).

The federal government has not been oblivious to the argument that only those with substantial incomes can meaningfully engage in rehabilitation. Robert Weaver, Secretary of the Department of Housing and Urban Development (HUD), has stated that "under current conditions many of the low-income residents see in . . . [rehabilitation] dislocation or economic problems."[37] Urban renewal legislation has slowly focused on this issue as seen in Section 312 of the Housing Act of 1964, which provides for loans granted directly from HUD to certain owners at 3 percent interest, and Section 115 of the Housing and Urban Development Act of 1965, which authorizes the LPA to make grants of up to $1,500 to hardship low-income homeowners for purposes of rehabilitation. And the Rent Supplement program is, in part, an effort to help the site tenant deal with the increased rents produced by the rehabilitation process.

The other argument that demonstrates the middle-class bias of neighborhood renewal concentrates on the sociopolitical characteristics of the low-income residents. Here, the focus is not on the quality of the individual's home or amount of his income but on his inability to comprehend or accept the sacrifices and time perspective inherent in the renewal process. James Q. Wilson makes perhaps the most categorical statement on this point when he asserts that "public regarding" residents will support urban renewal while "private regarding" residents will accept it, if at all, only after "protracted, subtle, and assiduous wooing of neighborhood sentiment."[38] "Public regarding" people, to be equated with middle-class attitudes and incomes,

have a high sense of personal efficacy, a long time-perspective, a general familiarity with and confidence in city-wide institutions, and a cosmopolitan orientation towards life. In addition they are likely to possess a disproportionate share of organizational skills and resources . . . precisely those attributes which are likely to produce "citizen participation in urban renewal" that planners and community organizers will consider "positive and constructive"—this is, participation which will influence some of the general goals of renewal and modify a few of its details, but allow renewal to proceed.[39]

"Private regarding" people are lower-class individuals who "are more likely to have a limited time-perspective, a greater difficulty in abstracting from concrete experience and unfamiliarity with and lack of confidence in city-wide institutions, a preoccupation with the personal and the immediate."[40] The result of this split in attitudes and capacities between the "public regarding" middle classes and the "private regarding" lower classes is, Wilson feels, a situation in which

the view . . . a neighborhood is likely to take of urban renewal . . . is in great part a product of its class composition. Upper- and upper-middle-class people [public regarding] are more likely to think in terms of the general plans, the neighborhood or community as a whole, and long term benefits (even when they might involve

37 Weaver, *op. cit.*, p. 98.
38 Wilson, "Planning and Politics: Citizen Participation in Urban Renewal," *op. cit.*, p. 247.
39 *Ibid.*, p. 245.
40 *Ibid.*

immediate costs to themselves); lower- and lower-middle-class people [private regarding] are more likely to see such matters in terms of specific threats and short-term costs.[41]

As the economic argument implies, one reason middle-class people can appear more enlightened is that they incur less of the burden of clearance, as they can afford to keep their homes from falling into disrepair, and of rehabilitation, because what repairs their homes do require are less of a drain on their total income. Moreover, critics of Wilson have pointed out that "in general the middle class has not docilely accepted the high 'costs' of renewal as the price of a 'better world' ";[42] when personal costs become too severe, the middle class also will object to the urban renewal process.

While Wilson attributes the reluctance of the lower class to mobilize for urban renewal to disagreement with the goals of the program, others have argued that the critical point is not the conscious unwillingness of members of the lower class to accept renewal but their inability to articulate their opinions when bargaining is going on between the neighborhood and the LPA. The dual problem of mobilizing the poor and then making them heard in renewal negotiations has been the focus of numerous studies.[43]

As partial solutions to the economic problems of neighborhood renewal have filtered their way into legislation, so have recommendations for overcoming the sociopolitical barriers to involvement of the poor been injected into the renewal process. The Community Action Program of the Office of Economic Opportunity represents an organized effort in this direction, with its much-discussed goal of "maximum feasible involvement of the poor" in decision making.[44] Another method for engaging lower-class people is represented by the advocacy planning concept, which involves taking on the lower-income residents of a neighborhood as clients and gearing planning solutions to their needs.[45]

THE PROBLEM OF DEFINITION

Up to this point we have described aspects of the view of residential rehabilitation as a middle-class game. However, to talk of the middle class and the lower class and of the inclusion of one and the exclusion of the other in the business of planning neighborhood revitalization obscures as many issues as it clarifies.

41 *Ibid.*
42 "Citizen Participation in Urban Renewal," *op. cit.,* p. 598.
43 See Paul Davidoff, "Advocacy and Pluralism in Planning," *Journal of the American Institute of Planners,* Vol. XXXI, No. 4 (November 1965), pp. 331–338; Bernard Frieden, "Towards Equality of Urban Opportunity," *Journal of the American Institute of Planners,* Vol. XXXI, No. 4 (November 1965), pp. 320–330.
44 "Citizen Participation in Urban Renewal," *op. cit.,* p. 600.
45 See book review by Walter Thabit in *Journal of the American Institute of Planners,* Vol. XXXII, No. 3 (May 1966), pp. 181–182.

Does the low-income neighborhood have no way of making its needs felt in renewal negotiations?[46] Or is the key issue the fact that the poor within a neighborhood do not find their way to the negotiating table?[47] Both views ignore the possibility that some of the poor may participate in negotiations some of the time; consequently, proponents of both views fail to seek in renewal situations and in the characteristics of the poor themselves the critical differences that may determine whether or not the poor are involved in renewal and the extent of their involvement.

To discover the exact causes of exclusion from or limited participation in the rehabilitation game is not an easy task. One must first consider the nature of the sociopolitical and economic limitations of those who lack representation. Economic handicaps are generally more easily identifiable, but even here there are problems. There may be situations, for example, in which low-income residents participate in the planning process and voice their approval of the plan at a public hearing with the understanding that they will be able to carry out the economic demands placed on them by rehabilitation. Then, during plan execution, they discover that bringing their property up to code standards may be a far more costly operation than had originally been envisaged. Such a situation may not result from deception on the part of the LPA but simply from changes in the cost of labor and building materials, from more rigorous application of the building code than the LPA had anticipated, or from a host of other factors that raise rehabilitation costs. The economic problems facing the poor as a result of the rehabilitation game are, then, not necessarily correlated to the political exclusion of the poor from planning for their neighborhood. Likewise, the moves necessary to correct the economic problem are categorically different from those steps necessary to get the poor into the negotiation in the first instance.

As soon as one tries to define the sociopolitical characteristics of the poor —the characteristics that cause exclusion from the renewal game during its planning stages—the problems become even more complex. All one has to do, to get some idea of the difficulty, is to look at the current stack of literature discussing the salient characteristics of the poor.[48]

46 This is essentially Herbert Gans's position in *The Urban Villagers* and seems to be the base from which "Citizen Participation in Urban Renewal" argues. That article states that "One method of compensating for agency bias is to provide the lower-class neighborhood with a spokesman from the middle class." "Citizen Participation in Urban Renewal," *op. cit.*, p. 599.

47 Many critics take the point of view expressed by Walter Thabit, himself an advocate planner, who says, "Solving the organizational problems of gray [poor residential] areas . . . doesn't solve the problems of the poor in those areas . . . physical improvements have been or are to be made at the expense of . . . poor families forced to move out of each area." Thabit, *op. cit.*, p. 181.

48 S. M. Miller, in a perceptive study, "American Lower Classes: A Typological Approach"

The most significant alternative to Wilson's dichotomy between middle class and lower class is that of sociologists like Gans who see the lower-income population divided into two distinct camps, the "working class" and the "lower class":

The former consists of semiskilled and skilled blue collar workers, who hold steady jobs and are thus able to live under stable, if not affluent conditions. Their way of life differs in many respects from those of the middle class; for example, in the greater role of relatives in sociability and mutual aid, in the lesser concern for self-improvement and education and in their lack of interest in a good address, cultivation and the kinds of status that are important to middle class people. Although their ways are culturally different from the dominant middle class norms, these are not pathological, for rates of crime, mental illness and other social ills are not significantly higher than in the middle class. . . .

The lower class, on the other hand, consists of people who perform the unskilled labor and service functions in the society. Many of them lack stable jobs. They are often unemployed. . . . Partly because of occupational instability their lives are beset with social and emotional instability as well and it is among them that one finds the majority of the emotional problems and social evils associated with the low-income population.[49]

While Gans posits a wider range of class structure than Wilson, he concludes that not only are lower-class people unable to engage actively in renewal planning but working-class people have an "inability to participate in formal organizations and in general community activity," with the result that during the process of negotiating the redevelopment of Boston's West End, "the West Enders could not defend their interests and the redevelopment agency was unable to understand their needs."[50] On the other hand, Wilson, for all his emphasis on the unwillingness of "private regarding" residents to go along with the sacrifices called for by the renewal process, maintains that while an enormous amount of negotiation is involved, "there are many stable working class neighborhoods where indigenous leadership can be developed and involved in urban renewal."[51] Gans and Wilson are far more concise in their definitions than most critics of the renewal program, for whom "the poor" is a generic term that seems to include anyone who is adversely affected by clearance or rehabilitation. Obviously, many of those relocated from a residential project do have low incomes, but "the poor" and "those who have to relocate" are not synonymous.

(in Shostak and Gomberg, *op. cit.*, pp. 22–39), constructs a two-by-two matrix with economic characteristics on one axis and familial (what might be called sociopolitical) characteristics on the other. He emerges with four different "types" of poverty, each of which poses a different policy implication. Miller's rigorous delineation of variances within that sector of the population called "the poor" stands in sharp contrast to much of the literature in the field.

49 Herbert Gans, "Social and Physical Planning for the Elimination of Urban Poverty," *The Washington University Law Quarterly,* February 1963, reprint p. 7.

50 Gans, *The Urban Villagers, op. cit.,* pp. 264 and 266. See also Floyd Dotson, "Patterns of Voluntary Association among Urban Working Class Families," *American Sociological Review,* Vol. 16 (1951), pp. 687–693, for another study of the absence of working-class participation in formal organizations.

51 Wilson, "Planning and Politics: Citizen Participation in Urban Renewal," *op. cit.,* p. 246.

THE DIVERSITY OF NEIGHBORHOOD

Definitional problems aside, generalized description of the rehabilitation planning game usually fails to consider the diversity of neighborhood within which the game can take place. While the basic purpose of the game—negotiation between neighborhood people and the LPA of a plan for the area's physical future—remains the same, the characteristics of the players and the strategy employed by each team vary from match to match. Ultimately, the extent to which the local team represents a cross section of the project area is a function of the socioeconomic structure and political dynamics of the neighborhood for which planning is being negotiated. In every case, however, the local team is composed of the neighborhood powerful[52]—those local people who are able to negotiate for the future of their neighborhood. One can structure the concept of neighborhood diversity and neighborhood power around the following hypotheses. The ecology of a large city promotes residential districts that contain diverse socioeconomic interest groups, the kind, number, and compatibility of which vary from area to area.[53] The configuration of an urban neighborhood's powerful people is a function of the socioeconomic dynamics of the area,[54] and the local renewal team is then a vehicle for the powerful in the residential rehabilitation planning area.[55]

If one assumes that, regardless of the social complexity of the district undergoing renewal planning, the "middle-class people" constitute the only interest taking part in the planning process and benefiting from the rehabilitation game, then one can posit that, for the purposes of the game, the configuration of power in the community is the same as the distribution of "middle-class" individuals. On the other hand, if, as is maintained here, one argues that areas picked for residential rehabilitation are complex social units in which communication, activity, and interest group identity often

[52] Defining the concept of "power" is one task that has kept political scientists and sociologists gainfully employed for years. (See Lawrence D. Mann, "Studies in Community Decision Making," *Journal of the American Institute of Planners*, Vol. XXX, No. 1 (February 1964), pp. 58–65, for a concise summary of the literature on community power from the point of view of a city planner.) "Power" is here used to mean the capacity to be for or against urban renewal, the ability to make one's presence felt on the local residential rehabilitation planning team.

[53] See Walter Firey, *Land Use in Central Boston* (Cambridge: Harvard University Press, 1947).

[54] Rossi does not go quite this far, but he implies such a conclusion, in Peter Rossi, "Power and Community Structure," in Edward C. Banfield (ed.), *Urban Government* (New York: The Free Press of Glencoe, 1961).

[55] One might argue that the composition of the local team can be structured by either the LPA or powerful individuals within the neighborhood, and thereby represent something other than the natural rising to the surface of the neighborhood powerful. Yet in order to remain politically viable during the long planning period, the local team must be molded around the contours of local power. Otherwise, those vocal interests excluded from the structured team will, at some point, make themselves known by demanding a place on the community team. If they fail to gain entry to the local planning structure, they will oppose the renewal negotiations.

cut across income, education, and occupation lines, then the interests likely to take part in the renewal game involve more than the middle class. Thus an understanding of those included and excluded from representation on the local renewal team can come only from an examination of the socio-political and economic dynamics of the individual area in which renewal negotiations are taking place.

The social complexity of neighborhoods has been the focal point of several studies, all of which emphasize the impact of local environment on individual attitudes and behavior. Bell and Force maintain that a person's participation in formal associations is a function not only of his social status as measured by income, education, and occupation but also of the socioeconomic characteristics of the neighborhood in which that individual lives. These neighborhood characteristics may "define a set of general societal expectations"[56] which significantly influence the extent of individual involvement in local organizations. Thus under certain neighborhood conditions an individual whose class rank alone would indicate low participation in organizations may be deeply involved in local affairs.

Several studies have demonstrated the importance of recognizing individual neighborhood characteristics in determining the involvement of local residents in matters affecting the area. A survey in San Francisco, for example, of neighborhood attitudes toward urban renewal underlined the significance of clusterings of socioeconomic traits for explaining the variation, among different areas of the city, in questionnaire responses.[57] In another study, Carle Zimmerman found it necessary to establish a distinction between "nominal" communities, in which the "chief form of integration . . . is largely mechanical proximity,"[58] and the "realistic" community, in which integration is not a geographic phenomenon but rather a sense of belonging to "one community . . . that stands out by itself as a clearly defined integrating factor."[59] Thus when anticipating the composition of the local planning team, the type of neighborhood becomes an independent variable which must be considered equally with class and population characteristics.

Moreover, the capacity of local teams to marshal resources, organize and allocate tasks among team members may differ significantly. These capabilities are not necessarily tied to middle-class characteristics but are equally dependent upon relationships among the neighborhood powerful and between the neighborhood and the rest of the city.

[56] Wendell Bell and Maryanne Force, "Urban Neighborhood Types and Participation in Formal Associations," *American Sociological Review*, Vol. XXI, No. 1 (February 1956), p. 34.
[57] Arthur D. Little, Inc., *op. cit.*, p. 32.
[58] Carle Zimmerman, "The Evolution of the American Community," *American Journal of Sociology*, Vol. 46 (May, 1941), p. 809.
[59] *Ibid.*, p. 812.

In focusing on the diversity of power and interest groups in urban neighborhoods, one might hypothesize two limited types of local teams. The first is a team whose members represent only one interest group within the planning area, an interest powerful enough to control the renewal game and to produce a positive turnout at the LPA public hearing. In such a case, residential groups living within the project district might be excluded from the renewal game because their presence is not deemed necessary for political affirmation or because they themselves have little or no capacity to demand a place on the local team. The second, and opposite, situation focuses on an area with such homogeneity of population that the local team must reflect such homogeneity if it is to function at all. A variation of this extreme is a residential district with a number of interest groups, each so capable of mobilization that each would demand and receive a place on the neighborhood renewal team.

On the assumption that people who are involved in the rehabilitation planning game will fight to preserve their own property as well as that owned by the interest group they represent, the logical outcome of a renewal planning game in which the entire community is vociferously represented would be one involving little residential clearance. On the other hand, in the planning game in which one interest group is able to dominate the proceedings, a far greater latitude for demolition would exist.

THE PLANNERS AND THE REHABILITATION GAME

Up to this point, little attention has been given to the characteristics of the other team involved in the rehabilitation planning game: the Local Public Agency. Here, the critical focus is not on the complex of factors which determines who is on the team but on the assumptions that can be made about the attitudes, goals, and strategy that the LPA planners employ in their efforts to evolve a physical plan for a residential neighborhood.[60]

The planner's role—historical and potential—is open to a variety of interpretations and descriptions. In *The Death and Life of Great American Cities*, Jane Jacobs employs the image of the city planner as a middle-class bureaucrat who wants to sterilize the city by eliminating its diversity and by rooting out any buildings which fail to meet the local housing code standard.[61] Her description is a caricature of what can be called the objective

---

[60] "Planner" is here used as a generic word to cover those members of the LPA who are actively engaged in negotiations with the neighborhood team. In addition to professional city planners, the LPA teams may include lawyers, community organizers with social work backgrounds, and public administrators. To call them all planners is to describe their situational opportunities, constraints, and attitudes rather than their particular professional training.

[61] Jacobs, *op. cit.*, pp. 3–25.

planning style—a style in which aggregate physical characteristics, standards, and relationships constitute the basis for determining the characteristics of a renewal plan.

In contrast to the image of the bulldozing planner making decisions while sheltered in City Hall is the picture (currently drawn by the liberal wing of the planning profession) of the advocate planner, who seeks out the people of the neighborhood with which he is dealing and helps to design a plan that is in keeping with local wishes for the district's future. The advocate planner is basically a mobilizer of public opinion. He may provide advice and technical information, but the contours of the plan are essentially the product of negotiation at the neighborhood level, expressive of neighborhood goals and needs as seen by local residents.[62]

These two portraits can be said to represent the two end positions along a spectrum of roles which the planner can conceivably play. While the planner working directly for a local neighborhood organization is, by definition, far closer to the advocate end of the spectrum than the planner employed by the LPA, wide latitude may exist within the organizational constraints of an LPA. Where along the objective-advocate spectrum the individual LPA planner settles will be the result of the interaction of three pressures: the professional norms of the planner and his agency, the city-wide political and bureaucratic forces, and the demands imposed upon the planner by the neighborhood team with which he is negotiating.[63]

Those who observe planners engaged in the urban renewal process tend to concentrate on one source of pressure while excluding the other two. For instance, Gans and Paul Davidoff criticize the middle-class value system of the "planning and care-taking professions."[64] Davidoff states:

Planning agencies are likely to reflect the dominant values of their society. In general, planning has supported the status quo, and this is particularly evident in situations where planning agencies have supported regulations which exclude income groups and racial groups from gaining access to a community and where agencies have dislocated low income families in order to help families in lesser need.[65]

On the other hand, Scott Greer, quoting a harried renewal administrator, focuses on the pressures generated toward the LPA at the city level:

Look, your community is whatever your political structure will let you get done. The community makes up its mind . . . and you have to work with it.[66]

Greer concludes that planners have little leeway to consider neighborhood demands, with the result that

62 Davidoff, *op. cit.*, pp. 331–338.
63 See Nancy Arnone, "Urban Renewal in Boston: A Study of the Politics and Administration of Social Change" (unpublished Ph.D. thesis, Department of Political Science, M.I.T., February 1965). The work constitutes a detailed study of what Miss Arnone calls "the politicized municipal bureaucracy," p. 173.
64 Gans, *The Urban Villagers, op. cit.*, p. 174.
65 Paul Davidoff, quoted in "Citizen Participation in Urban Renewal," *op. cit.*, p. 127.
66 Greer, *op. cit.*, p. 117.

the residents of declining areas have very little weight in . . . decisions. These are usually neighborhoods of the bottom dogs: they lack expertise, organizational skills, and association with the powerful.[67]

Concentrating on the position emphasized by Davidoff, one sees the planner in the rehabilitation game imposing on neighborhood discussions his middle-class view of the "good city," which may or may not reflect the attitude of the neighborhood team with whom he is negotiating. In Greer's view, the planner is the captive of city-wide political forces that circumscribe the opportunity area within which he can operate and thus make neighborhood values or goals of little significance in deriving a plan for the area.

Others view negotiations at the neighborhood level as the critical force acting on the planner. They believe the neighborhood plan has no absolute worth as a "planning solution" unless related to the needs and desires of the people living in the area.[68] Such a solution may or may not be related to sound middle-class planning principles or the demands of the city-wide political forces that allow renewal to operate in the first instance.

The last two points of view are not necessarily incompatible. One can conceive of a neighborhood planner, bounded by certain city-wide pressures but, in the opportunity area afforded him, free to bargain with the neighborhood team.

The critical question here is: Does the LPA team, within the latitude allowed a bureaucratic agency by its city-wide political support, financial constraints, and the dictates of HUD's urban renewal guidelines try to impose its middle-class values and "good planning principles" on the local community regardless of local desires or needs? Or does the overriding goal of the LPA at the neighborhood project level become a successful plan as measured by local political approval? We have argued that the structure of the residential rehabilitation game requires a plan that not only can withstand a public hearing but also can enlist support during the execution stage. One might transfer Greer's description of political feasibility from the city to the local level and hypothesize that the LPA's neighborhood plan is a manifestation of "whatever your political structure will let you get done."[69] Thus a successful plan becomes one approved by the political forces in the neighborhood, within the limits prescribed by the coalition supporting renewal at the city-wide level.

In order to assure local support, the planners will be intent on cultivating "local power" representatives of different interest groups within the project area. As one author puts it, the LPA team will

67 *Ibid.*, p. 120.
68 "Citizen Participation in Urban Renewal," *op. cit.*, p. 601.
69 Greer, *op. cit.*, p. 117.

attempt to counter opposition by preventing its effective mobilization; to co-opt community leadership . . . to negate opposition before it arises.[70]

To do this, the LPA team must gain a clear understanding of the socio-economic structure of the area in which it is operating, must pinpoint the politically significant interests in the district, and must adapt its style and plan to the demands of those interests. Failure to deal effectively with the sources of power in the renewal district will result in conflict and the possible breakdown of the rehabilitation planning game.

A SUMMING UP

The concept of residential renewal as a game in which two teams negotiate over the expenditure of public and private resources has been derived from general consideration of the rehabilitation process and the planning structure that seems logically to flow from that process. Yet it would be incorrect to assume that every rehabilitation project automatically produces such a game. For example, if one turned to the 187 rehabilitation projects on the federal books at the end of June 1966, one would find that many are small "pocket" projects involving only a city block or two. In such cases public investment is minimal, and the need for local support is restricted to families on a few streets. In other rehabilitation situations an LPA might be so unwilling to accommodate the demands of the local area that it would hold back a renewal project rather than bargain over its contents. The bitter deadlock over a plan for Cooper Square on Manhattan's Lower East Side is an example of this unwillingness on the part of the LPA to shape its plan to the political demands of the local neighborhood.[71]

Thus what would seem to be the internal logic of the rehabilitation process may not always result in a planning game. However, there are enough renewal situations reflecting that logic to justify a study of residential rehabilitation planning as a game situation in which the unique characteristics of individual neighborhood dynamics determine the composition of the local team, the course of planning negotiations, and the content of the renewal plan.

In this chapter it has been argued that the composition and thus the goals and attitudes of the citizen team is a function of the socioeconomic dynamics of the area delineated for revitalization and that the goal of the LPA team becomes of necessity that of plan approval at the local level within the opportunity area afforded by city-wide political and planning considerations as well as by the rules and resources of the federal government. As a result of this process, the plan which emerges at the neighborhood level is, in Ban-

[70] Arnone, *op. cit.*, p. 127.
[71] "Citizen Participation in Urban Renewal," *op. cit.*, p. 510.

field's terms, a matter of "political influence" in which "resultant solutions" and "decision-choices"[72] reflect the demands of the local power system, tempered with limitations imposed by the LPA's city-wide environment.

The composition of the renewal team, based on the socioeconomic dynamics of the community, determines which groups are excluded from the bargaining process and, consequently, most severely penalized by the effects of renewal. A local renewal team, if structured on a narrow social or physical base, is responsible to only a limited part of the community, and the neighborhood interest groups that are absent from the bargaining table suffer the penalties always incidental to exclusion from the political process.

[72] Edward C. Banfield, *Political Influence* (New York: The Free Press of Glencoe, 1965), pp. 337–341.

2
The
Planning
Game
in Boston:
Three
Neighborhoods

A One-City versus a Multiple-City Approach

The rehabilitation planning game can be studied by examination of neighborhoods in different cities or various areas in one city. On behalf of the multiple-city approach, one can argue that rehabilitation situations drawn from a single city do not give a fair sample of the variation possible in the rehabilitation planning game. While limiting a study to one community makes it difficult to argue that the results of the investigation have universal application, having the case studies located in the same "control system" is of decided advantage for comparative analysis. Problems of comparability created by regional factors, by city size, by variation in economic and social dominance among urban areas, and by the goals and strategies of different LPA's are avoided. The single-city approach provides a solid base for comparing the differences among residential districts and the manner in which those differences influence the form and content of the rehabilitation planning game. Thus, in the balance, the one-city strategy seems to offer the more useful approach to studying the diversity of neighborhood and the relationship of that diversity to the planning game.

BOSTON AS A SETTING FOR THE REHABILITATION PLANNING GAME

Boston provides an ideal case study for the rehabilitation game. With City Council approval in November 1965 of a renewal plan for Boston's South End, the LPA had successfully negotiated comprehensive renewal plans for three of the city's major residential areas: Washington Park, Charlestown, and the South End. (See Figure 2.1.) The size of the neighborhoods—each over 500 acres—suggests a major rehabilitation effort; approval of the projects by the City Council indicates political support at the neighborhood level.

There are reasons for turning to Boston's rehabilitation planning games other than the fact that the city provides the opportunity to make a comparative study of three areas. Boston's renewal program is one of the largest in the country. *Fortune* magazine has stated that "Boston is being turned into a laboratory demonstration of renewal techniques, which . . . may affect 25 percent of Boston's area and 50 percent of its population."[1] Wolf Von Eckardt has characterized Boston's program as one of "our better urban renewal efforts."[2] *Architectural Forum* has devoted an entire issue to the Boston program and called the rehabilitation planning approach "one of the most inventive in the nation."[3] Boston's massive economic and political investment in urban renewal and the city's sophisticated approach to the process indicate a city serious about resurrecting its central business district and ensuring the future of its old neighborhoods. Moreover, the strategy with which the Boston Redevelopment Authority (BRA) has approached the revitalization of the city's residential neighborhood is an early essay into the kind of massive assault on city problems envisaged by the Model Cities Program.

The Boston experience has already provided a basis for comments on the nature of the rehabilitation planning process. Constance Williams' "Citizen Participation in Urban Renewal—The Role of the Resident" evaluates the Washington Park and the Charlestown renewal experiences:

The different goals wanted from the renewal program in Washington Park and Charlestown reflected different characteristics among the citizens who were the spokesmen in each area. Those who favored the plans for urban renewal as pro-

1 Walter McQuade, "Boston: What Can a Sick City Do?" *Fortune*, Vol. LXIX, No. 6 (June 1964), pp. 132–134.
2 Wolfe Von Eckardt, review from *Library Journal* quoted on the back cover of the paperback edition of *The Good City* by Lawrence Haworth (Bloomington: Indiana University Press, 1966).
3 *Architectural Forum*, Special Issue: "Boston," Vol. 120, No. 6 (June 1964), p. 124.

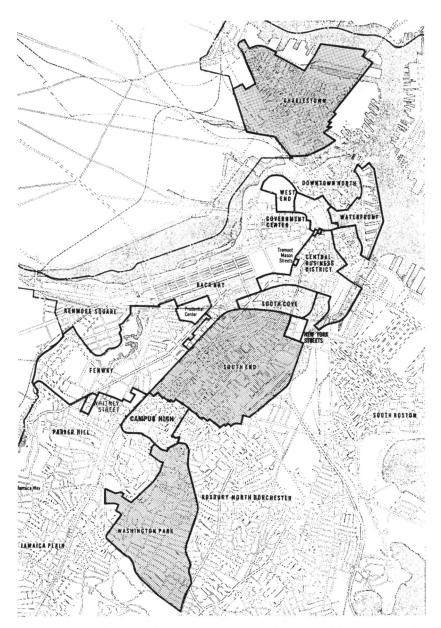

FIGURE 2.1 THE THREE NEIGHBORHOODS IN THE GENERAL SCHEME OF THE BOSTON URBAN RE-NEWAL PROGRAM

posed by the Redevelopment Authority were in general persons who looked forward to higher incomes and who tended to put high values on housing *per se*. This has been summarized by several people as representing a middle-class orientation as compared to a working-class orientation.

In Charlestown . . . there was emphasis on wanting to keep the income level appropriate for "working class people." . . .

In Roxbury . . . it is believed that there was at least a larger number who looked forward to higher incomes and welcomed the prospect of better housing and assumed they could afford it. . . . The lower-income families who were less articulate in Roxbury, on the other hand, held attitudes more like the majority of Charlestown.[4]

Miss Williams examines Charlestown through only the first public hearing, a hearing which produced that bane of all renewal games, the negative local response. Yet her basic analysis is clear. The majority of Washington Park planning game participants were middle-class; therefore, they supported residential rehabilitation. The majority of participants in Charlestown were working-class; therefore, they opposed renewal.

James Wilson, writing at about the same time as Miss Williams, sees the Boston urban renewal process in terms of his "public-private regarding" dichotomy:

The Boston Redevelopment Authority . . . has been put to the test in two neighborhoods selected for renewal. In one [Washington Park] . . . it was able to win from the middle-class Negroes who would benefit from the plan consent "in principle" to a rehabilitation program. . . . In the other case, [in] Charlestown, an old, lower-middle-income Irish neighborhood, . . . the citizens . . . knew their own interests well enough to cripple, at a public hearing, the proposed renewal plan with a flood of objections and conditions which, at least for the time being, the renewal authorities could not meet.

If one's goal is urban renewal on any really large scale in our cities, the implications of these observations are disturbing. The higher the level of indigenous organization in a lower-class neighborhood, the poorer the prospects for renewal in that area.[5]

Wilson, too, saw the success of Washington Park and the failure of Charlestown in class terms. The "public regarding" (middle) classes of Washington Park would support residential rehabilitation, the (lower-class) "private regarding" Irish of Charlestown would not.

David Stern in his Harvard honors thesis examines the South End and concludes that a small band of homeowners called the shots in the renewal negotiations there and that the planning process was built around the desires of middle-class homeowners at the expense of the vast majority of South End residents.[6]

[4] Constance Williams, "Citizen Participation in Urban Renewal—The Role of the Resident" (unpublished M.C.P. thesis, Department of City Planning, M.I.T., May 1964), pp. 84–85.

[5] James Q. Wilson, "Planning and Politics: Citizen Participation in Urban Renewal," *Journal of the American Institute of Planners*, Vol. XXIX, No. 4 (November 1963), pp. 246–247.

[6] David Stern, "Citizen Planners for Urban Renewal" (unpublished Honors thesis, Department of Social Relations, Harvard College, April 1966).

For each of these three commentators the critical division in response to rehabilitation planning occurs between the middle and the lower classes. Determining the extent to which their appraisals represent an accurate interpretation of the events of the rehabilitation planning games in Charlestown, Washington Park, and the South End will constitute a major point of emphasis in the investigation of planning in these Boston neighborhoods.

THE CONTEXT FOR REHABILITATION PLANNING:
BOSTON'S POLITICAL CHARACTER

The city that found John F. Collins an upset victor in the mayoralty election of 1959 has since been the subject of numerous reports on the political, socioeconomic, and physical problems throttling it at the time of that election.[7] Subject to all the unhappy vicissitudes plaguing the American central cities at mid-century—declining tax base and soaring tax rate, fleeing middle-class residents and businesses, deteriorating housing stock and faltering public services—Boston's problems were magnified by the city's particularly exacerbated relationship with its metropolitan hinterland and state legislature.

Boston is an old city built for another century, as her narrow winding streets, abandoned waterfront, and weed-filled railroad yards testify. Despite her age and relatively small size, Boston is not a geographically or historically integrated community: she grew during the nineteenth century by annexing independent towns on her borders, towns that have kept their original names and, often, their sense of separate identity. These geographic divisions are heightened by the ethnic parochialism which characterizes Boston's social system. While Yankees, Jews, Irish, Italians, and Negroes maintain their own enclaves within the city, the dominant sociopolitical characteristic of Boston at the time of John Collins' election was Irish.

How the Irish immigrants wrested political power from their Yankee overlords and went on to rule the city of the Lowells and the Cabots has been the subject of commentary, fictional and historical.[8] In tight command of Boston's political system by 1910, the Irish have dominated Boston's nine-man city council and have returned an Irishman to the mayor's office with unceasing regularity.

[7] See Murray B. Levin, *The Alienated Voter: Politics in Boston* (New York: Holt, Rinehart and Winston, 1962); McQuade, *op. cit.*; Nancy Arnone, "Urban Renewal in Boston: A Study of the Politics and Administration of Social Change" (unpublished Ph.D. thesis, Department of Political Science, Massachusetts Institute of Technology, February 1965); Martin Meyerson and Edward C. Banfield, *Boston: The Job Ahead* (Cambridge: Harvard University Press, 1966); *Architectural Forum, op. cit.*
[8] See Oscar Handlin, *Boston Immigrants* (Cambridge: Harvard University Press, revised edition, 1959), for a moving account of the Yankee–Irish immigrant confrontation; Edwin O'Connor, *The Last Hurrah* (Boston: Little, Brown, 1956), for a fictional account of James

Boston has had a long history of corruption, of reform movements that blossom momentarily, only to fade from sight, of city agencies swollen with recipients of political patronage, of estrangement from city government of the "responsible" people—the financial, business, and newspaper communities. Collins' surprise upset of John E. Powers was an event of enormous significance to Boston. Collins was a relative unknown when catapulted into office; his election was more a vote against his opponent, characterized as a "power politician," than an affirmation of his own capabilities or program.[9] Unshackled by pre-election promises to individuals or organizations, Collins entered office virtually a free agent, and his renewal program must be seen in the light of this unencumbered position. For urban renewal would become the issue around which John Collins would stake his political future. "Ambitious and honest,"[10] extremely energetic, possessor of a "steel trap mind,"[11] Collins would attempt to blend the political base afforded him by his roots in Boston Irish culture with a concern for efficient good government that might woo back the Yankees alienated from the central city's public affairs since their loss of political power at the turn of the century.

Prior to Collins' election, urban renewal and city planning in Boston reflected the dominant sociopolitical culture of the city. Isolated from the highly politicized arena in which development decisions were actually made, planning was weak and ineffective. Redevelopment, carried on by the Boston Redevelopment Authority (BRA), created in 1957 from a division of the Boston Housing Authority which had been the LPA to that point, "displayed . . . shallow opportunism . . . [and] basically . . . was a real estate speculation."[12] In theory, the nine-man City Planning Board was to delineate renewal projects in line with the objectives of the city's comprehensive development plan evolved in 1950. It was the job of the BRA to carry out such projects. In practice, the linkage between the BRA and the Planning Board was virtually nonexistent. Under constant pressure from one or more of its five board members, the BRA—with little regard for the objectives of the Planning Board—went about the business of picking off prime real estate packages scattered throughout the city.

The 1950 "General Plan for Boston," a backdrop against which planning and renewal priorities were supposed to be established, allocated 2,700 acres of developed land within the city for clearance and redevelopment, of which

Michael Curley, the prince of the Irish pols; and Richard J. Whalen, *The Founding Father: The Story of Joseph P. Kennedy* (New York: N.A.L.–World Book, 1964; paperback Signet Books, 1966), for a study of Yankee-Irish relationships at the turn of the century.
9 Levin, *op. cit.*, p. 14.
10 *Architectural Forum, op. cit.*, p. 81.
11 Author's interview with Edward J. Logue, April 28, 1966.
12 *Architectural Forum, op. cit.*, p. 66.

1,100 acres "where conditions are particularly bad were typed as 'high priority' redevelopment areas."[13] The Planning Board's method of determining areas for clearance was extremely straightforward.

A number of approaches were made to determine the location and extent of these clearance areas, based on earlier studies made by the City Planning Board. Factors of blight that could be measured included: 1. The condition of residential buildings (based on 1940 census counts of dwellings needing major repair or without private bath); 2. The age of buildings; 3. The rent (low rent having been demonstrated to be closely related to such substandard housing conditions as lack of sanitary facilities or central heat). . . . These data, analyzed block by block, resulted in the marking out of areas so clearly substandard in building conditions and spacing that sweeping clearance of buildings is the only way they can be restored to social and economic health.[14]

The West End project, immortalized in Herbert Gans's *The Urban Villagers*,[15] was an operational example of the planning philosophy expressed in the 1950 "General Plan for Boston." Now the classic symbol of the way urban renewal should not be handled, the total clearance of a vibrant neighborhood to make way for luxury apartments was one of several occasions in the 1950's when Boston used the bulldozer approach to urban renewal.

Logue's BRA: Strategy and Rules for the Rehabilitation Planning Game

It was, then, against this background of disjointed clearance projects that Collins chose urban renewal as the standard around which to rally his administration. Renewal was to be the mechanism to reverse Boston's physical and economic slide into despair, to end the alienation of the Yankee business elite from the city's Irish political culture, and to give John Collins a foundation upon which to build a political reputation. To put together a program of sufficient scope and imagination, Collins called on Edward J. Logue, the chief of New Haven's extensive renewal effort.

Destined to become "more controversial, more discussed, more fervently admired and fervently hated than any [Boston] personality since James Michael Curley,"[16] Logue came first as a consultant. He would not agree to take on the job of administering Boston's renewal program until he was granted "the most massively centralized planning and renewal powers that any large city has ever voted one man."[17] From Logue's nine months of consulting emerged "The 90 Million Dollar Development Program for Boston,"[18] a proposal for radically changing the face of the city while re-

13 Boston City Planning Board, "Preliminary Report—1950: General Plan for Boston" (Boston, December 1950), p. 40.
14 *Ibid.*
15 Herbert Gans, *The Urban Villagers* (New York: The Free Press of Glencoe, 1962).
16 *The Boston Sunday Herald,* December 5, 1965.
17 *Architectural Forum, op. cit.,* p. 82.
18 "The 90 Million Dollar Development Program for Boston," reprinted from the *City Record,* September 24, 1960.

structuring the organization of the Planning Board and the BRA to bring them both under the control of one agency headed by Edward Logue. The political fight over the reorganization plan was a classic example of the old order's reluctance to give way to the new. Only after a protracted battle in the fall and winter of 1960–1961 was Logue granted the enormous power he had demanded. As Development Administrator responsible to both the Redevelopment Authority and the Mayor, he was to propose and execute renewal plans and to evolve comprehensive development plans for the city and capital improvement programs for all of Boston's municipal departments. Under Logue, planning and execution were joined in one powerful agency.

The impact of Logue's technically oriented, rational planning operation on Boston's tradition-bound sociopolitical system has been studied in Ph.D. theses and discussed in the popular press.[19] What concerns us here is not the system of alliances and coalitions which enabled Logue's BRA to survive in a basically hostile political environment but rather the political and planning assumptions which Logue brought to bear on the complex issue of neighborhood renewal.

Logue began his career in 1948 as a Philadelphia lawyer. He soon went to work for Chester Bowles, then governor of Connecticut. After accompanying Bowles to India, he returned to New Haven to handle Mayor Richard Lee's urban renewal program and, as *Fortune* magazine comments, "Between them the two wrote renewal history by accomplishing more with less cash than was done in almost any other U.S. city."[20] As a result of his national connections within the Democratic party Logue had a direct line to Washington bureaucrats, the "Feds" as he calls them, and especially to officials administering the urban renewal program.

Characterizing himself as a "collector of cities as some collect works of art,"[21] Logue is an action-oriented political pragmatist who has little use for general plans and city planners lacking the political power to realize their designs. For Logue, planning and politics are inseparable, planning being the art of the politically feasible, from the vantage point of City Hall. "I won't sit back . . . and let my political support go down the drain,"[22] said Logue when he campaigned for John Collins' successful re-election in 1963.

During his six-year stint as Development Administrator,[23] Logue built

19 See Arnone, *op. cit.*, for a systems analysis of the BRA and its relationship to the sociopolitical environment of Boston.
20 McQuade, *op. cit.*, p. 136.
21 *The Boston Sunday Herald*, December 5, 1965.
22 *Architectural Forum, op. cit.*, p. 82.
23 Logue resigned from the BRA in the summer of 1967 in order to run for mayor of Boston. His bid for elective office was unsuccessful: he finished fourth in a field of ten in the mayoral primary election.

the BRA into the city's largest and most influential public agency through his political acumen, capacity to draw on federal resources,[24] and support from Mayor Collins and Boston's Downtown interests—the financial, real estate, and newspaper communities. While the BRA staff, which came to number almost 500 during Logue's administration, was involved in a myriad of operations, all lines of authority still led to Edward J. Logue, for there was not one piece of the renewal system about which Logue did not have his own ideas. Holding the view that creative answers are forced out only by bringing issues to a head, Logue, a believer in the "self-fulfilling prophecy," takes on problems which a city planner's analysis would deem impossible of solution.

While Logue's "90 Million Dollar Development Program for Boston" includes reviving the central business district, the key to his program is in Boston's graying residential neighborhoods and their potential for physical rehabilitation and social reconstruction.

Logue's strategy for residential renewal demonstrates the extent to which planning and politics are fused into one action system; and the guideline axioms that follow represent an effort to sum up Logue's approach to residential rehabilitation. While derived for the most part from statements made publicly or privately by the Development Administrator and members of his staff, some of the axioms come from examination of Logue's program in operation.

1. Renewal must be done wholesale if done at all. Logue's program called for ten renewal and six improvement areas. Only "a big, bold, fast moving program"[25] could pull Boston back from its physical and social decline.

2. The key to urban renewal is residential rehabilitation. Eight of the ten renewal areas focused on rehabilitation.

3. The urban neighborhood is the framework around which to organize rehabilitation. Mayor Collins pointed out that "the ultimate success of this whole program depends on whether we can bring back these old neighborhoods."[26] "Ultimate success" was defined in the BRA's "1965–1975 General Plan for the City of Boston and the Regional Core" in the following way:

The Policy of the Development Program . . . is . . . to promote stability in the size of Boston's population while increasing the diversity of its composition so that it more nearly reflects the composition of the Region's population as a whole. This would, of course, entail a reversal of present trends towards increasing proportions of low-income groups and non-whites in the core City. However, this cannot be accomplished unless a positive effort is made to make residential Boston attractive to families at the time when they acquire the economic means to move elsewhere. For that reason an important objective of the Development Program must be to preserve

24 See McQuade, op. cit., for a description of Logue's enormous capacity to get federal renewal funds for Boston.
25 "The 90 Million Dollar Development Program for Boston," op. cit., p. 5.
26 Architectural Forum, op. cit., p. 103.

the stability of residential neighborhoods in Boston and make them, in as many respects as possible, competitive with surrounding cities and towns in housing, schools, and public services.[27]

This program, then, calls for a generous input of public services, improvement of housing conditions, and "complete refurbishing of the City's physical and cultural image."[28]

4. Rehabilitation areas should be picked on the basis of visibility and operationality. These criteria are typical of Logue's fusion of planning and politics. In his early days in Boston while still on a consulting basis, Logue met with the staff of the City Planning Board, which at that time was drawing up what it called "district plans" for each of the major areas of the city. The statistical information collected for the "district plans" became the basis for Logue's neighborhood renewal proposals, but the areas to be chosen for immediate planning purposes were determined, in the words of one of the planners at the session, "not necessarily by criteria of social or physical blight but rather in terms of renewal's political acceptability within the neighborhood and the visibility of the project area in the city as a whole."[29]

5. Physical renewal cannot operate without social renewal. As the 1965–1975 General Plan states, "Development of human resources in Boston will be vital to the success of the entire Development Program."[30] Logue was the generating force behind the Boston Community Development Program, later to be called Action for Boston Community Development (ABCD), which "was to run interference for Logue's renewal program,"[31] by evolving social plans for each rehabilitation area as well as by taking charge of organizing the area's team for the rehabilitation planning game.

6. Local citizen teams constitute the key device in generating plans for neighborhood revitalization. Mayor Collins said,

I would expect that neighborhood committees would have a key partnership role in the preparation and carrying out of renewal plans. I would call it planning *with* people instead of planning for people.[32]

Within each neighborhood an organization representing the different interests in the area should be set up, if one is not already in existence, to whom the "renewal mandate" would be given, that is, the right to negotiate a plan for the area with the BRA project team. No public hearing would be held on the rehabilitation plan until the mandate organization had given its formal public assent to the plan. The mandate group legitimizes the renewal plan for the neighborhood and provides the formal arena within

27 Boston Redevelopment Authority, "1965–1975 General Plan for the City of Boston and the Regional Core," November 1964, p. vi–2.
28 *Ibid.*, p. vi–3.
29 Author's interview with Richard Bolan November 12, 1965.
30 Boston Redevelopment Authority, *op. cit.*, p. v–3.
31 *Architectural Forum*, *op. cit.*, p. 83.
32 "The 90 Million Dollar Development Program for Boston," *op. cit.*, p. 2.

which differences of opinion can be resolved and conflict neutralized. Thus, it is important to select or set up an organization which is sufficiently representative of the residential, business, and institutional interests in the community to ensure that no group with the capacity to mobilize local opinion is excluded from the planning process.

7. It is important to get an overwhelming vote of approval from the local community at the BRA public hearing. That hearing is an indication of the success with which the BRA staff has co-opted the leadership and has neutralized opposition. A positive turnout lends an aura of acceptability and legitimacy to the entire planning process.

8. One reason for centralizing so much power in the office of the Development Administrator is to have it to give back to the people living in the rehabilitation neighborhoods. Each community should have the right to decide the contours of the physical plan for its area. As Logue says, "I don't think the people of West Roxbury have any right to decide what goes on in the South End. That is for the people of the South End to decide."[33] Yet if neighborhood people make decisions Logue considers "unwise," he believes in fighting those decisions unless doing so would jeopardize the entire planning effort.

9. The emphasis on neighborhood and neighborhood planning necessitates a highly decentralized operation with independent BRA teams in each project area. The individual project chief serves the residents of the neighborhood as their spokesman in any discussions with Logue and the BRA planners concerned with city-wide problems and pressures. In this way the central office will be kept aware of the political and social demands generated at the project level. While Logue has the final word and will intervene in renewal negotiations if overwhelming problems arise, the project chief tries to negotiate alone with his eye focused on the BRA public hearing, when his success at bargaining with the neighborhood team is measured.

10. About 20 percent of the residential structures in each project area should be cleared. While negotiation can take place around the 20 percent figure, Logue's view is that less clearance makes little impact on a community's physical condition and more than 20 percent demolition creates a negative image and risks organized opposition. In a city geared to think of renewal in terms of the West End clearance, the bulldozer approach is a political liability.

The amount of clearance possible is to a large degree a function of the manner in which project lines are drawn. With judicious tailoring of boundaries, clearance areas can be increased without raising the specter of

33 Author's interview with Edward J. Logue, April 28, 1966.

opposition. While taking down a total neighborhood may be unfeasible, the total residential demolition resulting from a rehabilitation project may, in fact, equal the total clearance of the West End. What is important is the context within which clearance takes place, not the clearance per se.

11. After negotiations with the neighborhood team about the nature of a physical plan for their district, the BRA draws up three possible renewal plans. While all three have similar inputs of public facilities and new private development, percentages of clearance vary from below 20 percent, to about 20 percent, to 30 percent. It is assumed the mandate group will compromise and choose the middle plan, the one that Logue views as the equilibrium point between the planning demand for a sufficiently reconstituted physical community and the political demand that clearance threaten no more than one family in five.

12. Boston's existing housing stock is the prime source of supply for families relocated from renewal areas. From Logue's point of view such an approach is realistic because of the number of units left vacant by the city's ever-declining population. When public housing is an absolute necessity, it should be built in small clusters integrated into existing neighborhoods. Another reason for avoiding public housing whenever possible was Logue's feeling that the Boston Housing Authority was unable to rise to the challenge of an action-oriented program.

These twelve axioms build a general framework for the residential rehabilitation game. The degree to which they are followed varies from project to project; and what is of prime concern in this study is the extent to which the general strategy is bent, molded, and realigned to meet the particular demands of the individual rehabilitation game.

THREE REHABILITATION PLANNING GAMES: AN OVERVIEW

The next chapters study the South End, Charlestown, and Washington Park from the time in each area at which renewal became an issue up to the BRA public hearing. Analysis of the individual renewal games has been similarly structured. The first section of each chapter describes the project area in detail as a social system and delineates its history, physical character, interest groups, and the extent of its social integration. Based on analysis of interest groups and their interaction, projection is made of the likelihood of each group's direct or indirect participation on the local team.

The analysis then focuses on the manner of renewal's entry into the area, the maneuvering to establish a base of operation, the tactical moves made by the citizen team and BRA staff to produce a politically acceptable plan, and the extent to which the area's spectrum of interest groups was or was not involved in the planning process.

Next, the plan that emerges from the renewal game is evaluated in terms of its impact on interest groups in the community, by showing which groups benefit from what physical changes, who is hardest hit by the clearance pattern, the relationship of clearance to housing considered deteriorated by objective planning standards, and the projected impact of rehabilitation costs on owners and renters.

These essays in neighborhood rehabilitation planning end at the point at which a planning proposal has run the gauntlet of neighborhood opinion and survived. Ideally, the studies would proceed beyond the point of plan approval in order to match the assumptions of the plan against the actual pattern of events during execution. There is little doubt that such a comparison would illustrate the resemblance of urban renewal planning to "the best laid schemes o' mice an' men." Yet, at the time of researching this study, only one of the three projects under examination had actually been in operation long enough to match the results of execution against the assumptions made at the time of plan approval. Moreover, I would argue that the point of political affirmation is a valid place to conclude a study of the rehabilitation planning game, for decisions which local residents make as to whether or not they will support a proposal are based on their understanding of the plan as plan, not as executed reality. In this sense the rehabilitation planning game is a self-contained process; as such it offers a distinct insight into the variety in urban neighborhoods and in their responses to the renewal planning process.

At one level, these studies report three rehabilitation planning games: they record the names, dates, and maneuvers critical to the process of negotiating a plan through each community. Yet my aim is not to write the definitive history of rehabilitation planning for three of Boston's ten renewal areas. Rather, I am concerned primarily with those aspects of the renewal story in each project area which relate the course, characters, and content of the renewal game to the socioeconomic and political characteristics of the district in which the game is played.

In view of the issues raised in Chapter 1, my examination of the renewal planning process in each district is structured to shed light on the following questions:

1. Are there significant differences in the quality and quantity of "the powerful" in old urban neighborhoods? Is there, in fact, a diversity of interest group constellations among the project areas? To what degree can the socioeconomic dynamics of those constellations be identified?

2. Does the origin of the renewal planning team, its emerging structure, and the manner in which members gain positions on it vary from area to area? Can one relate that variation to differing socioeconomic structures among Boston's residential districts?

3. To what extent does the concept of residential renewal as a game in

which two teams bargain over the content of a physical plan provide a useful framework for analyzing the planning process in three large rehabilitation areas?

4. Do the differences in socioeconomic character of the three areas under study produce renewal planning games that are located at different positions along the spectrum of possible games, discussed in Chapter 1?

5. To what extent does the concept that residential renewal planning is a middle-class game characterize those on the local team? Does Wilson's "public regarding–private regarding" dichotomy provide a satisfactory framework for describing those included in renewal planning as well as their objectives?

6. Are some neighborhood groups excluded from representation in the planning process by default, or are there potential conflicts between groups which preclude certain of them from having a hand in determining the outcome of the district plan?

7. Can one distinguish between those who may be excluded from the benefits of the rehabilitated neighborhood for economic reasons and those whose exclusion is due to sociopolitical conflict?

8. To what extent does the Boston Redevelopment Authority adapt its style and goals to the demands of the team with which it is negotiating? Can it be said that the agency's goal becomes that of neighborhood approval within the opportunity area afforded by city-wide political and planning constraints?

9. Do the comprehensive plans emerging from different renewal games vary in objectively quantifiable aspects, such as extent of residential clearance, provision for relocation housing, and estimated rehabilitation costs? Can these objective differences be related to the character and goals of the local team negotiating the proposal?

10. What are the implications for the city as a whole of a planning process that delegates decision making to the level of the individual neighborhood?

11. What lessons for the Model Cities Program can be learned from the rehabilitation planning game?

3

The South End

Part One

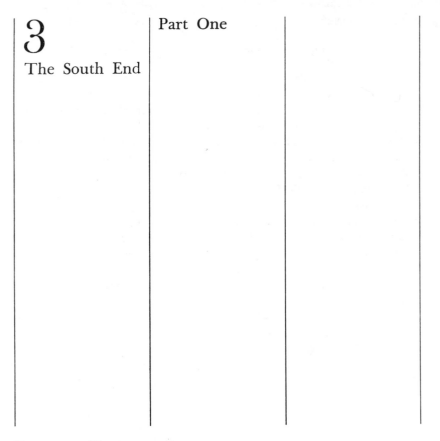

THE PEOPLE, HISTORY, AND GEOGRAPHY
OF THE SOUTH END: AN OVERVIEW

Boston's South End is one of the best-studied urban districts in America. For over sixty years its complexities have been analyzed and reanalyzed by social scientists, social workers, and novelists. J. P. Marquand beautifully captures its early grandeur and swift decline in *The Late George Apley*. To Apley, the proper Bostonian, the sight of a man in shirtsleeves on the stoop of a neighboring house was a clear indication "that the days of the South End were numbered."[1] Whereupon Apley promptly sold his home.

The area from which Apley fled with such rapidity was for the most part filled land salvaged from tidal marshes during the first half of the nineteenth century. While its initial development was slow,

beginning with the fifties it rapidly grew into a region of symmetrical blocks of high-shouldered, comfortable red brick or brownstone houses, bow-fronted and high stooped with mansard roofs, ranged along spacious avenues, intersected by cross

[1] John P. Marquand, *The Late George Apley* (New York: Pocket Books, 1944), p. 26.

streets and occasionally widened into tree-shaded squares and parks, whose central gardens were enclosed by neat cast-iron fences.[2]

Not all of today's 600-acre South End is laid out in elegant town-house fashion (see Figure 3.1). The area holds long stretches of monotonous bow-fronts built along straight cross streets, several pockets of flat-faced tenement housing, and much land devoted to commerce, industry, and institutions. There is, however, a visual unity in the "hard core" South End which is due to the careful way its squares and parks were laced together in the second and third quarters of the nineteenth century.

Union Park, always the "gold coast" of the district, gives some indication of what the area must have been during its prime. Well-kept bowfront houses sweep around a central park, from which rise enormous elms and maples. The street is quiet, the atmosphere faded but warm, and the South End's physical potential for gracious town-house living extremely apparent. Once-lovely Chester Park, however, has the misfortune to be on a cross-town highway. Here crumbling bowfronts curve around an oval park split by a four-lane boulevard. Boards vie with glass for dominance in window frames. The trees are gone, and traffic races by the two small arcs of grass, all that remain of the original park.

As Apley's exit suggests, the most significant fact about the South End in the last quarter of the nineteenth century was its quick tumble from respectability. Many events contributed to the fall—the newly created residential streets of the Back Bay, the railroad line that had to be crossed in order to get to downtown Boston. But the taproot of the South End's demise was the Panic of 1873, which threw many local real estate operators into bankruptcy. With banks selling foreclosed houses for what they would bring on a glutted market, property values dropped, Brahmins fled, and bowfront homes were taken over by immigrants and lodging house proprietors.[3]

The Crash of 1873 set the stage for the South End of today, the home of 5 percent of Boston's population and "95 per cent of its problems."[4] By the 1890's the character of the area was sufficiently defined for Robert Woods to entitle his study of the district *City Wilderness*.[5]

While the South End continued to be a City Wilderness into the 1960's, the social and historical forces of the twentieth century were molding the district into a wilderness of quite different thorns and brambles from that of Woods's day. The end of the great European migrations, the gradual assimi-

[2] Walter M. Whitehill, *Boston: A Topographical History* (Cambridge: Harvard University Press, 1959), p. 122.
[3] Albert Benedict Wolfe, *The Lodging House Problem in the City of Boston* (Cambridge: Harvard University Press, 1913), p. 15.
[4] *Architectural Forum*, Special Issue: "Boston," Vol. 120, No. 6 (June 1964), p. 104.
[5] Robert Woods (ed.), *The City Wilderness* (Cambridge: Houghton Mifflin, 1898).

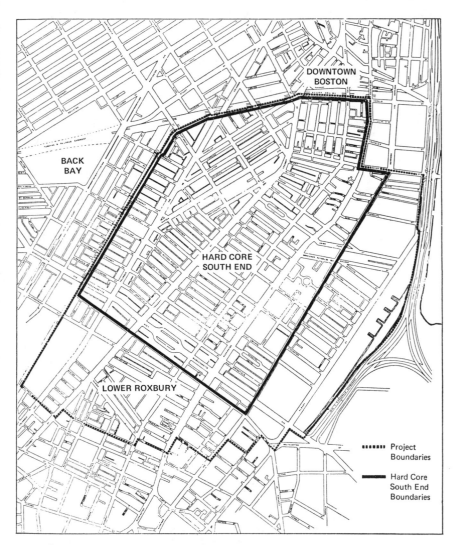

FIGURE 3.1 THE SOUTH END URBAN RENEWAL AREA

lation of ethnic groups into American life, the change from rural whites to rural Negroes as in-migrants to the central city—all of these national trends affected the composition of the South End's population.

In 1947 Walter Firey found, scattered through the South End, ethnic enclaves that had "remained rather solidly with their respective value systems; they have their own churches, lodges, and other organizations, and they generally live in family units."[6] Some of Woods's "struggling but sturdy working class" remained.[7] However, a radical transformation had occurred in the rooming house population. Firey found that the young rural Yankees and Canadians who had dominated this group at the turn of the century had been replaced by older members of the same ethnic stock, "mainly middle aged or elderly, and more male than female."[8] Lodging houses no longer catered to people on the threshold of their productive lives but to those grown old who by their very presence in the South End demonstrated a lack of success in meeting the challenge of an urban society. The number of bars had grown since Woods's day, as had the South End's identification with prostitution, numbers, and dope.

Table 3.1 gives a quantified account of the extent to which the South End of the early 1960's deviates from the Boston average in characteristics that directly or indirectly indicate old age, poverty, and solitary living. While the district holds only 5 percent of the city's population, it soars above its rightful share of the Boston total in practically every category describing social and economic problems.

Turning to census tract data for a more detailed picture of the socioeconomic characteristics of the South End, one sees that the 1960 pattern is relatively similar to 1950. While the South End population decreased at a far more rapid rate than in the city as a whole, there was no concomitant change in the area's socioeconomic profile. The South End consistently has maintained a population which has included Negroes, the aged, the poor, and the unskilled. While the area's nonwhite population stood at 40 percent in 1960, the South End's percentage increase in nonwhites for the 1950–1960 decade was less than in the city as a whole. Numerically there were fewer Negroes in the South End in 1960 than in 1950.[9]

6 Walter Firey, *Land Use in Central Boston* (Cambridge: Harvard University Press, 1947), p. 301.
7 Woods (ed.), *op. cit.*, p. 100.
8 Firey, *op. cit.*, p. 301.
9 In 1960 three South End census tracts had characteristics that set them apart from the general South End profile of solitary, old, poor people. One tract is next to the South End's hospital complex and, therefore, houses many young professionals. Another is dominated by the Cathedral Project, a public housing complex with many children. The radical shift in racial composition from 1950 to 1960 in this area (significantly, the only one in which such a shift occurred) results from the reshuffling of the Cathedral Project from 30 percent to 80 percent Negro occupancy between census takings. The third tract is only partially in the South End project area and has high familial characteristics because it contains the Lennox-Camden housing project and because this area is closer to Lower Roxbury, an area populated by large, young, poor Negro families, than it is to the lodging house "core" of the South End.

TABLE 3.1 AREA CHARACTERISTICS

	South End	City of Boston
ECONOMIC CHARACTERISTICS		
% unemployed—1960	8.7%	5.0%
Median family income—1960	$3,650	$5,757
% of families with incomes under $3,000—1960	40.5%	16.7%
% of families with incomes over $10,000—1960	4.2%	13.6%
HEALTH CHARACTERISTICS		
Death rate of infants per 1,000 under one year old—1961	57.7	26.1
% of Boston cases of pulmonary tuberculosis—1961	29.6%	100.0%
HOUSING CHARACTERISTICS		
% units owner occupied—1960	9.1%	27.7%
Population per household—1960	1.9	2.9
% sound dwelling units—1960	46.0%	73.3%
Median gross montly rent—1960	$51.00	$78.00
POPULATION CHARACTERISTICS		
Total population—1960	33,735	697,197
% decline from 1950 population	40.0%	12.5%
% population nonwhite	40.7%	9.8%
% numerical increase of 1960 nonwhite population over 1950 nonwhite population	−22.0%	60.0%
% of 1960 population under 18	21.6%	28.7%
% of 1960 population 65 and over	16.8%	12.3%
Families (2 persons or more) as a % of all households	34.0%	73.0%
Families (2 persons or more) with children	60.0%	63.0%
WELFARE CHARACTERISTICS		
Population as % of total city population—1964	4.5%	100.0%
% of city welfare cases in area—1964	11.3%	100.0%
% of city Old Age Assistance cases in area—1964	14.0%	100.0%
% of city AFDC families living in area—1964	8.0%	100.0%
% of city General Relief cases in area—1964	30.8%	100.0%
YOUTH CHARACTERISTICS		
% of Boston's youth 7–17 living in area—1960	3.9%	100.0%
Youth court appearances 1959–1961 as a % of Boston's total	9.9%	100.0%

Source: Statistics compiled by Anti–Poverty Planning Unit, ABCD, Winter 1964–1965, and "Social Facts by Census Tracts—1960," data compiled by United Community Services.

On the basis of aggregate statistics one cannot say much about the nature of the local team that might be put together to negotiate residential renewal. However, the age, poverty, and social pathology of the South End's residents do not seem conducive to the fielding of a squad capable of strong bargaining with the BRA project staff. Yet to categorize the South End as a poor neighborhood, and therefore according to one point of view, a district incapable of mounting a renewal offensive, obscures as much as it clarifies about the South End's social dynamics. Of the three areas under study, the South End offers the widest array and the most involved interrelationship of interest groups. Although the district has a certain architectural and historic unity, it is not an integrated or homogeneous community. As one observer commented, "This place is like a city. It has a little bit of everything as well as too much of one thing—problems."[10] What follows is an effort to give qualitative and quantitative dimensions in interest group terms to that "little bit of everything."

THE PROBLEM INTEREST GROUPS

THE NIGHT PEOPLE

A 1965 *New Republic* article called the South End the "land of the white hunter":

> . . . a top-flight Boston slum, the center of the city's colored vice . . . a network of streets and alleys interpenetrated by pathology . . . [where] towards the end of day the legitimate life ebbs away, locks its doors, retires into neighborhood meetings, or goes home to other parts of the city. And then the bars and dens come alive. Cars cruise dark streets. . . . Prostitutes emerge from rooms and apartments and find, along with Lesbians, homosexuals and pimps, their way to their favorite bar.[11]

While this description of the Night People is overdrawn, the South End is a haven for illegal activities. Participants are diverse, but bound by a mutual interest in keeping the South End a City Wilderness. While obviously the Night People would oppose urban renewal, the hatred other groups in the area feel for them and for the illegal character of their activities precludes formal involvement of their "interest" in the neighborhood renewal negotiating team.

SKID ROW

The South End contains 116 establishments with liquor licenses, one for every 270 people in the district. Many of these outlets cater to the racially integrated Skid Row community—predominantly sad, shuffling old men, yet with a solid number of younger adherents—located along the northern arc of the district. These men are not to be confused with the Night People. The interests of the two groups are different, and the attitude of society toward their antisocial behavior is distinct. There are yet to be groups that attempt to deal with prostitutes in the way Christian missions, doctors, and social workers try to handle Skid Row, for, unlike alcoholism, vice and dope are rarely recognized as diseases. While the denizens of Skid Row can be cate-

---

10 Author's interview with Thomas Dealey, July 1, 1966.
11 Joan Colebrook, "Boston's South End: Land of the White Hunter," *The New Republic*, March 6, 1965, p. 8.

gorized in many ways, it seems valid for our purposes to include most of them in Gans's "lower class"—individuals who are unemployed and are over-burdened with social and emotional problems.

It is easier to pinpoint the size of the South End Skid Row population than the number of people directly or indirectly involved in the activities of the Night People. A 1961 study estimated Boston's homeless alcoholics between 5,000 and 8,000 men.[12] During the eleven-month period of the study, 8,037 arrests for drunkenness were reported at Division Four headquarters, the police station covering the South End. The figure represents more than one third of Boston's yearly arrests for drunkenness and is, with one exception, eight times as great as that recorded by any other police division in the city.

While there is nothing illogical about having representatives of Skid Row on the neighborhood renewal team, the probability of finding spokesmen is low. In terms of inherent capacity to pursue and defend their interests in the South End, the Skid Row people (and the flophouses, soup kitchens, and halfway houses which service them) would have to rely on the area's social welfare and hospital complex to champion their cause.

THE NONPROBLEM INTEREST GROUPS

Night People and Skid Row are the two groups in the South End that are clearly "problem" interests. The groups described in this section have problems, like aged tenants in need of financial and medical help or "hardcore" multiproblem families, but these groups do not manifest extreme antisocial behavior.

THE LODGING HOUSE INTERESTS

The extent to which lodging houses[13] dominate the residential pattern of the South End is made clear by these 1963 BRA findings:

Our preliminary studies . . . show that there are 923 licensed lodging houses in the South End. Our preliminary estimates place some 10,000–12,000 residents in licensed lodging houses. This represents about 28–33 per cent of the South End population. Our estimates of unlicensed lodging houses vary from 400–900 additional units which is approximately 4,000–8,000 additional people residing in them.[14]

[12] Harold Demone and Edward Blacker, "The Unattached and Socially Isolated Residents of Skid Row" (Boston: Action for Boston Community Development, July 1961), p. 13.
[13] "Lodging house" is defined by Massachusetts law as "a house where lodgings are let to five or more persons not within the second degree of kindred." It requires a license for "such fee, not exceeding two dollars, as the city council . . . may establish." Failure to procure a license supposedly results in "a fine of not less than one hundred dollars nor more than five hundred dollars or by imprisonment for not more than three months." Commonwealth of Massachusetts, "Condensed Summary of Laws Relative to Innholders and Common Victuallers," June 1957, p. 5.
[14] Project Director Richard Green, in a letter to Charles Jordan, August 27, 1963.

Thus, the maximum estimate of South End residents involved in lodging houses includes over half the area's 30,000 people.

The lodging house population comprises diverse and potentially conflicting interests. A division must be made between owners and tenants, then between resident and nonresident owners and between "good" and "bad" tenants.

LODGING HOUSE OWNERS

Lodging house operators in the South End range from the resident female proprietress concerned about her home and tenants, many of whom have been with her for years, to the fabled absentee slumlord who owns a string of ramshackle lodging houses and milks his property dry. While these two extreme portraits are perhaps overdrawn, there is statistical verification for the BRA assertion that "As a general rule the owner occupied units tend to be of higher quality than those owned by an absentee landlord"; for while 12.8 percent of lodging houses without an owner occupant are in need of "major repair," only 5 percent of the owner-occupied dwellings fall into this category.[15] Ownership of the 923 licensed lodging houses is fairly evenly split, absentee landlords making up 55 percent.

In terms of social class the 400 licensed resident owners run the gamut from old-line Boston Negro women who emulate the Brahmin standards and values, to aged couples whose roots are deep in ethnic working-class society. Many have low incomes; for some the lodging house is their sole source of income. The unifying element in what is otherwise a disparate group is the significance of the lodging house as a form of economic security. Any public policy which would ensure steady-paying, reliable tenants would be viewed as a blessing by the resident landlords. They would support a renewal program that would rid the area of "bad" tenants and landlords without closing out the rooming house business.

Not all 512 absentee owners live outside the South End. Almost half of them live elsewhere in the South End.[16] For the most part, they can be assumed to have the same outlook toward their property as the resident owners. It is the owner from outside the area who represents a divergent point of view and profits by taking as much out of tenants and putting as little back into buildings as possible. Not living on the premises, he has no

[15] Boston Redevelopment Authority: South End, "Specifications for the South End Urban Renewal Plan as Presented to the South End Urban Renewal Committee on October 5, 1964," pp. 1–2.
[16] City of Boston, City Council, "South End Urban Renewal Area: Before Committee on Urban Renewal," November 10, 1965, p. 558.

compelling personal reason to care about the behavior of his roomers or the condition of his building. Were public policy to require him to invest in his property, he would probably sell rather than repair.

Identifying absentee owners with lack of concern for the condition of their property and its surroundings and resident owners with commitment to the area is, of course, an oversimplification, but as a projection of response to demands for rehabilitation, probably a valid one to make.

THE TENANTS

One can conservatively estimate that there were about 14,000 lodging house tenants in the South End in 1964. While many tenants fall into Gans's "working class" category, the majority, burdened down with age, poverty, and lack of social contacts, are representatives of his "lower class" concept.

To distinguish quantitatively between "good" and "bad" tenants would be a hopeless task because the terms are objective only in the mind of the beholder. Different lodging house owners have diverse views of what should be tolerated in tenant behavior. The obvious "bad" tenants are the ones who do not pay rent and who, in the words of one South End resident, "slop up the place."[17] Beyond these characteristics the qualitative distinction between the two types would depend more on the attitude of the individual rooming house operator than on any other factor. Obviously, a tenant whose main tie is to Skid Row or the Night People will not be tolerated by many resident owners. Bad housekeeping habits, old age, senility, and the occasional bender, however, are for the most part accepted as an inherent aspect of the lodging house business.

The rooming house dwellers are in the South End for many reasons: the anonymity the district provides, the cheapness of the rooms, the proximity of City Hospital, and the bars. Some of the tenants have lived in "the same room on the same street for twenty or thirty years."[18] For the most part they seem incapable of organizing to defend their interests in the renewal planning game. While it would be in the interest of all tenants to maintain the South End as a low-rent district, the "good" tenants would not miss the bars or the Night People. The tenants, "who are more like one of the family than anything else,"[19] probably would have a spokesman in their landlord or are themselves involved in some small way in a neighborhood association. The others who "slop up the place," would have to rely on the welfare agencies.

17 Author's interview with Royal Cloyd, January 6, 1966.
18 "The South End Today," Boston, October 1965, p. 56.
19 Katherine Swenson, in a letter to Edward J. Logue, May 23, 1963.

THE URBAN VILLAGERS[20]

Although census data for the South End are not fine enough to indicate the ethnic neighborhoods remaining in the area, pockets of ethnic community can be found. What Firey pointed out in 1947 is largely true of the population today:

Except for the Canadians and the Irish these foreign born persons do not constitute part of the South End's rooming house population. Rather they live in tenements scattered throughout the side streets of the district, generally in cohesive subcommunities of their own.[21]

A careful analysis of the Bradford-Shawmut area reveals a residential area with stores, restaurants, and clubs catering to the resident Syrian population. Here one finds children on the street, neighbors who know each other, and familial ties. Communication and residential stability is high relative to the rest of the South End. While many of the second and third generation have moved away, they will often stop in at the local cafés on their way out Shawmut Avenue to their suburban homes. Perhaps the clearest indication of the unique community to be found in this small area is that the cafés are not hangouts for Skid Row people or prostitutes but resemble the "local pub" of British tradition.

Greenwich Street, deep in the heart of Lower Roxbury is surrounded by decaying buildings and deserted fields. Yet it is an oasis of blue-collar Negro homeowners who fill their windows with flower boxes and take obvious pride in their modest but well-kept homes.

Sometimes these pocket neighborhoods are oriented along class values. Worcester Square, an area near City Hospital, has many resident rooming house operators who have been described by a South Ender as "a bunch of hard-nosed lower-middle class Yankee types who say 'we have made it—we own the joint' "[22] Here the lodging house interest takes on geographic shape and combines with a sense of neighborhood to reinforce commitment to the South End.

For groups like these, with roots deep in the South End, a renewal program that would improve the quality of the schools, get rid of the "dives," and generally revitalize the district would be wholeheartedly accepted. However, the Urban Villagers would vigorously oppose any plan that would threaten the integrity of their neighborhoods.

THE PUBLIC HOUSING PEOPLE

The South End has over 2,500 residents living in the area's 886 public hous-

[20] This designation, borrowed from Herbert Gans's book of the same title, is used to signify small pocket neighborhoods that have the pattern of communication and close relationship that Gans records in his study of the West End.
[21] Firey, *op. cit.*, p. 300.
[22] Author's interview with Melvin King, January 6, 1966.

ing units located in two projects, the Cathedral Project in the "hardcore" South End and the Lennox-Camden Project in Lower Roxbury. Both developments have a high percentage of Negro occupancy. The Cathedral Project changed racial composition abruptly between 1950 and 1960 and by 1960 included a large number of multiproblem families among its occupants.

In general, one would not expect the project people to become particularly involved in the renewal game. No matter what renewal did to the people around them, the public housing residents would not be displaced. Thus, the project people lack the impetus to personal involvement generated by concern for one's property or rent level.

NEGROES AND WHITES

Negro-white relationships cut across many other interest groups—Skid Row, the Night People, public housing, the Urban Villagers, and the resident homeowners. The following figures give the quantitative differences between white and Negro populations in the South End in 1964:

POPULATION	White	Nonwhite[23]
1. Population in households	16,397	13,569
2. Families	2,927	2,964
3. Unrelated individuals	9,032	3,431

If one eliminates "unrelated individuals," the number of white and nonwhite families are just about the same. The main difference between the white and Negro population is that whites far outnumber Negroes as tenants of the lodging houses.

While public housing underwent a racial transformation in the 1950's, there was no significant rise in racial friction in the South End. While race would be an important factor in any renewal game, at the moment of urban renewal's entry into the area interest groups other than race per se appeared to be more critical for the form and shape of the local planning team. In making this statement it is important to bear in mind that the time we are speaking of is 1960, not the present. Without question, far greater emphasis would have to be placed upon the racial issue were one evaluating the potential of the South End for urban renewal in 1968.

THE NEWCOMERS

The South End of the early 1960's drew Newcomers of varied financial

23 BRA: South End, "Specifications . . . October 5, 1964," p. 2–1. "Nonwhites" includes an ever-increasing number of Puerto Ricans and Chinese. Thus while "nonwhite" and "Negro" are used synonymously, here they, in fact, are not one and the same category.

status. The poor arrivals were rural Negroes and Puerto Ricans. Both groups suffered from the problems facing low-income in-migrants anywhere—lack of job skills, low income, large families, and few institutions able to integrate them into the neighborhoods in which they settle. (The Puerto Ricans faced the additional barrier of language.) Burdened by problems of day to day survival and having little identification with the affairs of the South End, the Southern Negro and Puerto Rican arrivals could be expected to show little capacity or will to become involved in the rehabilitation planning game.

Better off in terms of income and community ties were the Chinese families who had moved into the South End's Syrian neighborhood after having been dislocated by a highway built through Boston's Chinatown. The Chinese relocatees constituted a self-sufficient group and would become involved in the planning game only if threatened by demolition.

The significant Newcomers for the renewal game were the Urbanites. At the risk of yet another generalization, the Urbanites are young, white, professional, middle- or high-income people who have decided to buy houses in the South End and convert them back to their original single-family use, "not because they have to but because they want to."[24] The typical Urbanite has looked at the mosaic of activity in the South End, filtered out the Night People, Skid Row, and the plight of the old tenants in the upper floors of the rooming houses, and has seen only "a colorful potpourri of ethnic and religious groups . . . which makes the South End a little U.N."[25] The Urbanite sees the city as the frontier and the South End as "a great urban adventure."[26]

At the time that the BRA came on the scene this group constituted a handful of people scattered through two areas in the South End. The emergence of the Urbanites as a real rather than a potential interest occurred during the course of the five-year renewal planning period.

There was no question that the attitude of this group toward Logue's renewal would be highly positive. They viewed "the good city" as ethnically and racially heterogeneous; the extent to which they would promote or accept economic and social heterogeneity was, however, another matter. With their high social rank in terms of occupation, income, and education, their ability to organize for community improvement, their lack of sympathy for garbage, prostitution, and Skid Row, and their pride in and commitment to the positive elements in the South End—the Urban Villagers, the ethnic heterogeneity, the architectural unity—these Newcomers would constitute a key element in any team negotiating for the future of the South End.

24 "The South End Today," op. cit., p. 39.
25 The Boston Globe, April 10, 1964.
26 Ibid.

NONRESIDENTIAL INTEREST GROUPS

INDUSTRY AND INSTITUTIONS

The South End is a center of employment for 17,347 people. A large part of the area is devoted to industry and commerce, and many of the firms are large-scale operations, such as the biggest shoe-manufacturing plant under one roof in the United States.[27]

The vast complex of Boston City Hospital and Boston University Medical Center, a multimillion-dollar operation with significance for the entire metropolitan area, dominates the southeast corner of the district.

Like many other institutions locked into an urban setting, the hospitals and big industry are cramped for space. In their expansion efforts they have chipped away at the streets around them, thereby alienating residents who have seen parking lots, warehouses, and medical facilities replace their neighbors' homes. They have made an enemy of the local state representative who sees his political support ebbing away with each new nonresidential use.

Big industry and the hospitals, while dissimilar in their functions, are similar in the nature of their demands at the bargaining table and in the capacity and resources they could bring to bear on the renewal team. For these big operations renewal could offer space while cleaning up the characteristics of the South End that make it difficult for nurses to live in the area and workers to park near their jobs. While a "cleaning up" would appeal to many South End interests, the demand for space, should it impinge on residential areas, would further exacerbate a long-standing feud.

CHURCHES

The establishment churches that came to the South End during its brief moment of glory were followed by churches catering to the many ethnic groups that poured into the area after 1873. One could probably derive a pattern of ethnic movement through the South End by checking the building dates of the 33 churches that dot the district.[28] Today, as for the last sixty years, the South End has no dominant religious group. That the South End houses the Cathedral of the Holy Cross, the official center of Catholicism in Boston, is ironic as the district is far less a Catholic preserve than other areas in the city. In the South End are Lutherans, Methodists, African Methodist Episcopalians, Syrian Orthodox, Episcopalians, Greek Orthodox, and a number of Negro gospel sects, as well as several storefront churches serving the Spanish-speaking Puerto Rican community.

At the time of renewal's entry into the South End there was little com-

27 BRA: South End, "Specifications . . . October 5, 1964," pp. 1–3.
28 *Ibid.*

munication across this broad religious front. As one local clergyman put it, "The churches in this area have never been united on anything. Everyone has taken care of himself and gone no further."[29] Given the wide range of residential interests represented by the churches, a unified attitude toward renewal might be difficult to promote. Each organization would want to be sure its congregation was not scattered directly or indirectly by rehabilitation, while each would, of course, welcome an increase in parishioners. The great social and theological gap separating activity behind the awesome Gothic doors of the Cathedral of the Holy Cross and the ministrations of the storefront gospel churches, for example, might preclude a united religious front in the renewal game.

THE SOCIAL WELFARE INSTITUTIONS

The City Wilderness is saturated with welfare services. Various estimates put the number at forty, but the addition or deletion of the marginal mission or soup kitchen changes the absolute figure from year to year.

Four substantial missions cater exclusively to the needs of Skid Row. Operating at a more general level of concern are United South End Settlements (USES), Ellis Memorial Settlement House, Morgan Memorial, Salvation Army, South End Boys Club, and Robert Gould Shaw House. While an interagency organization provides the major groups with a forum for communication and joint activity, the task of rigidly defining agency goals has never been successfully completed. The problems in the South End—the lonely and destitute aged, the high school dropouts, the unwed mothers, the poor Newcomers, Skid Row—are so overwhelming that the efforts of the agencies are often scattered, remedial rather than preventive, and overlapping.

These institutions would welcome any program that would bring additional resources to bear on the multitude of problems in the South End. If they felt renewal to be a threat to their organizational integrity and to their clientele, they would fight it or try to rechannel it. Many of the agencies have been operating in the City Wilderness for years with the backing of some of the most influential public-minded citizens in the metropolitan area. Thus these organizations could draw on significant resources once renewal negotiations got under way. Committed to the area and to seeking solutions to the area's problems, the welfare interest group would be a significant player in the neighborhood renewal game.

THE SOUTH END AS COMMUNITY

As should be clear from the preceding description of interest groups, the

[29] Author's interview with Reverend Royden Richardson, January 3, 1966.

South End holds within its boundaries a wide assortment of people with potentially conflicting views as to a desirable end product to the planning game. In ecological terms, the district can be viewed as one in which several incompatible users of urban land are competing for control of the same space. Prior to renewal an equilibrium of sorts had been worked out among Skid Row, the Night People, the tenants, the owners, the poverty Newcomers, the Urbanites, industry and institutions. As the district's relatively consistent 1950–1960 socioeconomic profile suggests, that equilibrium existed for some time. Yet to assume these groups were ultimately content with one another is false. The resident landlords and concerned tenants had waged a half-century struggle against the crime, liquor, decay, and neglect that permeated the district. The battle had become almost a way of life, more a token protest than a concerted effort to wipe out the City Wilderness. And given the role of the South End in Boston's residential pattern, there was little chance of success. As the dumping ground for the aged, the poor, the sick, and the criminal, the South End had problems that were simply overpowering to the rooming house operators, the Urban Villagers, and the "good" tenants (the groups that would answer to the title "South Ender"). But with renewal the balance of power might change.

At the moment of renewal's entry into the district, the South End's composition in class terms was a mixed bag. Skid Row, Night People, and many roomers are clearly what Gans would term "lower class." On the other hand, "South Enders" tend to be solidly "working class" in their attitudes, occupations, and behavior. The Urbanite Newcomers filtering into the community constitute the most obvious representatives of middle-class sensibility and capability.

It would be misleading to suggest that the South End is nothing but a potpourri of competing, uncommunicative interest groups. Interests cut across group lines: there is the resident Negro rooming house operator living in an enclave of working-class Negro homeowners, or the aged Syrian roomer living in the midst of the Syrian community. However, what one must look for are integrative elements in the South End that may bind quite different geographic areas and interests together. These elements create the horizontal integration in the South End.[30]

30 Roland Warren, in *The Community in America* (Chicago: Rand McNally, 1963), pp. 161–162, introduces concepts that deal with the degree of organization, interaction, and interdependence within a community and between that community and its environment. "Horizontal integration" is concerned with "the structural and functional relationship of [the community's] various social units and subsystems to each other." "Vertical integration" deals with "the structural and functional relation of [the community's] various social units and subsystems to extra-community systems." While Warren is talking about community at the level of the town or city, his terminology is applicable to the residential rehabilitation area and provides an analytic tool for considering the nature of that area's

In 1960 the unifying aspects of architecture and history made "The South End" a meaningful phrase to the people living in what has been described as the "core'" of the project area delineated by the BRA for rehabilitation renewal. Beyond history and physical unity, the United South End Settlements stood as the one mechanism for tying together the polyglot district of the project area. Area-wide clubs and fraternal organizations played little part in the life of the South End. The organizations that did exist catered to ethnic interests. But USES saw the entire district, its businessmen, institutions, and residents, as the organization's responsibility. South End House, founded by Robert Woods in 1891, has been ideologically committed to viewing the South End as one community.[31] Its union in 1960 with four other settlement houses within the boundaries of the City Wilderness provided a firmer geographic base from which "to encourage, teach, organize for mutual support . . . and in every way work from within the community for its social development."[32]

Woods began by organizing several blocks into associations. He united them in 1907 with an area-wide South End Planning Council, which for fifty years

carried on its activities through committees for health and sanitation, liquor control, housing and recreation. Membership on these committees was drawn from the churches, schools, social services, and neighborhood associations which sent the delegates to the Council.[33]

Despite the addition to the council's framework in 1950 of Interagency, an association of social service professionals working in the area and of the South End Businessmen's Association, a USES worker recently wrote

A decade ago there was only a moribund district-wide Council which has existed in one form or another since 1907. There were struggling neighborhood improvement associations and few experienced local leaders. There was apathy, frustration, and discouragement about accomplishing anything through City Hall.[34]

While the community organization system supported by USES was fragile at best, it was nonetheless a potentially significant mechanism for linking various interest groups and providing one of the few forums in a district devoid of formal organizations.

---

internal dynamics as well as its relationship to the larger urban community of which it is a part.

[31] To Woods the neighborhood was the proper unit of social community. See Robert Woods, *The Neighborhood in Nation Building* (Cambridge: Houghton Mifflin, 1923).

[32] United South End Settlements, "United South End Settlements: The Story and the Scope," Spring 1965, p. 2.

[33] William Loring, Frank Sweetser, and Frank Ernst, *Community Organization for Citizen Participation in Urban Renewal*, prepared by the Housing Association of Metropolitan Boston for the Massachusetts Department of Commerce (Cambridge, Mass.: Cambridge Press, 1957), p. 63.

[34] Charles Fraggos, "A Settlement's Role in Community Development: A Decade of Experience," paper presented at the National Conference on Social Welfare, Atlantic City, May 26, 1965.

The network of organizations staffed and supported by USES, the South End Businessmen's Association, Interagency, and the Planning Council provided a focal point for those who wanted to "do something" about the district, to build on its strengths and deal with its problems. For those relatively few involved in the neighborhood associations, the Planning Council represented a way of life, a source of prestige, and a means of communicating with like-minded people.

The Planning Council cut across interest groups. It was composed primarily but not exclusively of property owners, the "oldtime South Enders": Urban Villagers and resident lodging house owners, black and white. There were also a number of "good" tenants. In fact, only Gans's lower class was unrepresented on the Council. Many members themselves knew or had known poverty and tolerated the problems of the poor and the elderly. All Council members, whatever their differences, were united against the area's liquor and vice—the two interest groups that had, for over a half-century, provided a rallying point for those few people with the capacity and the desire to revitalize the South End.

While USES provided a framework for horizontal integration, there seemed to be few vertical ties operating between the South End and the society around it; for, despite the efforts of the social welfare agencies and the residents within the South End Planning Council, the liquor licenses remained, as did the Night People, the shoddy public services, the dilapidated buildings, and the general environment of a City Wilderness.

In theory, political process provides linkage into the community outside the district's boundaries. Yet beyond the figures that indicate, not surprisingly, a relatively low degree of political participation by South End residents lies the fact that the district is cut off from power at both the city and state level. Boston's at-large Council representation ensures that the more populous districts of West Roxbury, Dorchester, and South Boston will dominate the council. In fact, "no single major political figure appears to be a resident of the South End."[35]

At the state level the isolation of the district is even more inevitable, for the district is cut into five wards, each of which has the weight of its political base well outside the South End. Thus, no one representative has concern for even a large piece of the area. In 1960 the district was spread among four senators and eight representatives in the State House. The result of this diffusion of responsibility has historically been one in which the district is simply bypassed in the distribution of parks, playgrounds, city services, and other goods and services that politicians provide for their voters. The insig-

35 USES, George D. Blackwood, "Politics and the South End," February 26, 1959, p. 1.

nificance of the South End as a power base meant that few in the area had had any experience with formal politics or politicians. Indeed, perhaps the only significant linkage to the larger city and metropolitan system was provided by the prestigious boards of the social service and hospital complex, Morgan Memorial, and USES.

THE SOUTH END AS A PATTERN OF POWER

Power, the capacity to articulate approval or disapproval in the renewal planning game, would appear to have been a rare commodity in the South End of 1960. All statistical indices point to a low capability to mobilize for participation on the residential rehabilitation team. Moreover, a careful look at different interest groups indicates that the numerical majority of the residents in the South End—the roomers, the Night People, and Skid Row—were in all probability unwilling or unable to participate personally in the game. The Urban Villagers, representing tenants and homeowners, the resident lodging house operators, speaking for themselves and their tenants, the Urbanite Newcomers, the social service agencies, the hospitals, and big industry were the groups most likely to jockey for the right to negotiate with the BRA.

Community-wide leaders in the South End were few in number, and there was, in fact, little vying for position. More often than not, USES had to impose leadership functions on reluctant residents. As a homeowner said, "In 1960 this place was a power vacuum. The real question was not whether people would fight over who would run things but whether or not you could put together enough leadership from enough different places to put a plan through."[36]

A 1960 diagram of power distribution in the South End would show a geographically scattered pattern, with the South End Planning Council the one shaky linkage between the pieces and USES the one organization viewing the South End in unitary terms.

Despite local efforts, the City Wilderness of Woods's day was still a pronounced reality in 1960—5 percent of the population of Boston with 95 percent of the city's problems. When the South End stood on the brink of renewal, it was a neighborhood more by definition of history, geography, architecture, and the effort of USES, than because of any inherent unity of interest. The history of the renewal planning game in the South End became essentially a story of mobilizing these few pockets of power that existed, reconciling their divergent interests, and overcoming their mutual suspicions to weld the City Wilderness into a unit capable of planning for its own future and willing to support a renewal plan.

36 Author's interview with Royal Cloyd.

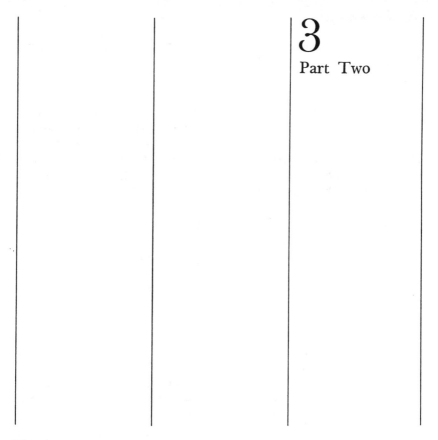

3

Part Two

The Advent of Renewal:
Origins of the Rehabilitation Planning Team

Given the state of organization and leadership in the South End, it was understandable that the first murmurs of urban renewal would come from the USES-staffed Planning Council. From the moment word filtered from City Hall that a massive renewal plan would be part of the Collins administration, the South End Planning Council (SEPC), led by USES began preparations for the challenge. As early as January 1961, a meeting was held to discuss the way to set up an urban renewal committee. The extent of USES domination of the Planning Council at this point is seen in the fact that five of the six people at the discussion were employees of USES, the sixth being the president of the SEPC.[37]

The BRA's progress was slow, and not until late 1960, when Logue and Collins made their dramatic proposal for "The 90 Million Dollar Develop-

[37] Urban Renewal Committee of the South End Planning Council, Minutes, January 12, 1960.

ment Program for Boston," did some form of renewal for the South End become more than an idea.

Logue spoke in the South End twice before his appointment, and, not surprisingly, his main point of contact in the area was with USES and its director Charles Liddell. Logue's view of USES as the one institution in the South End capable of rallying the district to involvement in renewal, plus his friendship with Liddell, made it inevitable that when a committee was formed for citizen participation in the South End, USES became its guiding force. ABCD formally recognized USES' position by making Charles Fraggos, head of the USES community organization staff, "ABCD District Community Co-ordinator."

Formed in mid-1961, the South End Urban Renewal Committee represented something of a cross section of the nonproblem South End interest groups. Royal Cloyd, a resident homeowner, took on the task of committee chairman after much urging from USES. One of the earliest Urbanites, Cloyd was also one of the most articulate. Liddell was one of ten members of the USES-dominated committee. Ex-officio were Charles Fraggos and Russell Traunstein, the BRA project director with a social work background and prior experience in urban renewal in New York.

Starting in September 1961, this twelve-man South End Urban Renewal Committee met weekly for four months. The period was a time of far-ranging and ambitious thought as to what renewal might mean for the South End. "Guidelines," "goals," "framework for analysis," and many other concepts dear to planners' hearts were much discussed.

The chairman's concern for a broad view was expressed when he proposed that members of the Committee read as background material for the discussions Lewis Mumford's *The City in History* and Jane Jacobs' *The Death and Life of Great American Cities.* Charles Liddell made clear from the first meeting the extent to which he felt social and physical planning must go hand in hand if there was to be real improvement in the quality of life in the South End for the people currently living there. Liddell was also a moving force behind the idea of expanding the Committee to a broader-based organization, saying, "Whatever decision might be made it should involve participation of all the people in the South End."[38]

In late October 1961, Russell Traunstein drew up a lengthy statement that summarized in detail the fundamental issues with which his staff and the South End Urban Renewal Committee were dealing. In the report he declared the capacity of the Committee to speak for everyone in the South End by characterizing it as

[38] South End Urban Renewal Committee, Minutes, September 25, 1961.

an articulate, representative, and authoritative group drawn from the residential, institutional, business, and professional community. It speaks directly and knowingly for the concerns of practically all South End interests.[39]

While the Committee did not as of yet speak for all South End interests, the list of concerns that evolved from its deliberations as reported by Traunstein took into consideration a broad spectrum of South End groups.

> The concentration of taverns and liquor licenses is too great . . . a community center complex is needed . . . a great deal of new and rehabilitated housing is required for the elderly . . . facilities must be provided for homeless men. . . . There should be a cross-section of socioeconomic levels in the community. . . . It is recognized that some of the traditional social problems will most probably remain, and should be realistically considered in the planning process. . . . Vice and criminal activities must be eliminated.[40]

As social workers, Traunstein and Liddell saw that solutions to the South End's problems required more than physical change. Moreover, they were ideologically committed to including in the Urban Renewal Committee as many interest groups as possible. Only the Night People were ruled out. The future of Skid Row and of the elderly tenants was still open to solution within the South End, and answers were expected from the combined efforts of the BRA, ABCD, and USES.

In 1961 hard decisions on particular issues did not have to be taken in the South End, and there was great optimism as to the capacity of all local groups to benefit from the renewal process. As one member of the Committee stated, "It was a good-humored year. Everything seemed far away. No one was under attack, and all things seemed possible.[41] At the end of 1961 the path of renewal's entry into the South End—through the small USES-supported Urban Renewal Committee—was broadened to make for a larger and, it was hoped, more inclusive organization.

A neighborhood team was formed which translated the social and physical planning tandem into organizational terms. To the original Committee were added representatives of the neighborhood associations, the South End Businessmen's Association, SENRAC (the South End Neighborhood Renewal Action Committee), an organization representing South End institutions, and Interagency. This expanded organization was broken up into two subcommittees, one on physical and one on social planning. With the formation of a forty-member Committee, the South End Urban Renewal Committee became the legitimatized renewal bargaining agent for the district.

---

[39] "South End Project–Project Director Planning Statement," mimeograph, October 27, 1961, p. 3.
[40] *Ibid.*, p. 5.
[41] Author's interview with Royal Cloyd.

THE SOUTH END TEAM PLANS FOR RENEWAL:
ROUND ONE

The expanded URC (Urban Renewal Committee), as convened in December 1961, was made up of 5 businessmen, 5 professionals, 5 people from South End institutions, and 23 residents. All of the formal organizations in the district concerned with the South End as a place in which to live, work, and do business were represented. Royal Cloyd, after explaining to the group its origin and what was expected of it, went on to say:

> We do not represent all of the interested people in the South End, but we have taken advantage of what we have and hope to expand to include those not represented but who should be. . . . At the moment there is no plan for the South End. . . . In our planning for the South End we would not want to see it as one vast social agency or a bright new place which was not more than a museum.[42]

Cloyd announced that the first job of the Committee was to see that existing and newly created neighborhood associations held two meetings, one on social and one on physical planning goals for their neighborhoods. The desire to include all of the South End in sampling opinion on renewal goals meant that association boundaries were expanded to take up the no man's land that existed between organizations. Thus the meetings held in the winter of 1962 broadened the base of involvement and were the first step in establishing neighborhood associations as a significant component in the South End renewal team.

The results of the thirty meetings—two in each of fifteen areas—provided a geographically well-distributed sample of opinion. However, the 434 people who went to the meeting on social planning and the 297 answering the physical questionnaire did not represent a cross section of South End interest groups.[43] For example, in the physical questionnaire 65 percent of the 267 people who answered the question, "Do you own your own building?" replied in the affirmative, yet in 1960, only 9.1 percent of the total occupied dwelling units in the South End were owner-occupied. Even allowing for the duplication of husband and wife in answering, the overrepresentativeness of homeowners is apparent. The response to the ownership question gives good indication of what USES, the URC, and anyone concerned with the South End felt intuitively—that property-owning families had a disproportionate capacity and willingness to become involved in the renewal process.

The answers to the two questionnaires, while not representative of all South End interests and skewed toward homeowning families, nonetheless present a clear picture of contrasting opinion on many issues basic to the form that renewal should take in the South End. Along with many suspi-

---

42 South End URC, Minutes, December 11, 1961.
43 South End URC, Results of Questionnaire, Winter 1962, Appendix, p. 3.

cious comments about the aims of the BRA and the City the following points of view emerged:[44]

1. On who should live in the South End

Some felt that professional, middle income, and younger people should be encouraged to come into the area. . . . Others thought planning should encompass present residents only.

2. On public housing

Low cost rental housing was considered the most important need . . . public housing was approved by some . . . [yet] some disapproved of public housing.

3. On rooming houses

Some worry was expressed that modernizing buildings in the South End would . . . drive out present tenants . . . [yet some felt] a reduction in the number of rooming house singles and the concentration of rooming houses in one section were desirable.

4. On Skid Row

While there was general agreement that there were too many liquor stores in the South End (371 out of 386 said there were liquor stores in their neighborhood),

Many said "get rid of the winos," but a number had suggestions for treatment and rehabilitation of these men. . . . A few felt that the problem of skid row could not be dispersed and there is no hope of completely removing "derelicts" from the South End.

The results of the neighborhood questionnaires highlighted the diversity of opinion on the critical issues of renewal even among those representing a highly biased sample of the South End's interest groups. Thus, the need was apparent to find a mechanism for negotiating differences within the interest groups in the South End if a united front were to be presented to the local BRA team.

Throughout the winter of 1962, the URC and its Physical and Social Planning Committees gathered monthly with Traunstein and his staff. Given its quantity and quality in the URC, leadership was spread too thinly in too complex a system when Physical, Social, Steering Committee, and plenary gatherings occurred each month. Moreover, the difficulty of determining the distinction between social and physical planning problems hampered the work of the committees, and much time went into defining areas of responsibility.

Whatever its structural weakness and reluctance to make specific decisions in the winter of 1962, the URC existed as a potentially strong mechanism linking the weakly joined components of the South End social system. The demands of the renewal planning game were forcing life into the limping neighborhood associations and the URC was recognized throughout the city as the formal South End renewal team. As *The Boston Globe* recorded,

44 *Ibid.,* pp. 2, 4–5, 11.

"Emerging from the dismal picture is a grass-roots union of citizens with potentially strong leadership, a community wide representation."[45]

It is a significant comment on local politics in the South End that throughout this planning period no one protested the right of the URC to speak as the renewal negotiating team for the district. Yet there is no question that at this stage in the South End's renewal history, despite the questionnaires, only a small percentage of the local population had the vaguest idea of what renewal was all about.

And, indeed, it would be difficult to call the interaction in 1962 between Traunstein's South End BRA team and the URC headed by Cloyd and backed up by Liddell and the USES staff, a bargaining process in which team lines were firmly drawn or issues clearly established. Traunstein urged the URC to take the initiative, but the URC was reluctant to do so. Liddell was prodding the Committee to come up with a clear operational statement of social and physical goals for the South End against which specific proposals could be measured. However, reaction to events in the community, plus the problem of role definition in an overstructured organization, kept the group from being a hard bargainer.

THE FIRST SOUTH END PLAN:
THE COMMON WAY OR "GREEN STRIP"
While the URC was groping for a modus vivendi, the BRA team was going ahead with studies of the South End and coming to its own conclusions as to the needs of the district.

The BRA planners had recognized from the start that the South End was not a single community. Their solution was to posit two South Ends, one represented by families and those with whom families could be compatible and the other made up of Skid Row and poverty-stricken elderly tenants. While these two categories have a much finer breakdown, the critical decision for the BRA was their conclusion that both major groups could be planned for. The BRA had initially assumed that these two communities separated themselves geographically within the South End, but a quick survey demonstrated there was no such division. The planners had originally hoped to divide physically the "problem" South End from the "family" South End, while drawing both South Ends together around a band of community facilities to be located along a line through the center of the area. This proved impossible: the physical community could not be restructured to deal with the social needs and locational requirements of these two major interest groups in the area.

45 *The Boston Globe*, June 4, 1962.

The inability to meet social needs by bending physical components posed a classic dilemma. Some of the planners felt the only solution was to slow down designs for the South End until the problem of Skid Row could be solved by means other than simply locating it elsewhere in Boston or beyond the city limits. But Logue, who had made the South End a high priority area in 1960, had no wish to delay: "Some social planners say clear up the problem [the alcoholic] first before you do anything else. I say the hell with them."[46] As usual, Logue's position carried the day, and plans for the South End forged ahead. The dual community reflected in the original BRA thinking was replaced by focusing on the multiplicity of groups that used the area, with no reference to Skid Row or the Night People. While negotiations for renewal would continue to produce bartering over the relative weight of the impoverished elderly and migrants, there never again would be discussion of physically structuring a part of the South End to serve the area's "problem people."

Grinding inexorably onward, the BRA schedule called for a preliminary sketch plan in the fall of 1962. The plan, according to Traunstein, would incorporate the ideas presented by the original ten-man URC, the efforts of the expanded forty-man group, the expression of feeling by residents in the physical and social questionnaires, and the opinions articulated at a BRA hearing held in April 1962. The sketch plans, however, showed the usual three clearance percentages (15, 20, and 30 percent) and were the result of not much more than a month's whirlwind activity by an urban designer from South Africa who had been assigned to the South End team in September 1962 specifically for the purpose of drawing up a renewal sketch.

As anyone in the BRA is now quick to say, the designer had little personal knowledge of the South End as a social, political, or physical entity. That he didn't understand it socially and politically is indicated by the fact that he proposed a swath of clearance through the heart of the Syrian community. That he didn't understand it physically is clear from a tour he and Logue took of the South End, during which Logue asked him why he had made certain proposals. At several points the designer had to admit he hadn't realized buildings, in one case a multistory industrial structure, existed on particular locations.

The proposal was oriented around a common way or "green strip" as it came to be known, which ran the length of the South End. The function of the common way was to provide a spine of activity which would pull together the two halves of the South End and focus activity around a highly central, highly visible axis. In the center of the project area across from the "green strip," was to be the heart of new South End—a cluster of community and commercial facilities and new housing.

The area below Massachusetts Avenue, much of which was vacant land or spotted with remnants of former row housing, was to be almost entirely redeveloped, with an input of 2,500 units of public and elderly housing around the existing Lennox-Camden project.

The core of the South End residential community was to be rehabilitated and new schools, shopping and community facilities, and a circulation pattern that would radically reduce the amount of through traffic in the area were to be built. The core, it might be argued, was buffered by Massachusetts Avenue from the massive low-income public housing community. As one planner who had worked on the design said, "You could maintain, if pushed, that the sketch plan was a highly stylized and architectural solution to the problem of the South End as two communities."[47]

THE COMMUNITY REACTS TO THE
FIRST SOUTH END PLAN

The current view of both BRA staff and members of the South End community is that the common way plan, while imaginative and physically enticing, reflected little of what was discussed by the BRA, the URC, and the individual residents. The sketches were hastily drawn to meet the BRA schedule, which demanded a plan be circulated in the South End by the winter of 1962. Many members of the South End staff felt not only that the design was an unsuitable solution for the complex area, but also that the patterns of clearance to make room for the common way were bound to cause dissent. Nevertheless, Logue accepted the plan and, thus, cleared it for showing to the South End as a preliminary sketch proposal.

Now the question was what to do with the plan. And here the whole process by which it would be negotiated in the community came into question. Both the BRA and the articulate, concerned residents accepted the URC as the South End's official negotiating team, but exactly what the URC was supposed to do with the plan that it was handed in December 1962, was uncertain. Some maintained that the URC Steering Committee should "spend a few weeks looking into it to understand it, and then bring it to the whole Urban Renewal Committee to get their ideas."[48] Others felt that the proposal should go immediately to the neighborhood associations for their review. As one member stated, "People feel badly because of the lack of up-to-date information from ones in the know."[49]

47 Author's interview with Richard Bolan, January 7, 1966.
48 South End URC: Steering Committee, Minutes, September 11, 1962.
49 South End URC, Minutes, November 19, 1962.

After much discussion, the URC voted, with five dissenting, that the proposal be sent to the local organizations. Thus, the first BRA South End plan moved from the URC with no form of commitment from that body.[50] Throughout the lengthy debate on procedure, Traunstein continually stressed that the BRA would do nothing contrary to the wishes of the URC and that the sketch plan was "just a proposal" that could be changed.[51] But exactly how might it be changed? Would the neighborhood associations or the URC have the final say? In other words, what was the formal structure of the local renewal team? The confusion and disagreement at this stage of negotiation were as much over the lack of clarity in the structure of the planning game as over the substantive elements in the plan itself.

With the arrival of the sketches and the decision to present the 30 percent clearance map to the neighborhood associations for comment and correction, the BRA's area of negotiation was considerably broadened. As long as discussion remained within the confines of the URC, as it had during 1961 and 1962, the process of debating renewal in the South End was orderly. The URC members might complain that they didn't have enough facts to make judgments on issues such as public housing and demolition, and the BRA might express impatience with the committee's decision-making process; but, in general, cautious good will prevailed on both sides. With the release of the sketch plan to the neighborhoods, the BRA got a taste of the feelings that could be aroused in the South End. At several of the neighborhood associations, reaction was loud and violent. People who had never been to a neighborhood gathering before, who had never even heard of urban renewal, much less the URC, suddenly appeared. While the BRA, USES, and URC representatives tried, usually in vain, to clarify their different roles in the planning process, the well-structured meetings of the URC gave way to free-swinging sessions with a wide representation of South End interest groups. Yet not all response was negative, and many neighborhood meetings went through the process of examining the sketch and awaiting further information in the form of blownup maps of their own particular areas.

REAPPRAISAL

The spring of 1963 was a critical time for the BRA, USES, and the URC. Each sought to clarify its role vis-à-vis the others. Memoranda circulated within and among the organizations in an effort to figure out what was wrong and how it could be corrected.

In retrospect, several things seem to have been out of joint. The URC had

50 *Ibid.*, December 17, 1962.
51 *Ibid.*

been structured to give widespread South End representation, but throughout 1961–1962 there was little flow of information downward from the Committee to the neighborhood level. Good horizontal communication existed among leaders, most of whom had known each other from long years of work with the South End Planning Council; but the rest of the South End went its own disjointed way. Beyond filling in two questionnaires, the Urban Villagers, the old tenants, and the resident property owners who were not intimately involved with the URC either had not sought or had not been provided with much access to renewal negotiations. For them to be confronted suddenly with a sketch plan was a disturbing experience. As one resident stated, "When they came down here with that plan we had no idea what was going on. It was only after the shock of that thing that we figured we had better find out what renewal was all about."[52]

In addition to this communications gap were the objections to the sketch itself. Some saw the common way as just one more place for drunks to sprawl. Others maintained that, despite all talk of its unifying function, the common way was actually a subtle device for dividing the South End into two different socioeconomic communities. Many argued that the circulation plan's dead-end streets and angled bypasses were impractical and simply isolated one section of the South End from another. The volume of public housing poured into Lower Roxbury concerned those who contended that while facilities for low-income residents were vital, they should not all be located in one corner of the project area.

Furthermore, internal disagreement within the BRA resulted in the sketch being frequently altered. From the moment the plan was released, Logue began to tinker with it. Indeed, the sketch was rarely the same from one meeting to the next. Buildings appeared and disappeared in the sketch, and such maneuvering merely reinforced local suspicions about City Hall's intentions in the South End.

Further troubles arose from the way in which the BRA South End team was interacting with local residents in the spring of 1963. There was never any question that Traunstein, the BRA project director, was sincerely interested in producing a plan that would benefit as many groups in the South End as possible. He had written off the Night People early in the game, but as a social worker he was deeply concerned that all the other groups in the area benefit from renewal. Yet because he was not a physical planner it was difficult for him to express a professional opinion on the sketch plan. He hoped that with prolonged negotiation the "bugs" in the proposal could be ironed out, but eventually he became co-opted by a plan that he felt in no position to criticize.

While the URC had genuine trust and regard for Traunstein, they were uneasy about his staff planners who were making the rounds of the neighborhood associations to present the sketch plan. While several of the team came across as sincere and straightforward, others were middle-class professionals with all the liabilities that a style of cold, dry rationality would pose in a community not geared to such an approach. Often criticism of the plan at neighborhood meetings would be met by a defensive remark on the part of the planner. Frequently, the process of explaining emerged more as one of hard sell. And while there was continued insistence that "this is just a proposal," recommendations for change were often answered with technical reasons why things had to be the way they were shown in the sketch. Ironically, several of the BRA staff dutifully explaining the plan were themselves less than convinced of its wisdom.

Another problem with the Traunstein team's "style" was posed by a site office in the South End. While the bulk of the district staff was located in City Hall, a small group of "rehabilitation experts" were already in the area to provide owners interested in property rehabilitation with information about loans and technical advice on remodeling and construction. With their often conflicting advice and the office's air of uncertainty, the impression created by this small group was a negative one. Its members were viewed by some as incompetent, by others as lazy and even dishonest. The team's activities resulted in a black eye for the BRA, and one of Traunstein's major problems became how to overcome the image conveyed by his rehabilitation staff.

While the BRA struggled with its problems, USES, the bulwark of community organization in the South End, found itself caught in a cross fire between local citizens and the BRA. Some residents identified the settlement house staff entirely with the BRA; others felt the social workers were "gadflies—who do nothing but take notes and talk";[53] still others saw USES as just another interest trying to get a piece of the South End's renewal action. Meanwhile, the BRA felt that "USES kept pulling the rug out from under us at neighborhood meetings,"[54] and USES felt that the BRA was not clear on the settlement's role in the renewal proceedings. As one USES memo put it: "Some [BRA staff] seem incapable of understanding our role at all, others feel that we have a responsibility to sell BRA's line . . . this seems to

---

[53] USES, Interoffice Memorandum, "Still Another Point of View," April 26, 1963, p. 1.
[54] Author's interview, February 3, 1966. (The source wishes to remain anonymous.)

be the majority."[55] In planning game terms, players whose roles were clear were not sure which team USES was on—that of the URC and the neighborhood or that of Traunstein and the BRA.

The role of ABCD throughout this period of readjustment was equally hazy. Logue saw ABCD as the social arm of his renewal effort and, thus, as basically subservient to him and his projects. However, the newly formed ABCD quickly adopted organizational goals of getting out from under Logue's control and of not limiting its innovative activity solely to renewal areas. This conflict had repercussions in the planning games in all three areas under study. Liddell and Traunstein had great hopes for ABCD's capacity to match physical plans with social programs. With the gradual estrangement of ABCD from the renewal process, those hopes for quick action died.

As the sketch plan made the rounds of the neighborhood associations there were indications that some of the SEPC leadership was growing impatient with the URC. For example, several old-time SEPC members met with staff people from USES to discuss the fact that the "reputation of the SEPC was being jeopardized and its usefulness endangered by its complete submersion in the Urban Renewal Process."[56] This meeting, one of several, was symbolic of a growing disenchantment with the URC as the community mechanism with which to play the residential renewal game. Yet the people at these gatherings were not rival groups or newcomers trying to get on the renewal team but were themselves part of the leadership group involved in URC from the start. What was being sought was a restructuring of organization and command within the limits of the existing team in an effort to meet the demands of the planning game.

The toppling of the URC chairman was the result of these efforts to produce a more satisfactory approach to renewal negotiations. Royal Cloyd, the leader of the growing number of Urbanites, was replaced by George Farrah, South End born and bred. Farrah, who worked in the traffic department office at City Hall, was a young, articulate spokesman for the old-time South Enders, and especially for the Syrian Urban Villagers. With his City Hall connections, his roots in the South End, and his organizational and leadership capabilities, Farrah, it was felt, would be able to work effectively with many South End interest groups.

On the BRA side of the ledger disenchantment with the course of events in the planning game resulted in a similar shakeup; a few weeks prior to the reshuffling of the URC, Traunstein was removed from the South End project and replaced by Dick Green. This step was the result of a complex

55 USES, Interoffice Memorandum, "Still Another Point of View," *op. cit.*
56 USES, Interoffice Memorandum, May 1963.

interplay of forces. Behind the scenes, in a shadow image of the struggle going on in the URC, was a jockeying for position among USES, ABCD, and the BRA. The basic issue was the question of who was going to call the shots in the South End urban renewal project. USES increasingly felt that Traunstein was pulling away from them, that he was being co-opted by his own plan, and that the social-planning aspect of renewal, the job of ABCD, was being ignored. Several stormy meetings among Liddell, Traunstein, and ABCD personnel, centering on the "who does what in the South End" theme, resulted in a split between USES and Traunstein which, along with the bogging down of the plan, made the BRA project director's usefulness in the South End problematic. Whatever the relative significance of events and relationships, Logue felt a radical adjustment was necessary. Bringing in Dick Green was that kind of adjustment.

Dick Green was a city planner who had had an impressive career at the BRA while dealing with citizens' groups in the Boston neighborhoods of Charlestown and Dorchester. A former associate describes Green as "a person with momentum and enthusiasm. People go along with him because they say 'the guy has worked so hard there must be something to what he says.' "[57]

Green's professional status put him on equal footing with the city planners on the BRA staff. Furthermore, he had a reputation for holding little stock in the view that the planner alone should make judgments about land use. When he agreed to Logue's request that he go to the South End, he made two stipulations: that he be able to hire his own staff and that he have free rein to change the first plan as he saw fit. Logue agreed to both points. Although Green had the sanction to alter the proposal, he spent much of his time during his first months as project director in the South End trying to convince the designers and planners in the BRA central office that in fact the first plan should be dropped. Design and comprehensive planning concepts were popular with the BRA during this period, especially in the central office, which was totally isolated from the political and social realities of the individual project areas. Thus, Green's debut in the South End was spent fighting to be accepted in a suspicious and uncertain community while struggling to get rid of the original sketch plan.

As we have noted, Logue intervenes at the local level only when crises are in the wind. The spring of 1963 was such a time in the South End, and the Development Administrator was heavily involved in the area during that period of transition. In June 1963, just after Green was brought in and when it was apparent that Farrah would soon replace Cloyd, Logue met with the URC to discuss the rumblings in and between the South End and BRA teams.

Logue started off by saying that if anything of significance was to be done in the South End, it would depend on two public events, the BRA South End hearing and the City Council hearing. Characterizing the renewal process as "the most political event that can ever take place in the South End,"[58] he questioned how representative of the South End as a whole an observer would consider the URC. Yet when asked to define his yardstick for local involvement, Logue replied he felt "comfortable that the Urban Renewal Committee represented everybody it needs to represent so that we can say that what it approves is the right thing to do for the people in the South End."[59] "Everybody it needs to represent" was not spelled out. However, with its emphasis on elections and the significance of the BRA public hearing, the orientation of Logue's presentation was clear, and "needs to represent" can be interpreted here as that representation necessary to overcome the hurdles of the public hearing and the potential opposition of South End residents. Logue's ears were still ringing from the Charlestown hearing of January 1963, when his system for ensuring the neutralization of opposition broke down completely. He wanted to be certain he wasn't courting the same thing in the South End.

Logue went on to put the South End squabble in a larger political context:

We are electing a new mayor who will preside over a New Boston . . . we will find a ready audience to complaints in people running for mayor. There is a good negative fight especially in the hearts of everyone in this room.[60]

Only when he was sure that "negative fight" had been eliminated would Logue consider taking a South End plan to a public hearing of any kind. As the minutes of the meeting point out, Logue emphasized that there is

no rule book in planning with people. We [the BRA] are not interested in dealing with an Urban Renewal Committee that is not prepared to be responsible. When the revised plan is presented to this group it will only be with the understanding that we will study it, comment on it, and put it together and tell Mr. Logue we are ready to go to the neighborhood associations of the South End.[61]

The session with Logue constituted a critical juncture in the South End renewal planning game. The Development Administrator reaffirmed his willingness to give the URC the planning mandate for the South End. Moreover, his emphasis on the condition that he would not move a revised plan into the neighborhoods without the URC's approval placed even more reliance on that group as the mechanism through which renewal decisions would flow. The significance of this decision is heightened if one recalls that

58 South End URC, Minutes, June 17, 1963.
59 *Ibid.*
60 *Ibid.*
61 *Ibid.*

the flare-ups throughout the winter of 1963 assured Logue that the URC was not representative of all South End interests. But what were the alternatives? As one observer noted, "Logue had to make a decision as to whether or not he could go with the URC and have them produce. He decided that there was nowhere else or no one else to go to in the South End."[62]

Because of the paucity of leadership in the South End, the URC was the only possible choice. People were not struggling to wrest power from the URC or to get within its ranks. It was members of the URC itself who had threatened to find another forum within which to debate renewal when they felt that the URC was not providing them with that opportunity. With the shake-up of URC leadership, the dissidents could return to the fold. With a reshuffling of project staff, there was no longer an obvious BRA commitment to the sketch plan. By the summer of 1963, both teams had restructured to once again enter the lists to hammer out a plan for the South End.

The renewal game was still intact. Neither side had been alienated from the structure of the game or from the nature of the game itself. Royal Cloyd did not lead any splinter group away from the South End team but stayed on as an important member of the URC. The survival of the structure of the game at the expense of leaders on either side gave a certain venerability to the South End renewal game which it never lost thereafter.

To people looking back on it, the first plan for the South End had been "widely opposed"[63] and "condemned" by the URC, with the result that "Mr. Logue threw it out."[64] It was convenient two years later to think in such violent terms; a new plan had been devised, and it gave South Enders a sense of power to point out that they had knocked the BRA back on its heels during the first round of the planning game. There were those who would maintain that the first plan could have been gotten through the neighborhood associations without a political revolt, but that the mutterings in the South End as a result of the effort to explain the sketch made Logue decide that discretion was the better part of valor. Thus in the summer of 1963 the first round of the South End neighborhood renewal game came to a close with both teams regrouped for a second effort.

THE SOUTH END TEAM PLANS FOR RENEWAL:
ROUND TWO
In September 1963, Green sent a memo to his staff in which he made the following points:

---

62 Author's interview with Royal Cloyd.
63 *New South End*, Vol. I, No. 3 (November 1965).
64 BRA: South End, "South End Urban Renewal Area before the Boston Redevelopment Authority," Mimeographed Transcript, August 23, 1965, p. 137.

It is impossible to do urban renewal planning without community support, and this in turn implies that we must recognize the needs of the community as it exists in order to gain support. . . . *The South End, as we are all aware, is a series of neighborhoods, all of which are different.* I think that it is important that we all recognize that the South End is an exceedingly complex community.[65]

The key to Green's success lay in his recognition of this complexity. He structured his approach to renewal to deal with the fact that there were many communal South End interests and that the mechanism for arbitrating among these different interests could be found in the neighborhood associations as well as in the URC.

Clearly, Green was broadening the base of negotiations while working within the existing renewal framework. At a URC meeting in September 1963, it was reported that "Mr. Green is now walking through the different neighborhoods to see for himself and to get the different reactions of the people."[66] Essentially this procedure, which came to be known as "walking the neighborhoods," was one in which the local organization would round up its stalwart members and set out with Green's staff to point out the strengths and weaknesses of the territory encompassed by their neighborhood association. The neighbors and the BRA team would go up and down the streets until it was felt the BRA had, as Green put it, "an on-the-spot feel of the neighborhood"[67] and knowledge of specific physical changes desired by local residents. Although there were URC charges that Green was "dividing the community in order to conquer it"[68] by negotiating with individual associations, he was giving people who had no idea what renewal was about and who had reacted violently to their lack of knowledge a sense of participation. Green thus made the neighborhood associations the basis of local team structure in the second round of negotiations.

The first BRA team had been baffled by the problem of devising a physical solution that would take into account the multiplicity of South End interest groups. The original plan treated the South End as a unitary whole, bypassing the issue of plural interests completely. Green's decision to use the neighborhood associations as the basis on which to build enough community support for the public hearing meant diverse interests were represented in the renewal game. For while it is quite true that neither all the lodging house owners nor all the Urbanites, for example, are clustered in one association, the paucity of leadership at the neighborhood level means that one or two dynamic, like-minded people probably will dominate the local organization. As a consequence, particularized interests are championed by individual neighborhood groups at both the local and URC level.

[65] BRA: South End, "Staff Memorandum No. 1," September 16, 1963.
[66] South End URC, Minutes, September 23, 1963.
[67] *Ibid.*
[68] Author's interview, January 5, 1966. (The source wishes to remain anonymous.)

While the sixteen neighborhood associations were vital to the second round of planning,[69] with few exceptions their official and unofficial membership during the planning period constituted a small percent of the adult population in the neighborhoods they represented. (See Figure 3.2.) By a most generous estimate, at one time or another during the four-year planning period 10 percent of the adults in the South End, about 2,500 people, had been to a neighborhood meeting of some kind. Perhaps 300 people were involved to the extent that they could be counted on to attend monthly meetings and to have significant knowledge of what was transpiring in the renewal planning process. About 90 percent of those 300 were resident property owners: Urbanites, rooming house operators, and Urban Villagers. Moreover, these 300 people were not spread equally among the associations. Where Worcester Square could get together 100 members for an important meeting on renewal, Six Points's membership was one conscientious and devoted South End resident. The crowds that had attended meetings to see the sketch plan had been drawn in by extensive advertising and were atypically large. With a few exceptions, the average monthly club meeting to deal with "neighborhood" issues did well to get twenty participants.

Of the sixteen organizations there were four well-organized, forcefully led groups with an active membership of fifty or more, eight with a less extensive grass-roots organization but with vocal leaders, and four decidedly paper organizations existing as convenient fictions between the few individuals who could be said to personify the organization and the BRA who wanted some kind of forum for neighborhood expression if a time came during the planning period when more neighbors felt a need to be heard. The disparity in the power and scope among the different neighborhood organizations must be borne in mind. For one thing, the associations were continually trying to broaden their membership, a process for the most part meeting with the frustrating results that one could anticipate in a district like the South End.

We noted earlier that the over-all capacity of the local residents to participate in the planning process was severely limited. The actual number of those involved in the associations vindicates this judgment. Yet these organizations did provide a forum for anyone who wanted to become involved at the neighborhood level, and from the point of view of co-opting power in the community—those who could assist or retard renewal—the associations were extremely effective mechanisms. What is surprising, given the composition of the South End and its aggregate capacity to mobilize, is the

[69] In fact, a BRA pamphlet of August 1965 describing the plan that was accepted for the South End is subtitled, "The Sixteen Neighborhoods Plan for a Better Community."

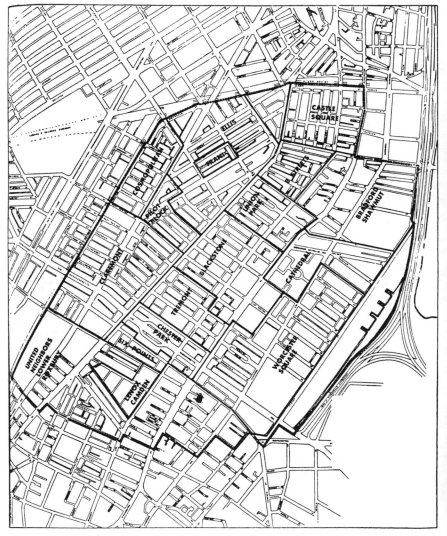

FIGURE 3.2   SOUTH END NEIGHBORHOOD ASSOCIATIONS

extensive representation of working-class, as well as middle-class, interests in the neighborhood groups.

While the neighborhood associations were on the rise during the summer of 1963, another component of the local renewal team was on the wane. USES, without which no renewal system could have been built in the South End, would never again be as powerful as when, according to some observers, it had been influential in the toppling of both Cloyd and Traunstein. USES' declining influence was attributable to several factors. Throughout the first round of planning USES had found itself caught between the BRA and the community—an uncomfortable setting for an agency not geared for conflict and committed to promoting the well-being of the South End as a whole. Traunstein, feeling that USES had helped to do him in, had warned Green to beware the same fate, and Green entered the planning game determined not to get trapped by USES or any other one group that sought to speak for the South End. As Green himself said, "I don't want any middle man between me and the community."[70]

Added to Green's reluctance to give USES prominence was the deep-seated antipathy of the new head of the URC toward USES. While willing to admit the significant role USES had played at the beginning of renewal, Farrah was not about to let the organization "interpret" renewal or the BRA to him or his committee.[71] Moreover, several of the neighborhood organizations had become capable of directing their own affairs and, with an infusion of new leadership from the new Urbanites, quite capable of dealing with the BRA without the help of USES.

During this period USES became another interest group with strong representation on the local team. Indeed, the basic structure of the renewal game (two discrete teams bargaining with each other) made USES' original role of catalyst and linking mechanism difficult to play successfully. As an interest group, USES spoke for many of those in the South End who were unable or unwilling to promote their own interests in the renewal game—the elderly, the roomers, Skid Row.

If bargaining and negotiation had not been an integral part of the first round of the renewal game, they were of the second. The URC was a more seasoned body. Farrah, a veteran of the infighting of City Hall, was firmly of the opinion that "because we hold the controls people should get together and assert themselves."[72] And Farrah knew the value of newsprint to improve the URC bargaining position. When negotiating the re-use of Castle Square, a part of the South End which had been slated for clearance in the

[70] Author's interview with Richard Green, January 18, 1966.
[71] Author's interview with George Farrah, January 5, 1966.
[72] South End URC, Minutes, January 6, 1964.

pre-Logue days, Farrah made clear to the press the determination of the
URC to have housing built on the site:

> If we lose Castle Square to industry, it endangers the whole renewal process in the
> South End. . . . We're willing to demonstrate that we will plan with the BRA. We
> want to see if they're willing to demonstrate they will plan with the people.[73]

The BRA policy of walking the neighborhoods and listening to local
demands was a clear indication that the BRA South End team was putting
most of its hope for plan acceptance on the residential community. Negotiation took place with individual businessmen, the South End Businessmen's
Association, the large institutions, the medical complex, and the churches,
but the key elements of the renewal system established by USES in 1961
were the neighborhood associations and a URC dominated by residential interests. Soon after Farrah was made president of the URC, the number of
delegates allotted to the neighborhood associations doubled. In the South
End women are afraid to go out alone at night, and raising the number of
delegates to two provided companionship. It also, of course, increased the
weight of the neighborhood associations in the URC. By June 1965, when
the vote approving a South End renewal plan was cast, neighborhood representation on the committee had increased from 38 to 63 percent of the total
representation. Nothing could be more symbolic of the expansion of the
role of the neighborhood association in renewal negotiations than this
change in percentages.

THE SECOND SOUTH END PLAN:
"THE CONCEPT"

By January 1964, the walks around the neighborhoods had come to an end.
Impatient at the lack of specific proposals from the BRA, the URC wrote a
letter to Logue in which it stated that the committee will "work in conjunc-
tion with Mr. Green but in the meantime we are formulating our own plan
for the South End."[74] Green reacted to this move by announcing what came
to be known as "the concept." (See Figure 3.3.) This outline for the restructuring of the South End was the result not only of URC pressure but
also of the demand from design technicians in the BRA central office that
Green demonstrate his acceptance of a "total planning solution" for the
South End to take the place of the sketch proposal that he had rejected.
"The concept" was well received by the URC, who felt it reflected many of
their suggestions.[75] The central office designers were so pleased with "the
concept" that before long they were criticizing Green for his straying, in
specific plan proposals, from his own guidelines.

[73] *The Boston Herald,* July 21, 1963.
[74] South End URC, Minutes, January 6, 1964.
[75] *Ibid.,* January 20, 1964.

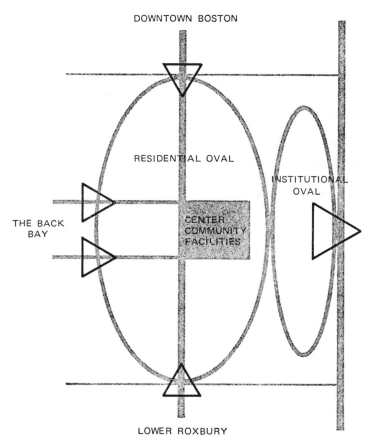

FIGURE 3.3 THE SOUTH END CONCEPT

When the first planning team divided the area into two South Ends, it based its division on two residential groups—the problem and the non-problem people. Yet because of the difficulty of fitting physical form to social needs, the first sketch plan had not clearly articulated such a division. "The concept" also postulated a division, but it was now the separation of the residential from the institutional and industrial community, a separation far more conducive to physical planning.

"The concept" did not spell out who would live in the housing oval or what kinds of businesses and institutions would be included in the smaller oval. Thus, at the design level, the conflict between residential groups was avoided, while focus was directed toward a point of real friction in the South End, the conflict between institutional and residential use of land.

"The concept" provided the framework within which the concrete elements of the renewal plan could be negotiated. Green and his staff took the design to the neighborhoods during the spring of 1964 in order to fill it in with specific demands of these local constituencies. "The concept" traveled to 155 meetings, and by the fall of 1964 the BRA was ready with a second plan. The negotiations that went on from the emergence of "the concept" to the point of plan approval by the URC in June 1965 were concerned essentially with which interest groups would be represented in the residential oval. The questionnaires filled out at neighborhood meetings during the Traunstein administration had pointed out four critical areas of dispute among South End residents: public housing, Skid Row, rooming houses, and the role of middle-income people in the renewed South End.

Although Traunstein had maintained that, excepting the Night People, benefits might accrue to all groups in the area, he left the project before there had been any specific resolution of the potential conflict over these four issues. The first sketch plan, while it had initially contained 2,500 units of public housing, had not made any statement on rooming houses or Skid Row. Logue had quickly withdrawn the 2,500 figure, and the restructuring of the renewal game had kept the issue from being pursued further. The fundamental issue raised by "the concept" was to what extent was the South End to remain Boston's prime repository of the old, the poor, and the problem-ridden. How high a toleration of these groups was compatible with the resurrection of a vital and self-sufficient South End which would not only hold its current residents but also draw families from suburbia? Was it possible to create a South End that would be neither "one vast social agency" nor "a museum piece"?

Green's adherence to the bicameral system of URC and local neighborhood associations as the basic structure of the local planning team provided a mechanism by which to work out a politically viable compromise on the issues of rooming houses, Skid Row, public housing, and facilitating the inflow of Urbanites.

THE INTEREST GROUPS NEGOTIATE

ROOMING HOUSES

In the fall of 1963, while Green and his staff were still walking the neighborhoods, the future of rooming houses thundered forth to remain a "privileged problem" for the duration of the planning period.[76]

Royal Cloyd, representing the Union Park Neighborhood Association, the area into which Urbanites had been filtering in growing numbers since the

76 Albert O. Hirschman, *Journeys Towards Progress* (New York: Doubleday, 1965), p. 305.

start of renewal planning, put forward the Urbanite position when he blasted rooming houses as "contributing much to the deterioration of the area."[77] His charge was answered strongly by several URC members who were themselves rooming house operators:

We must cope with the problems and work towards a solution for rehabilitating rooming houses. We must keep in mind that we are working under the assumption that we are planning for the people *now* living in the South End; this includes roomers and we must deal equally and fairly with all types of property. . . . Of prime importance here . . . is consideration of the types of persons living in rooming houses; many are not at all detrimental influences on families living near-by. It is the flop-house type of rooming house which caters to transients and all sorts of undesirables that is a liability to good residential neighborhoods.[78]

Eventually the resident owners, defending their occupation and their "good" tenants, overcame Urbanite opposition. After this discussion the URC took the position that "rooming houses are here to stay and do, very definitely, have their place in the total picture of the South End."[79] "Bad" rooming houses, however, with their "undesirable" tenants were written off and, like liquor establishments and the Night People, became a group that the entire URC and all the neighborhood associations agreed should be eliminated from the renewed South End.

From this point, the exchange on rooming houses was carried on between the URC and the BRA, with the BRA constantly being urged to find ways of making the rehabilitation of the "good" rooming houses economically feasible. The FHA does not insure rooming houses, and the BRA spent much time convincing reluctant Boston bankers to state formally that financing would be readily available for owner-occupied rooming houses. At the time, most URC members were cautiously optimistic about the outcome of these BRA efforts.

SKID ROW

There was general agreement by the URC and the neighborhood associations that the South End had too many liquor licenses for bars and package stores. As Green and his staff came to realize when discussing "the concept" at the neighborhood level, any move to get rid of a liquor license would be greeted with enthusiasm by local residents. Logue himself made the all-out war on liquor licenses clear when he said

Either booze has got to win or the decent families of Boston—particularly those of the South End of Boston—have got to win. We have chosen sides. We are on the side of the families.[80]

At the same time there was the realization that while many of the 113

77 South End URC, Minutes, October 21, 1963.
78 *Ibid.*
79 *Ibid.*
80 *The Record American,* July 13, 1964.

licenses could be gotten rid of (in fact more than 50 were removed in the final plan), the South End would continue to have a large number of liquor outlets and thus in all likelihood a good percentage of Boston's Skid Row element.

As the questionnaire had indicated, there were mixed feelings in the South End as to the extent to which the renewal plan should consider the needs of Skid Row. The URC did not touch this problem until well into the winter of 1964, at which time Farrah announced that the South End's public bathhouse would be set up as a temporary screening and diagnostic center for alcoholics. The news set off a whirl of argument. One URC member, an Urbanite, declared, "we are being cursed by everyone's problems —this is a state and not a city problem."[81] In reply, Liddell "urged that we not lose sight of the fact that the majority of community needs must be met . . . the total view must be foremost in our thinking."[82] Others concurred that the South End did, in fact, have some responsibility for Skid Row problems and agreed to support the screening facility provided that it was only temporary.

The Urban Renewal Committee thus served as a forum for reconciling widely divergent views on responsibility of the South End for its Skid Row population. It produced a solution that, while not as comprehensive or enduring as members of the hospital and social welfare interest groups felt necessary, was more substantial than many Urbanite and rooming house interests desired.

PUBLIC HOUSING

Insistence on the neighborhood level of planning established sanctity of "turf"—the right of the individual neighborhood associations to determine land use for their areas. The acceptance of this right by the members of the URC provided renewal with a mechanism for resolving goal conflicts for the South End as a whole. For example, the Worcester Square Neighborhood Association, dominated by the increasingly articulate and forceful leadership of residential rooming house operators, was adamantly opposed to additional public housing in the South End. The Worcester Square group disapproved because it feared the competition of public housing to lodging houses and because public housing meant additional Negro occupants in a white neighborhood on the edge of the Negro residential area. While fighting to keep public housing out of the area of its jurisdiction, the association recognized that it could plead self-determination only if it granted the same privilege to its neighbors. Thereupon, Worcester Square quickly stopped

81 South End URC, Minutes, January 4, 1965.
82 Ibid.

criticizing the Tremont Neighborhood Association, which, dominated by a liberal minister, had recommended housing for the elderly within the Tremont boundaries. Thus did sanctity of "turf" provide a means of satisfying potentially conflicting points of view between neighborhood associations.

At the level of the South End as a whole, it was Green who seized the initiative and proposed that the URC accept 500 units of housing for the elderly and 300 units of scattered-site public housing, 50 units to a location. Liddell and others from the social welfare community wanted to double each category, but the overwhelming majority of the URC would not support an increased amount of public housing. Yet people knew that some public housing was necessary to meet the needs of the vast number of low-income people in the South End, and rehabilitation of tax foreclosed properties by nonprofit corporations was put forward as a possible alternative to new public housing. The creation of three such corporations buoyed the hope that a significant amount of low-rent housing would emerge from the renewal process.

Thus while many URC members were opposed to any public housing, the committee also had avid supporters of more units of subsidized housing. The URC held that "from the very beginning this Committee has committed itself to work for the best interests of the entire South End. The fact remains that we have a large percentage of low-income families and we would be remiss in our duty if we did not try to get decent, safe, and sanitary housing for these people."[83] The URC served as the mechanism for legitimatizing the aggregate amount of subsidized housing to be brought into the area under renewal, and the process of negotiation at the neighborhood level provided locations for that housing.

THE URBANITES

The manner in which the BRA handled the Gray Trust indicates the extent to which the structure of the URC and the neighborhood associations dictated that the BRA plan with those already living in the South End. The Gray Trust was a real estate firm that had accumulated over sixty pieces of property in one neighborhood association area. The managers of the organization wanted BRA support for their enterprise. The BRA, rather than deal directly with the Trust, insisted that the Trust work through the URC. Efforts on the part of the Trust to get representation on the URC resulted in a battle between the Urbanites who saw Gray Trust as a positive force for converting more of the district into a solid single-family home area and the rooming house operators, representatives of the welfare community, and

83 South End URC, Minutes, April 5, 1965.

Urban Villagers who wanted nothing to do with the high rents that such an operation would produce and who felt that people should not be able to steer their way onto the URC simply "on the basis of money or property they possess."[84] Eventually the Urbanites backed down, and the members of the Gray Trust were told the only way they could be included in the renewal structure would be as members of the Ellis Neighborhood Association, the organization covering the area in which the Trust owned property. Neither Green nor Logue was willing to jeopardize his relationship with the URC to facilitate significant rehabilitation of the South End with private money. The nature of the renewal game in the South End precluded such obvious strategy to bring in upper-income groups.

The Gray Trust incident is food for thought for those who would argue that renewal in the South End is simply a cover for middle-income home-owners who do as they please at the expense of the rest of the community. While all but one of the residential representatives on the URC were home-owners, they held divergent points of view as to what renewal should do for the area. Furthermore, if all URC members had been middle-income owners, they would have unanimously welcomed the Gray Trust.

A list of the many issues over which bargaining took place between the BRA team and South End residents would indicate the significant extent to which the Urban Villagers and other representatives of the working-class community were able to influence the direction of planning in their neighborhoods. Even public housing tenants joined in the planning game. For example, in the final round of negotiations a strong alliance was struck between the tenants in the Cathedral public housing project and the Worcester Square Neighborhood Association for the purpose of promoting housing rather than commercial re-use, as the BRA proposed, for the area directly north of the Cathedral Project. The alliance was strong and vocal enough to convince the BRA to change the re-use to housing—a change which the BRA team was extremely reluctant to make but which it realized was necessary if serious conflict were to be avoided.

SOCIAL PLANNING
Traunstein and Liddell had emphasized from the start that physical renewal in the South End would be meaningless without parallel effort in the social sphere. Indeed, the entire URC structure was oriented around a dual effort. ABCD was entrusted with the bulk of social planning but was unable to meet the expectations that had been held for the organization. The problems ABCD faced in its relationship to the neighborhoods and to the BRA

constitute a long and complex story made more involved by the War on Poverty, which diverted ABCD's attention from the particular needs of the South End urban renewal program. While ABCD had innovated job training and educational programs in the South End during the planning period, the impact of the programs had been slight at the time of the renewal hearing. Late in the winter of 1965, a large-scale community action program was funded for the South End. Concerned with the entire range of problems facing the district's poor, the program gave much promise of serving the area's needs. Yet because the program came late in the planning period and was initiated outside the formal framework of the renewal game, it carried little weight at the BRA public hearing.

Whatever might be the impact of social programming during the project execution period, the contribution of social planning to the rehabilitation planning game was limited and disappointing to those who had seen such an input as fundamental to a comprehensive program for the South End.

The Image of the BRA

While working through critical issues at all levels of organization, Green created an image of an individual who could intervene between the "downtown BRA," viewed with suspicion if not hostility, and the needs and desires of the people of the South End. One observer went so far as to include Green in the list of the ten most significant South End leaders, an interesting comment on the open-ended leadership pattern in the district, as well as on the extent to which the project director was seen to represent the South End's interests.

Green gained the trust of the people with whom he worked and minimized the intervention of the central office in his operation. Logue respected Green's judgment; and while Logue often was curious to know "what's going on down there" and impatient over the length of the planning period, he let Green make the decisions. Green's relationship with Logue and the central office throughout the planning period is perhaps the best vindication of the Logue system. A powerful project director fought for his constituency —the local project area—in the central office while ultimately remaining loyal to Logue and to the BRA goal of steering renewal projects through to execution.

With few exceptions, Green's staff reflected his style. There was a unified image about the BRA project team during the second round that had not been present during the Traunstein era. Moreover, where Traunstein had found himself bypassed by members of his own staff and his scope of prerogative gradually chipped away by Logue's handing small pieces of the South End project to someone else in the BRA, Green never allowed his team to bypass him and never surrendered any aspect of the South End project.

By the time of the BRA's draft plan for the URC in the fall of 1964, Green and his staff were deeply committed to producing something that would meet the demands of the vast number of interest groups with whom they were dealing. As one member of the staff put it, "We got to the point where we were going for 100 percent approval—we really began to believe that we could get through without a voice of opposition. And we almost did just that."[85]

This time, when the plan was ready to move from the BRA offices to the South End, the process by which it would be reviewed was carefully spelled out. In September 1964, Logue appeared with Green before the URC and stated, "As soon as the URC is satisfied the BRA will take it around to the people."[86] At the next URC meeting to discuss the plan, held without the BRA, it was agreed that the plan reflected what the neighborhoods had requested.[87] Despite this general approval the URC, remembering the first plan with its constantly shifting pieces, demanded to see specifications and blowups of individual neighborhoods before it would vote on the proposal. The BRA, which had used the hard sell very little during the second round of planning, was obviously anxious to get the plan approved and out to the neighborhood associations. Thus, Green stated that specifications and blowups could be forthcoming only after the URC approved the proposal. After much letter writing, telephoning, and general negotiation among Logue, Green, and the URC, the BRA backed off, produced the specifications, and agreed to ask the URC not for "conditional acceptance" of but rather for "general endorsement" of the ideas represented in the proposal.[88] By sitting on the plan for several months, the URC got its specifications without committing itself 100 percent to the plan. Once again it would be up to the individual neighborhood associations to barter over the specific details before approving the plan at the neighborhood level and then at the URC.

General endorsement, however, was far more than the URC had given to the first plan. While the URC was careful not to bind itself too tightly, the BRA was equally determined to get some kind of commitment from the formal negotiating agent before going out to neighborhood meetings. The second plan might be far more the product of the neighborhood associations than the first, but nonetheless some kind of URC sanction was demanded.

With URC "general endorsement," the BRA went to the neighborhoods, the churches, the institutions, and virtually every organization in the South

85 Author's interview with David Meyers, January 20, 1966.
86 South End URC, Minutes, October 5, 1964.
87 *Ibid.*, November 13, 1964.
88 *Ibid.*, November 23, 1964.

End. As one BRA staff member put it, "We took that plan to every local group we could lay our hands on."[89]

THE POLITICS OF RENEWAL AFFIRMATION

At the November 1965 meeting of the City Council to hear the renewal plan, approved by the BRA Board at an August public hearing, Dick Green gave this account of how the proposal had been devised for the South End:

We took this concept which really was the community's concept out to 155 organized meetings, and we asked at the end of every meeting: are we moving in the right direction for South End planning and the answer was at the end of every meeting 'yes, you are.' Then we went to the Urban Renewal Committee and asked them . . . to do their own planning first, to do a plan they felt their own neighborhoods should have, and we told them we could not be committed to everything they did simply because nobody really wants sometimes a school right next to them . . . but they stated simply and in many instances quite strongly in maps, in drawings, and in statements, and in some verbal presentations what they felt the best community in their neighborhoods should be. Based on this we put together the first draft of the Urban Renewal Plan, and we took this out again to 155 organized meetings, and based on the reaction from that plan, we told the Urban Renewal Committee and their neighborhoods and all the other people associated in the South End that we wanted their reaction, and based on their reaction, we would be able to change the plan to develop a final plan. And we got the reaction, and I think we maintained a pretty good batting average. Where we had to give on an item because the community felt it was necessary . . . we generally did, but not always, and if we did not we gave them a complete and detailed list of reasons why it could not be done.[90]

Green's description of the bargaining was simplified but accurate. Step by step he and his staff moved from the generalities of "the concept" that threatened no one to the specific decisions on the location of public housing and schools and the demolition of buildings. Green made every effort to accommodate the demands of the individual neighborhoods, and it is the opinion of all observers and participants in the bargaining sequence that the product of his efforts, which finally was approved by a vote of 41 to 6 at the June 1964 URC meeting, was a "political plan" hammered out in the community,[91] "a compromise plan in which neither side got all of what they wanted."[92] The final South End plan was a series of neighborhood designs soldered together into a proposal for the area as a whole. Concern for design criteria or over-all concept went by the boards in the drive to gain the approval of individual organizations.

The plan called for the rehabilitation of more than 3,000 structures and the construction of over 3,000 new private rental units under the 221 d3 federal housing program. While BRA estimates indicate that rehabilitation

89 Author's interview with Sylvia McPhee, February 9, 1966.
90 City of Boston, City Council, "South End Urban Renewal Area: Before Committee on Urban Renewal, November 9, 1965, pp. 5–6.
91 Author's interview with Charles Liddell, January 5, 1966.
92 Author's interview with George Farrah.

is economically feasible for 70 percent of the structures in the South End,[93] a BRA working paper on rehabilitation admits that the "South End probably represents the greatest challenge to the Authority's rehabilitation effort."[94] The total number of families and individuals to be displaced was 3,550, 19 percent of South End households. Just over half the displacees are single-person households. The number of structures not taken though in need of major repair or extensive minor repair far exceeded those actually slated for demolition.

Of the relocation plan, phased over seven years, Green could say at the BRA public hearing, "anybody who wishes to stay in the South End we believe we have adequate facilities for them."[95] While this point would be contended by many in the South End, BRA figures do make formal provision for rehousing all relocatees within the South End.

For all the fanfare attendant upon the scrapping of the first plan, the product that emerged from the URC in the spring of 1965 was not radically different from its predecessor. The clearance areas are similar in the two proposals. While less residential property is to be cleared in the second plan, the major differences are that in the second plan the Syrian community along Shawmut Avenue has been spared and there have been increased takings along Tremont Street and Columbus Avenue, for the most part made possible by the existence of liquor licensed establishments in the buildings. The circulation pattern has been simplified. Fewer streets are blocked off or made to take oblique angles. The community center complex that figures so prominently in the first sketch is present in the final plan. School locations have not been varied drastically. Beyond the absence of the Green Strip in the second plan, the main difference between the plans lies in the use of land in the institutional-industrial oval. But even here the demands of the two neighborhood associations for housing behind the Cathedral Project and the several other patches of residential usage break up the purity of "the concept's" concern to keep residential and industrial-institutional uses separated.

What is significant about the second plan is that the arrangement of pieces is different, as is the rationale behind that arrangement. The pieces in the first plan—the schools, the "common way," etc.—came from one individual planning in a political vacuum. The location of components in the second plan resulted from an intricate bargaining procedure at a number of levels.

93 BRA: South End, "Project Area Report: Application for Loan and Grant Part I: Final Project Report," Fall 1965, R–221.
94 BRA, "A Working Paper on Rehabilitation," Winter 1964–1965, p. 46.
95 City of Boston, City Council, "South End Urban Renewal Area: Before Committee on Urban Renewal," November 12, 1965, p. 558.

Clearly, in Banfield's terms, "social choice" had replaced "central decision making" as the mechanism for determining land-use patterns in the South End.[96]

During the second round and the drive to the public hearing, the BRA listened to every voice raised. There was someone at the bargaining table representing, to some extent, the South End people who were a priori alienated from the planning process—the old tenants, the rural Negroes, Skid Row. Public housing was to be built, 300 family units, 500 units for the elderly—not enough for some, too much for others. A temporary drying-out center for alcoholics was allowed to operate on Dover Street—too temporary for some, not temporary enough for others. Rooming houses were guaranteed financial help from the banks—a mistake from the point of view of some, not enough of a commitment from that of others. In essence, the variety of interests capable of mobilizing opposition in the South End ensured that the vocal people scattered throughout the area would be able to carve out a "political" plan among themselves.

It must also be recognized that all the interest groups characterized as having a stake in the South End were not dealt with equally in the final plan. It comes as no surprise, for example, that 46 of 116 liquor licenses were to be removed from the South End and that most efforts to deal with the problem of Skid Row were beaten back.

While the South End Businessmen's Association was an important element in the South End renewal negotiations, the process by which its members were accommodated took place for the most part on an individual basis outside the URC. "The concept's" provision of an oval for industry and institutions made it possible to expand without conflicting with residential uses.

Not surprisingly, individual churchmen rather than the churches as a unified body were influential in the second round of the renewal game. Churches in the South End tended to reflect the interest of their parishioners, and since there is a multiplicity of interests in the South End, one found some clergymen promoting public housing with a fervor, others fighting it with equal enthusiasm. Several clergymen were deeply involved in the renewal proceedings; others had nothing to do with them. In the spring of 1964, when "the concept" was making the rounds, Green and his staff realized that the neighborhood associations were not reaching most tenants in their areas. The BRA then made a strategic move to include churches in the review and from that point on kept in contact with many of the 28 churches. While by the August 1965 BRA hearing there existed a South End Clergy

[96] Edward C. Banfield, *Political Influence* (New York: The Free Press, 1965), pp. 324 ff.

Association which supported the plan, as a unified interest group the churches never made their weight felt in the South End planning process.

OPPOSITION

If the critical demand for a successful residential rehabilitation plan is the co-option of the majority of those in the community with the capacity to articulate approval or opposition at a public hearing, the BRA had the odds on its side when it went to the public hearing in the summer of 1965. At that hearing 149 testimonials were presented, of which only 20 were in opposition, and the majority of that 20 were not South Enders. South End opposition came from a few small businessmen who felt they were being dealt with unfairly and from a few residents who had formed a group called the South End Citizens Rights Association a few weeks before the public hearing and had managed to get 120 signatures in opposition to the plan. When their leader denounced the South End's planning game, crying "this is a steamroller meeting the BRA has developed to signify the sanctions of our residents,"[97] his words were overwhelmed by an outpouring of affirmation. While support for the hearing was carefully mobilized by the URC, the SEPC and the BRA, there is no question but that the plan had the approval of the vast majority of articulate South End residents. Green had negotiated the plan in enough ways and in enough places to ensure that at the time of the public hearing there remained no dissatisfied South End leadership capable of mobilizing significant opposition.

When the plan finally emerged from the bargaining process, the South End was proud that the rules of the renewal game had been followed. Negotiation for renewal had been carried on through the formal system laid down by USES in 1961. Majority decisions had been adhered to by the dissenting minority. The right of the URC to negotiate the renewal mandate was never again brought into question after the readjustment in the spring of 1963. While personal feelings often ran high, they rarely had interfered with the issue orientation of the majority of the participants in the renewal planning process. The use of renewal as a jumping-off point for other political activity never became a significant issue in the South End planning game. The overwhelming desire of those on the local team to do something about their area while abiding by the rules of the formal renewal system produced a plan backed by the majority of the articulate South Enders and left the community's social relationships unscarred by the process. There were threats of walkouts, and there was enormous pressure brought to bear in the neighborhood associations, but there never was an exit. As one associa-

97 BRA: South End, "South End Urban Renewal Area Before the Boston Redevelopment Authority," Mimeographed Transcript, August 23, 1965, p. 57.

tion president put it, "We fight for what we want, but we act on things democratically, and we go along with majority rule."[98]

The most significant population change during the planning period was the movement of Urbanites into the South End. Several neighborhood associations came to be dominated by these articulate spokesmen who saw the city as a new frontier. Yet, at least for the planning period, a delicate balance was worked out between old time SEPC people on the URC and the Urbanites. Royal Cloyd was most helpful in bringing together Newcomers and old-timers to explain the one to the other and to minimize potential conflict between living styles and concepts of organizational participation.

THE NEW SOUTH END:
"SOCIAL AGENCY" OR "BRIGHT NEW PLACES"?
The possibility that the South End would become, as Royal Cloyd had warned in the early days of renewal, a "shiny museum piece," operated by and for Urbanites concerned many of those planning for the New South End. Others countered that only with renewal was there any hope of preserving the heterogeneous racial and social residential population in the area—that without renewal there would be a gradual end to the rooming house population as owners sold out to Urbanites who would convert the bowfronts to single-family use. With renewal, the argument ran, there was hope of some public housing, housing for the elderly, and nonprofit 221 d3 housing, as well as relocation services for the dispossessed.

Others maintained that the threat of total inundation by Urbanites was vastly inflated and that their number was overrated due to their visibility and audibility in community affairs. Rather than limiting the spread of middle-class families and rents, the renewal process ensured that the district would be opened wide to Urbanites. Groups dependent on low rents would be squeezed out by the economics of rehabilitation and by upward pressure on property values—pressure that benefits the resident homeowner but not the renter.

Whether or not renewal would serve as a means of providing a better environment for families, "good" tenants, homeowners, and old people was still problematic at the point of plan approval. What is significant to us, however, is that throughout the planning process there was every intention on the part of the URC and the neighborhood organizations that such be the result of the renewal program. If as the plan moved into execution the economic demands of the rehabilitation process were to force out Urban Villagers and rooming house operators, their exit could not be considered part of the plan's original design. The people in the South End involved in

[98] Author's interview with Rose Mehegan.

the renewal game had no illusions about the BRA and its capacity to carry out all of the renewal plan's assumptions. Constantly South Enders maintained that they would "watch the BRA like a hawk" during the period of project execution.

Given the range of interests involved in negotiations for the South End plan, it is impossible to see the area's renewal planning game in terms of middle class versus lower class or "public regarding" versus "private regarding." Our study of interest group characteristics and the process by which those groups were or were not included in the planning game indicates that a more complex framework for analysis has to be utilized in order to explain the manner in which a renewal plan emerged from the South End. The view that a small band of middle-income homeowners pushed a plan through that benefits them and disadvantages everyone else in the district obscures the unique socioeconomic and historical characteristics of the South End, which ensured that groups other than the Urbanites—the most clearly identifiable middle-class group in the area—participated directly or indirectly in the rehabilitation planning game. The politics of renewal affirmation required a wider range of South End interests than those clearly defined as middle-class.

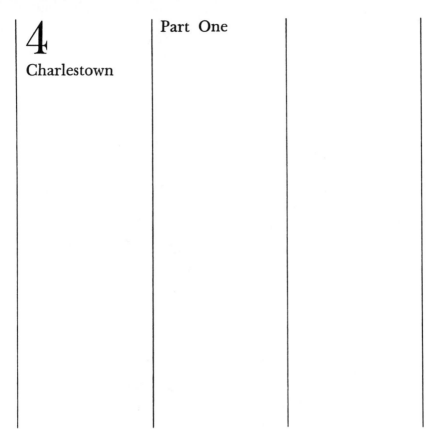

4

Charlestown

Part One

THE PEOPLE, HISTORY, AND GEOGRAPHY OF CHARLESTOWN:
AN OVERVIEW

Unlike the South End, which emerged from the sea during the nineteenth century, or Washington Park, which had no existence until created by the BRA project boundaries, Charlestown has a long, colorful, and self-contained identity. Today a "residential island surrounded by nonresidential use,"[1] cut off from the rest of Boston and other neighbors by wharves, water, and highways, Charlestown looks back on an origin that predates Boston itself. The core of residential Charlestown is built on the sides of two hills, one of which supports the Bunker Hill Monument. At the bottom of these hills housing has been withered by the traffic that races around Charlestown's boundaries and by the heavy industry that seems to be lapping at the base of the high ground waiting to climb into the still inviolate "heartland" of the Charlestown community. (See Figure 4.1.)

---

[1] Boston Redevelopment Authority: Charlestown, "Charlestown—Background Information," Winter 1962, p. 2.

FIGURE 4.1 CHARLESTOWN URBAN RENEWAL AREA

The housing that Charlestown has to offer is a mixed lot, harboring eight architectural styles from Post-Revolutionary to Georgian Revival among its polyglot row, three-decker, and freestanding housing stock. As charming residential settings, Monument and Winthrop Squares can compete with any of Boston's best neighborhoods. In contrast, the entire area locked between truck-dominated Rutherford Avenue and the Main Street Elevated shows what happens to a residential district sacrificed to transportation networks. There vacant land alternates with dilapidated houses, stores, and parking lots, creating a shabby pattern of misused land.

At the start of its long history and for many decades thereafter, Charlestown was a rural shipping village. Even after the dramatic events of the Revolutionary War, during which the British responded to the resistance offered them at Breed's Hill by burning the entire settlement, Charlestown remained a haven for some extremely venerable Yankee families. It was during the potato famines of the 1840's that the area blossomed forth as a refuge for Irish immigrants. The town, which had held a population of ten thousand in 1840, doubled in size by 1855, and most of the newcomers were from Ireland.[2] Unlike the South End, where ethnic heterogeneity has been a way of life since the area first became a City Wilderness, Charlestown was transformed rapidly from a Yankee village to a town with predominantly Irish population, and Irish it has remained.

A glance at the aggregate statistics of Charlestown around 1960 reveals a community almost 100 percent white, with Chinese constituting most of the nonwhite category.[3] Compared to Boston as a whole, Charlestown has a larger percentage of families with children, a better health and social welfare record, and less delinquency, though Charlestown trails Boston in education and in the percentage of professionals in the labor force. Charlestown labor force characteristics do not change much from 1950 to 1960.

While aggregate statistics do a good job of revealing the extent to which Charlestown adheres to the Boston norm on many fronts, three important statistical characteristics of the town are not revealed in Table 4.1.

1. While clear that Charlestown's population declined from 1950 to 1960 at a rate almost three times that of the city as a whole, one of the most significant aspects of that loss was its concentration in the twenty- to forty-five-year-old bracket, what has been called the "crucial productive age."[4] This group has fled in large part because, with only two private houses built in the district since 1902, there was little to choose from in Charlestown's

2 BRA: Charlestown, "Historical Data—Charlestown, Massachusetts," undated, p. 17.
3 *The Boston Herald*, December 2, 1965.
4 *Ibid.*

TABLE 4.1   AREA CHARACTERISTICS

	Charles-town	City of Boston
ECONOMIC CHARACTERISTICS		
% unemployed—1960	7.9%	5.0%
Median family income—1960	$5,350	$5,757
% of families with incomes under $3,000—1960	21.4%	16.7%
% of families with incomes over $10,000—1960	11.2%	13.6%
EDUCATIONAL CHARACTERISTICS		
% of persons 25 years or over with less than 8 years' schooling	19.6%	17.9%
HEALTH CHARACTERISTICS		
Death rate of infants per 1,000 under one year old—1961	11.4	26.1
% of Boston cases of pulmonary tuberculosis—1961	4.4%	100.0%
HOUSING CHARACTERISTICS		
% units owner-occupied—1960	28.0%	27.7%
Population per household—1960	3.3	2.9
% sound dwelling units—1960	70.7%	73.3%
Median gross monthly rent—1960	$58.58	$78.00
POPULATION CHARACTERISTICS		
Total population—1960	20,147	697,197
% decline from 1950 population	33.0%	12.5%
% population nonwhite	0.6%	9.8%
% numerical increase of 1960 nonwhite population over 1950 nonwhite population	−300.0%	60.0%
% of 1960 population under 18	35.5%	28.7%
% of 1960 population 65 and over	9.9%	12.3%
Families (2 persons or more) as a % of all households	75.0%	73.0%
Families (2 persons or more) with children	71.0%	63.0%
WELFARE CHARACTERISTICS		
Population as a % of total city population—1964	2.6%	100.0%
% of city welfare cases in area—1964	2.3%	100.0%
% of city Old Age Assistance cases in area—1964	3.4%	100.0%
% of city AFDC* families living in area—1964	4.1%	100.0%
% of city General Relief cases in area—1964	1.0%	100.0%
YOUTH CHARACTERISTICS		
% of Boston's youth 7–17 living in area—1960	7.0%	100.0%
Youth court appearances 1951–1961 as a % of Boston's total	5.8%	100.0%

* Aid to Families with Dependent Children.
Sources: Statistics compiled by Anti-Poverty Planning Unit, ABCD, Winter 1964–1965, and "Social Facts by Census Tracts—1960," data compiled by United Community Services.

housing stock that could compete with the lures of the single-family homes being constructed in suburbia.

2. A total of 1,149 of Charlestown's 5,978 housing units (or in 1960 about 4,500—20 percent—of the town's 20,147 inhabitants) lived in the massive

public housing project dominating the northeast corner of the district.[5]

It is crucial to separate the housing project statistics from those of the rest of the Charlestown community, because without the project averages Charlestown emerges as a middle-income, blue-collar, large-family town with a low incidence of welfare problems and extremely low rental levels relative to incomes. BRA figures estimate the median family income outside the housing project at $6,200.[6] While this figure seems inordinately high to some, the nonproject average is, without question, above the city mean of $5,757.

3. Less than half of the town's foreign stock is listed as Irish, while a conservative assumption would be that well over half of Charlestown's total population is of Irish origin. The explanation is that census statistics note only the overseas origins of first- and second-generation individuals, an approach that obscures the Irish origins of many Charlestown families.

The individual census tracts of Charlestown show that the social and economic characteristics of the town as a whole apply at the tract level as well. Excluding the three tracts that include pieces of the public housing project and are, therefore, lower in income, homeownership, and residential stability, there is only a small spread between the highest and lowest income tracts in all the indices recorded. On the assumption that income, homeownership, familial attachments, and absence of social welfare characteristics constitute some index of residents' capacity to participate in community affairs, one can say that the Charlestown population outside the project has a relatively high potential capacity for involvement in the rehabilitation game.

Unlike the South End, where social problems were every bit as critical as physical ones, Charlestown in 1960 was an example of a community in which a resolution of the district's physical blight and deterioration and an infusion of public services and community facilities would go a long way toward answering the needs of the area. Not content with cutting the residential community off from its waterfront, industry and transportation lines were eating into the housing stock, forcing it to be abandoned and allowed to deteriorate.[7] Charlestown had little recreation space for its numerous chil-

5 By 1965 Charlestown's population had shrunk to 17,400, so the housing project as a percentage of the Town's population was even greater; the 1960 figures are used because of the comparability of data.

6 BRA: Charlestown, "Analytical Summary of the Public Hearing Before the Boston City Council Regarding the Charlestown Urban Renewal Project," Spring 1965, p. 11.

7 Prior to 1961, the city of Boston was carrying about 250 parcels in Charlestown on its foreclosure roles. Of these, 50 were buildings. There had been a yearly average for about five years of forty buildings coming onto the foreclosure roles, with only five or six being auctioned off. The foreclosure rate on vacant land was about the same—forty parcels a year. While most of them were auctioned off, they usually became truck yards and parking areas for the Charlestown Navy Yard. In 1965 75 percent of the lots sold by the city were vacant. (BRA: Charlestown, "Analytical Summary of the Public Hearing Before the Boston City Council Regarding the Charlestown Urban Renewal Project," Spring 1965, pp. 4–5.)

dren. In a town passionately proud of its hockey team, there was no place to skate. Charlestown's shopping facilities were so meager that 85 percent of each homeowner's commercial shopping dollar was spent outside the district's boundaries.[8] Beyond the easily recorded indices of "blight" and "deterioration" which mark Charlestown was the significant fact that in 1960 the average nonproject income level in Charlestown was higher and the rental level lower than the city average.

From the physical and economic points of view Charlestown offered the perfect setting in which to test Logue's approach to residential rehabilitation: highly visible physical problems joined with a relatively low incidence of social ills, a homogeneous population, and a high rate of resident homeowners, many of whom had the financial capacity to carry rehabilitation costs.

From our description thus far, one gets no insight into the origins of the civil war the urban renewal issue caused in the town. To get at these roots, one has to look beyond aggregate statistics and into Charlestown's unique social and political characteristics.

INTEREST GROUPS

THE TOWNIES[9]

An outsider coming upon Charlestown for the first time feels like an anthropologist discovering a tribe in the highlands of New Guinea or a clan of Kentucky mountain folk still speaking pure seventeenth-century English, for in many ways Charlestown is an anachronism. Bypassed by the urbanization and industrialization that surround it on all sides, its physical isolation both symbolizes and contributes to its social uniqueness. While many of the Town's young people and socially mobile families flocked to suburbia after World War II, the enclave that remained is bound together by religious, ethnic, historical, and marital ties often stretching back for generations. The characteristics that commentators on urban life see plaguing today's city have not come to Charlestown: anomie, breakdown of the family, separation of work and residence, loosening of the means of socialization. Family life is the way of life in Charlestown. Old couples or individuals are more than

---

8 Author's interview with Frank Del Vecchio, Project Director of the Charlestown Urban Renewal Project, February 15, 1966.

9 By "Townie" I refer to a member of the Charlestown community whose life style is more or less as described in this section. This is not an attempt to define social structure or culture but, as Gans says, to "describe the quality of social life." (Herbert Gans, *The Urban Villagers* (New York: The Free Press of Glencoe, 1962), p. 4.) While the image of the Townie style may be as much in the mind of the beholder as in hard statistical data, with the advent of renewal planning the image assumed its own reality.

likely to have sons and daughters living elsewhere in the Town. It is estimated that 70 percent of Charlestown's men work on the docks or in the factories and warehouses in and around Charlestown.[10] The district's Catholic parishes, marked by the three spires on the Town's skyline, are headed by three Monsignori, an unusual concentration of powerful men of the Church. The overwhelming Catholic composition of the community means that the three churches, along with the two parochial schools and Holy Name Societies in each parish, are enormously important agents for socialization in the Charlestown community. Use of parish lines as a means of identifying oneself with a particular part of Charlestown is so persuasive that members of a protestant minister's congregation identify their part of Town as "St. Francis' Parish."

Yet the Irish-Catholic culture that statistically dominates Charlestown is not the sole unifying force in the Town. Irish working-class solidarity has over the years become interwoven with a loyalty to Charlestown—"Our Town," as residents call it—which transcends anything necessarily Irish or Catholic. Thus one can account for the fact that Charlestown's sizable Italian stock is well assimilated into the Town's society. As one observer puts it, "It is a lot better to be a Charlestown Italian Protestant than a North End Italian Catholic. Italians are Wops when they don't live in Charlestown, but they are Townies when they live here."[11]

Beyond ethnic, religious, and historical bonds with the Town lies another unifying strain typical of village life—intermarriage, which over five generations has knotted the community with family ties. The extent of those ties is difficult to document, but the view that "everybody is related to somebody in this Town" is one expressed by most observers of the Charlestown scene. The scope of the extended family in Charlestown is vividly illustrated by the following statement made at a renewal hearing:

I don't represent any organization here today. I just represent my family clan, which is ten sisters and brothers and their husbands and wives, 103 grandchildren and 60 great-grandchildren . . . this adds up to 185 that want to be recorded as against urban renewal.[12]

With all her social ties, it is readily understandable that Charlestown be characterized as a community with "instant communication." Combine a social setting in which everyone "either knows or is related to everybody else"[13] with the possibilities for speed offered by the telephone, and the social system's capacity to absorb and distribute information becomes almost limitless.

10 Author's interview with Frank Del Vecchio.
11 Author's interview with Reverend William Burnett, March 1, 1966.
12 BRA: Charlestown, "Charlestown Renewal Area: Public Hearing Held by BRA," Stenographic Transcript, March 14, 1965, p. 59.
13 Interview with Gene Hennessey, February 14, 1966.

A perhaps inevitable feature of an isolated homogeneous village like Charlestown is pinpointed by the resident who remarked, "This place is either a wonderful small town or a Peyton Place—take your pick."[14] The essential point is clear. Long years of isolation, a lack of new blood, and a multitude of points of involvement with others in the town have resulted in a situation in which "everybody has something on everybody else."[15] Personal feuds, gossip, and the pettiness of the small town alternate with the positive features of an urban village which engender such loyalty that graduates of the Charlestown High School return each year from the Boston metropolitan area and beyond for their annual reunion. Allegiance to Charlestown is strong, as the words of one who left the fold indicate, "You never find me in Somerville. I sleep there once in a while, and eat a meal there, but 90 percent of the time I am right here in Charlestown. It is the only town to be in."[16]

The society we have been describing in Charlestown is much like the working-class subculture detailed in great thoroughness by Gans:[17] the extended family, peer group society, and suspicion of the outside world. One could fruitfully compare in detail life in Charlestown to Gans's report of the West End. However, we are primarily concerned, not with the total Charlestown social system, but with those particular aspects of Townie culture which might affect the operation of the residential rehabilitation game.

It must be pointed out that the Townie interest group cuts across the categories of homeownership or tenancy, age, and income. Because the Townie interest is a composite of many observable aspects of the style of life in Charlestown, it is impossible to say how many people actually manifest all the characteristics we have emphasized here.

THE PROJECT PEOPLE

It is important to recognize groups in Charlestown that do not partake of the life style we have been describing. The most obvious such group is found in the public housing project that makes up roughly one sixth of the housing units in the Town. By and large, the project people are "set apart from the 'townies.' "[18] Despite this isolation, some long-time Charlestown residents have moved into the project. The fact that the second president of the prestigious Charlestown Federation was a former project resident indicates that the barriers between it and the rest of the community are not insurmount-

14 Interview with Marie Sweeney, March 8, 1966.
15 Interview with Michael Matt, February 9, 1966.
16 BRA: "Charlestown Renewal Area: Public Hearing Held by BRA," Stenographic Transcript, March 14, 1965, p. 235.
17 See Gans, op. cit., pp. 229–262.
18 The Boston Herald, December 2, 1965.

able. Yet Townies generally feel that many "transients" live in the project and that it has "gone downhill since the war."[19]

While the project people are the poorest enclave in the Town, they are the least likely to be adversely affected by urban renewal, for renewal does not threaten their homes through demolition or their pocketbooks through rehabilitation, and it offers the prospect of new schools, parks, and other public facilities from which the project residents would benefit.

THE NON-TOWNIES

A painstaking BRA survey of police listings revealed that there were 7,778 in-migrants over the age of nineteen to Charlestown during a ten-year period (1950–1959) in which the Town was undergoing a net loss of about 6,000 people.[20] The large number of in-migrants seems to contradict the image of a static urban village community rapidly being drained of its young blood. On the other hand, one must take into account that the housing project, representing about 4,500 people, has a 10 percent turnover rate per annum and thus in the ten-year period under scrutiny well over half of the 7,778 in-migrants could have been funneled there, leaving less than 4,000 people who actually moved into Charlestown proper. Obviously, not all the 10 percent was made up of people from outside Charlestown, but a large proportion of that turnover can be assumed to have originated from a location other than the Town itself.

There is no question that of the 7,778 in-migrants many were concerned not so much with the Town's social setting as with the extraordinarily low rentals offered in the area. The "transients," as many of the newcomers during the fifties were called, found lodging throughout Charlestown but were felt to be concentrated in the belt of deteriorating housing trapped between Main Street and Rutherford Avenue.

Looking elsewhere in Charlestown for non-Townie residential interest groups, one finds that, unlike the South End, there are only a few rooming houses scattered throughout the town. Moreover, while well-stocked with liquor licenses, Charlestown has a skid row that is said to consist of "fifteen professional bums who hang around City Square."[21]

When the deviations from the Charlestown norm are accounted for, the overwhelming fact remains that the majority of Charlestown's people are Urban Villagers in a secularized Irish-Catholic, working-class setting. Given this fact, it is important to concentrate on four aspects of Townie style

19 Author's interviews with Thomas Getherall, March 2, 1966, and John Grace, February 27, 1966.
20 BRA: Charlestown, "Demographic Analyses and Forecasts for Charlestown," February 16, 1962, p. 9.
21 Author's interview with Frank Del Vecchio.

which would have direct bearing on the manner in which the local renewal team might be constituted and might play the planning game.

ORGANIZATIONS

Unlike Gans's West End Urban Villagers, Townies are for the most part inextricably involved in formal organizations. With their Holy Name Societies and sodalities, the three parishes provide the institutional setting for much of the Town's social life. Moreover, the Town is filled with a vast number of "booster" clubs, ranging from the Lions and Kiwanis to the High School Boosters and the Friends of the Charlestown Library. Not everyone in Charlestown belongs to clubs, and it is difficult to pin an exact percentage on those who are involved in the organizational maze. What is significant for us, however, is that organizations, clubs, and sodalities constitute an integral part of the Townie life style. Prior to the founding in 1965 of the John F. Kennedy Multi-Service Center, there were few social service organizations in Charlestown, and before 1960 neighborhood associations and block organizations did not figure significantly among the host of formal groups in the Town.

ELITES AND EGALITARIANISM

At the beginning of the twentieth century, it was possible for an observer of the Charlestown scene to write:

Irish families were living in Monument Square, Winthrop Square and other sections which had been the homes of the elites of old Charlestown; and they had developed a social life that was comparable with the best of the past.[22]

This image of the elite at the top of the hill and the "poor" people down in the valley continues to this day. Aggregate statistics bear out the fact that incomes are higher and the percentage of professionals greater in the tracts around Monument Square. However, since World War II, Charlestown has offered little prestige for those "moving up in the world," and therefore the natural forces of social mobility have taken most of those seeking higher status out of the Town.

In *Beyond the Melting Pot,* Moynihan makes a statement that has great bearing on the Charlestown community in the 1960's:

The Irish American character was . . . urban and it was egalitarian. Where the Irish had been wild, they now became tough. Where they had been rebellious, it now became a matter of being defiantly democratic.[23]

22 William Cole, "Charlestown," Unpublished section of *Zone of Emergence,* by Robert A. Woods and Albert J. Kennedy, 1910, p. 10 (manuscript on file at United South End Settlements).
23 Nathan Glazer and Daniel Patrick Moynihan, *Beyond the Melting Pot* (Cambridge: The M.I.T. Press, 1964), p. 245.

Given the absence of a recognized elite and of a clear means of identifying a ruling class, the distinctions that exist in the Town between "important" and "unimportant" people are under constant surveillance by those desiring either to maximize or to minimize such differences. The tension between egalitarianism and drive for status permeates life in Charlestown.

TOWNIE POLITICS

Jockeying for leadership positions within Charlestown organizations constitutes a significant aspect of Townie style. Campaigns for the elected offices in the Knights of Columbus and the American Legion Post are fought over with real passion. The absence of a clearly defined leadership class and the existence of a vast array of formal organizations demanding leaders provide a framework within which individuals in the Town can vie for position. And, as one observer put it, "Status here is gained as much by knocking someone off a leadership position as by gaining that position for oneself."[24] A closed social system in which with a few exceptions social status in terms of the larger society can only be gained by leaving the urban village for the suburb results in a situation in which prestige can be gained in Charlestown only at the expense of some other Townie—a situation that breeds a system of personal rivalries and recollection of past political combat.

The Townie trait of jockeying for position within the community and its organizations is an aspect of the "immigrant style" of politics carefully recorded in Banfield and Wilson's *City Politics*.[25] The history of how the Boston Irish came to terms with their Yankee masters by wresting political power from them has been recounted many times. And there is no denying that the Charlestown Irish are hyperpolitical creatures. In formal terms this political awareness manifests itself in the high percentage of Charlestown's residents who are registered voters: 82 percent, the third highest of Boston's 22 wards, where the over-all registration average is 73 percent.[26] In the 1964 primary election for state representative, fourteen Townies ran for the Democratic nomination. With only one representative from Ward 2, this number of candidates represented the highest ratio of candidates to office of any ward in the city.

Many of those involved in the internal battle for leadership in Charlestown are playing the game of parlaying sufficient prestige in the complex of organizations within Charlestown to "run for Rep." Conversely, one of the

24 Author's interview with Michael Matt.
25 Edward C. Banfield and James Q. Wilson, *City Politics* (Cambridge: Harvard University Press and The M.I.T. Press, 1963).
26 City of Boston, Election Department Annual Report, 1964.

fears of those not involved in formal politics is that an individual will use the organizational system of the Town as a base from which to get into politics.

Gans's description of the Urban Villagers' attitude toward politicians is extremely relevant to Charlestown:

West Enders judge good government by peer group rules and by the extent to which its allocation policies fit their interests. . . . Government agencies have no reality; the city is seen as a congeries of individuals, most of whom are corrupt.[27]

The people of Charlestown possess an enormous political awareness. They know how to play the political game and have had vast experience at it. Yet like the West Enders, they maintain a certain ambivalence toward politics and politicians. Many residents find politics distasteful and are constantly on guard against being used for another's political advantage or being accused of using someone themselves. Such ambivalence, however, does not prevent people from personally taking advantage of the political system. As a BRA staff member put it,

You take the Representative from Ashburton [a small outlying Massachusetts town]. A guy from that town comes in and visits his Rep in the state house and the Rep shows him the hall of flags and the Senate chambers and the guy goes away very impressed with his Rep and what he is doing on Beacon Hill. In Charlestown the Rep is a personal messenger boy. People go into him and they don't buy any of the hall-of-flag crap. They say, "What have you done for me lately?" In this town a guy won't last more than three terms because he can't do everything for everybody and that is what is expected, and when he misses enough and builds up some enemies he gets knocked off the block.[28]

HOUSING AS AN INFERIOR GOOD

Census figures in 1960 indicate that while the city percentage average of annual income paid for gross rent was 16 percent, Charlestown residents, including project people, paid less than 13 percent. Fourteen dollars a month could be added to the Charlestown average to arrive at a ratio of rent to income that would be equal to the Boston average.

Obviously, despite the high median income, there are homeowners in Charlestown whose level of income precludes expenditure on home improvement. What is of concern to us here, however, is the number of homeowners who could afford to improve their property but have chosen not to do so. Moreover, like Gans's West End, when investment in housing is made, it is in terms of interior improvements and conveniences rather than exterior work and painting.

There are several reasons why families who could afford to have not put more money into the exteriors of their Charlestown homes. The primary issue is one of values. Those who have been particularly concerned with the

27 Gans, *op. cit.*, pp. 164–165.
28 Author's interview with Michael Matt.

quality of their housing and with housing as a status item have left Charlestown for suburbia. Rather than upgrading the quality of the exterior of their residences, families remaining in the town have chosen to spend their money on clothes, recreation, travel, and, in some cases, vacation houses. Moreover, allowing exteriors to remain shabby is viewed as a means of keeping down one's property tax assessment.

HORIZONTAL INTEGRATION

The very essence of Townie style is that religious, ethnic, and historic identification with a particular physical setting combine to link closely the majority of Charlestown's inhabitants into a unified community. The lines of the three parishes, St. Mary's, St. Catherine's, and St. Francis', serve as a more immediate frame of reference than the boundaries of the Town itself; but while these parish divisions do form the basis for some rivalry, they do not cut Charlestown up into distinct neighborhoods. Nor ultimately is the aura of social distinction that surrounds the "top of the hill" significant enough to detach that area from the sense of "one town" that permeates Charlestown. The public housing project represents the one large barrier to complete horizontal integration throughout the district. Yet even here there is not total isolation, for ties to the Catholic Church serve as a means for drawing many project people into the life of St. Catherine's Parish.

VERTICAL INTEGRATION

In 1630, one year after Charlestown's founding, John Winthrop arrived in town with a large band of settlers. After several months of vain search for easily accessible water, Winthrop decided to seek greener pastures and moved with most of his followers across the harbor to Boston. Historical accounts relate that, "He took also the frame of the house he had been constructing in Charlestown much to the discontent of those who remained."[29]

Winthrop's act started a pattern of events by which Boston consistently seems to benefit at Charlestown's expense. Even the act of annexation which joined Charlestown to the larger city in 1873 was marked by confusion and, from Charlestown's point of view, bad faith. Swayed by Boston's promise of municipal improvements, Charlestown voters narrowly approved annexation. The improvements were never forthcoming.[30] In 1901 the town was irreparably damaged when the Boston Elevated Company was granted the right to run tracks the length of Charlestown's Main Street. Within ten years, the first of many petitions was raised for the "El's" removal.[31] In 1942

29 BRA: Charlestown, "Historical Data—Charlestown, Massachusetts," undated, p. 3.
30 Ibid., p. 19, and author's interview with Frank Del Vecchio.
31 The Boston Herald, December 2, 1965.

Charlestown was hit again when the Boston Housing Authority ripped out a huge part of the Town's northeast corner to put in the public housing project. The demolition of housing and the dislocation of owners and tenants caused by this effort was made an even blacker mark against the city when payments for residential structures were set at assessed valuation plus 10 percent—a figure that, given the state of Boston's assessments, bore little relationhip to the market or replacement value of the houses. Moreover, prior to demolition, the Housing Authority made promises to rehouse all those uprooted by the construction in the new public units, promises it was unwilling or unable to keep.[32] The next time a public agency came into Charlestown was in 1950 when the Massachusetts Port Authority bulldozed dozens of homes to make way for access ramps to the Mystic River Bridge.

While few are left in Charlestown who remember when the "El" took over Main Street, many remain who watched the housing project and the Mystic River Bridge go up, while their homes and those of their neighbors went down. Given the natural suspicion that this urban village has for outsiders, distrust has been magnified a hundredfold by constant battering at the hands of the larger community. Where South Enders may feel that they have suffered from neglect at the city's hand, Townies have a vast housing project, a clanging elevated transit line, and a massive skyway to prove that they have been positively sacrificed to benefit the rest of Boston and the suburbs.

The immediate and proper conclusion to draw from these events is that Charlestown has little political power at the city or state level. While the community does not suffer from gerrymandering and has control of all of Ward 2, Charlestown's population loss has cut its representatives in the State House from two to one. Moreover, the Town must share a state senator with East Boston, an Italian district that has sufficient votes to determine who can and will be elected. The fact that Charlestown is almost totally Democratic means that once a state politician has gotten past the primary election, he has to make few efforts to be assured of the Charlestown vote. The single state representative is, as we have pointed out, under so much pressure from individuals in the Town seeking personal favors that he has little time to think or act for the Town as a whole. This lack of political muscle is reflected in the distribution of public funds to Charlestown, as astute Townies are well aware:

The state has spent millions in Southie [South Boston] . . . and while we don't begrudge any section their just due we still wonder why we never have any state funds spent in Charlestown. Or do we? All we have to do is add up the City

[32] Author's interview with David Walsh, February 25, 1966.

Councillors, the state reps and the Senators (and leave us not forget the Senators) and we have our answer.[33]

Cut off literally as well as figuratively from the larger urban system, the district has preserved its small-town homogeneity while being buffeted by an expanding metropolis. Inward-looking both physically and socially, Charlestown has never felt itself part of the city around it. This historical absence of positive linkages with the larger community constitutes a heritage that would have to be overcome before renewal planning could be successfully achieved in the Town.

CHARLESTOWN AS A PATTERN OF POWER

From the point of view of power in the rehabilitation planning game, the most significant characteristics of Charlestown are her egalitarian spirit, organizational capacity, and the xenophobic tribalism of the majority of the area's residents. Unlike the South End, the capacity to make one's voice heard is not a diffusely scattered ability but rather a deep-seated aspect of life in the Town.

Beyond the fact that power, as we are using the word, runs deep in Charlestown, one must consider the impact on renewal planning of the Townie game of knocking the leader from the top. For rehabilitation planning is predicated on finding leaders who can speak for their area, and the extent to which the Townie characteristics of social equality and love of political infighting might work against the structured bargaining process of the renewal game must be borne in mind when assessing the compatibility between Logue's planning strategy and the social dynamics of Charlestown.

At a larger scale one must also recognize that the xenophobia of the Charlestown urban village, coupled with its history of disastrous relationships with the larger community, creates a situation in which an outsider coming to Charlestown to "do" something for the Town would be viewed with suspicion and distrust. Any renewal team dropped into the community would have to demonstrate that it was not going to sacrifice Charlestown, as had been done so many times before, for the betterment of Boston and the metropolitan area.

In spite of all these aspects of Charlestown style and history which might have a possible negative impact on the renewal game, Charlestown in 1960 was in many ways an ideal community for residential rehabilitation. Basically the Town is an area in which the "communalist concept of the public interest can be said to operate [and where] the ends which the plurality entertains 'as a whole' are ends which its individual members universally or

[33] *SHOC Talk* (Self-Help Organization-Charlestown), Vol. 9, June 1961.

almost universally share."[34] The end "almost universally shared" in Charlestown is a positive attachment to the Town itself and its way of life. As one resident put it, "We know we can move any time we want to, because this is America; but we do not choose to. We are Townies, and we would rather fight than switch."[35]

In that hypothetical world of the central decision maker with total control over the course of events in the renewal rehabilitation game, the Charlestown project would have offered none of the complex issues of Washington Park or the South End. Planning with one Charlestown interest group in mind did not automatically preclude another, as was the case in the other two areas. In Charlestown, "the poor" were for the most part in the housing project, in which case they were protected from the costs of demolition or rehabilitation, or they were part of the Townie camp, in which case their interests would be well represented on the local planning team. While the transients might have a less secure position in the renewal game than the genuine Townies, there was nothing fundamentally incompatible between their life style and that of the average working-class Townie.

The actual course of events in renewal's confrontation with Charlestown would show how incidental was the objective nexus of Charlestown's problems with the capacities of the renewal process. For while it is true that preservation of the town and the resurrection of its physical structure could be said to be a universal goal among Townies, the real issue in Charlestown would be the means of achieving that goal. It is about the question of agreement on means that Ed Logue could correctly say, "I suppose there is one thing we would all agree on and that is that there is no unanimity in Charlestown about almost anything."[36]

[34] Martin Meyerson and Edward C. Banfield, *Politics, Planning, and the Public Interest* (New York: The Free Press of Glencoe, 1955), p. 323.
[35] BRA: Charlestown, "Charlestown Renewal Area: Public Hearing Held by BRA," March 14, 1965, p. 23.
[36] City of Boston, City Council, "Charlestown Urban Renewal Project: Before Committee on Urban Renewal," Stenographic Transcript, April 1965, p. 116.

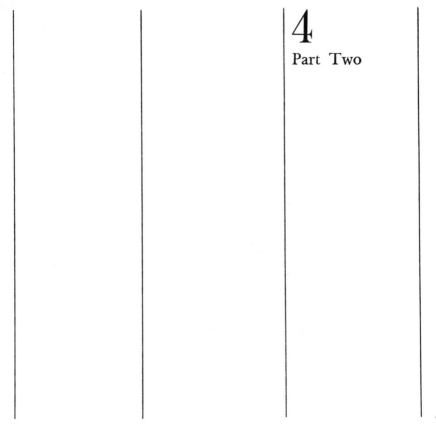

4
Part Two

THE ADVENT OF RENEWAL:
ORIGINS OF THE LOCAL TEAM

If Ed Logue had come to Boston one year earlier, he would have had difficulty finding a point of entry into Charlestown, that is, a group to whom he could have given the mandate for renewal negotiation; for despite its high level of social activity, in 1960 Charlestown had no tradition of community organization concentrating on the welfare of the Town as a whole. In April 1960, however, the scene changed radically with a letter to the *Charlestown Patriot*, the district's weekly paper. "Charlestown is in a bad way," it read. "How many feel concerned? . . . Isn't it time that all the people and all the organizations got together for common self-preservation?"[37] One person who was concerned and willing to translate that concern into action was the author of the letter, Leo Baldwin. Born and bred in Charlestown, Baldwin had been taken away from the Town by his engineering career for the eight years following World War II. He had been shocked at the physical condi-

37 *Charlestown Patriot*, April 7, 1960.

tion of the Town when he returned, but his drive to "get Charlestown moving again" did not start until 1960.

The response to his letter was enthusiastic. People from the churches volunteered to help, the state representative cheered the idea, and one week later Baldwin again wrote to the *Patriot,* urging the creation of "not an anti-anything group but a pro-group for Charlestown and anything that will improve the conditions for all the people of Charlestown."[38]

Baldwin's third letter made clear that the need for such a citizen's organization was not simply because the Town's physical condition required serious attention but also because urban renewal in the form of Ed Logue was coming to Boston, and Charlestown had better be ready for action.

We of Charlestown have no knowledge of what Mr. Logue is going to do for the correction of the slums and blight marching up our hills, and the way matters stand today we are liable to wake up some morning to the sound of bulldozers. Mr. Logue thinks big and bold. What would we do then? Run around and form a committee to save Charlestown? The people of the West End formed their committee when the West End was doomed. Have you seen the West End lately?[39]

Baldwin was clearly using the threat of the bulldozer as a way of rousing Townies to his call. His month-long effort resulted in a meeting in May 1960 at the Charlestown Knights of Columbus Hall, which drew more than 600 Charlestown citizens, including representatives from all the churches and fraternal and social organizations in the Town. When one considers that the total adult population of Charlestown in 1960 was about 12,000 people, a 5 percent turnout at a meeting promoted by one person for only a month gives some indication of the capacity of Townies to mobilize when the proper lines of communication are tapped.

At the meeting, Baldwin reiterated the points that he had made in the *Patriot.* Charlestown was falling apart, and wasn't it time Townies did something about that fact? Urban renewal was around the corner, and hadn't the Town better be equipped to minimize the threat and maximize the opportunity of that process? The creation of the Self-Help Organization-Charlestown, or SHOC, was the answer to these questions; and 350 of those present joined that night. SHOC was to be made up of individuals, not representatives of organizations, and any citizen of Charlestown was welcome to join.

Events of the next few months tell an extraordinary tale of citizen involvement in "doing something" about Charlestown. Baldwin's natural leadership, combined with the enormous enthusiasm with which SHOC was greeted by a large number of Townies, created a situation in which a grassroots movement for the betterment of Charlestown could flourish and grow.

It is important to emphasize that the need for a mechanism to deal with

38 *Ibid.,* April 14, 1960.
39 *Ibid.,* April 28, 1960.

urban renewal was as much a reason for SHOC's establishment as the organization's self-help aspect. Later on, the standard line of the hardcore anti-renewalites would be that SHOC was part of a plot to sell renewal to the people of Charlestown, that it had been formed in the back room of the mayor's office, and that the idea of SHOC had been promoted and accepted in Charlestown on the assumption that it was solely a self-help operation.[40] An examination of the record shows that this story was a total fabrication.

Within a month of its organizational meeting, SHOC was fleshed out with officers. Baldwin was president. An executive board that was to meet monthly was established, and seven zone captains were appointed, one for each voting precinct in the town. During 1960 the group expanded by leaps and bounds. By August there were 800 members. Rubbish drives, cleaning up vacant lots, pressuring City Hall to provide trucks for hauling away trash, blocking a liquor license—into all of these activities SHOC threw itself with enthusiasm. A "teen canteen" was established, block dances were held, and a monthly letter called *SHOC Talk* was published and widely distributed in the Town. The organization got the pledged support of all the Charlestown churches and prestigious organizations. Even those who later were in violent opposition to urban renewal and who felt that the creation of SHOC was simply a plot to sneak urban renewal into the community admit that it was a wondrous organization during its first year of operation.

From its beginning in May 1960, SHOC was not just a cleanup brigade and organizer of social functions. It was also the local team that would play the residential renewal planning game. That was clear from the start, for only four weeks after the founding meeting Dick Green, who was then working for the Boston City Planning Board (incorporated into the BRA when Logue took over in 1961), talked to the SHOC executive board about "the City's intentions insofar as the Charlestown area was concerned."[41] By July Baldwin was able to say that "The present members of SHOC have been told of urban renewal proposals and they have been told that they are the people—because they have shown the interest—who will be consulted when urban renewal plans are formulated for this town."[42]

A meeting with Logue in September 1960 confirmed in formal terms the relationship between the BRA and SHOC that had been presumed since May. Taking on the "great responsibility" of negotiating renewal for Charlestown's people was, said *SHOC Talk*, "not a job we relish, but it is

40 See statements by Marie and James Sweeney at City of Boston, City Council, "Charlestown Urban Renewal Project: Before Committee on Urban Renewal," Stenographic Transcript, May 1965, pp. 1238–1248.
41 SHOC, Executive Board Meeting, Minutes, June 6, 1960.
42 *Charlestown Patriot,* July 7, 1960.

the only hope in sight."[43] The bellicose terms of all SHOC's proclamations made clear that the organization would drive a hard bargain with the BRA.

Throughout the winter of 1960–1961, SHOC set about the task of structuring itself to deal with renewal negotiations. A Planning Council was created to serve as the organization's official body for dealing with the BRA staff. Using the *Patriot* to explain the role of the new group, Baldwin stated:

The Planning Council . . . will not make autonomous or independent decisions affecting Charlestown. The suggestions as to the desires and wishes of the people will be channelled through the Zone Captains and assistants to the Executive Board where they will be debated before being included in the plans as indicative of the wishes of the majority. Separate surveys will be made in each neighborhood . . . to determine the wishes of all concerned.[44]

The seven-man Council, with one representative from each zone, was to be moderated by Baldwin and advised by two members of the clergy, a lawyer, and the Charlestown state representative. Soon biweekly meetings were being held between Green and the Planning Council to discuss the specific elements of a plan for the district's rehabilitation. Thus, less than one year after Leo Baldwin's original letter to the *Patriot*, Charlestown had an operating renewal team based on broad community support.

THE CHARLESTOWN TEAM PLANS FOR RENEWAL:
ROUND ONE—THE ERA OF GOOD FEELING

Those who engaged in this early planning period look back to it through intervening years of strife and dissension as the Golden Age of citizen participation. Baldwin himself recalls the process with great approbation.

The [BRA] Charlestown Project Director listened, set down suggestions, consulted with other elements in the community. . . . Although some apprehension was exhibited by those who felt that they would become directly affected, on the whole, excellent community relations were maintained. The Project Director showed sincerity and concern for the myriad problems posed by the blight of sixty years. SHOC's open meetings kept those informed who wanted current information and most importantly the town was provided an outlet for blowing off steam and acquiring information.[45]

The Project Director was Dick Green, and he seems to have approached Charlestown with very much the same astuteness he was later to demonstrate in the South End. Many of those today in violent opposition to renewal in Charlestown were deeply involved in the early SHOC planning efforts with Green and feel that if he had not left the project, the civil war over urban renewal could have been avoided.

Charlestown is anything but a liberal community as its attitude toward Negroes indicates; however, the fact that Dick Green is Jewish was probably

43 *SHOC Talk,* Vol. III, September 1960.
44 *Charlestown Patriot,* February 21, 1961.
45 Leo Baldwin, "The C.U.R.E.: The Charlestown Urban Renewal Effort 1960–1965," unpublished manuscript, March 1966, p. 17.

to his advantage in his negotiations with Townies. That Green was not only an "outsider" but also a "non-Irish outsider" made it inevitable that people would have to explain to him "how things were" in Charlestown. He could be expected to make mistakes and not have ready solutions. Yet two of the things most vividly remembered about Green were his willingness to admit when necessary that he did not know the answer to a question and his persistence in tracking such answers down. Moreover, his open manner and constant availability to small and large groups gave him a reputation as a regular guy and a straight shooter, appellations that would not be granted many BRA personnel during the course of negotiations in the Town.

In view of the rapport that developed between Green and SHOC, it is interesting to note the planning assumptions against which his negotiations were couched when he first met with the organization in the spring of 1960. The District Plan for Charlestown, worked out by Dick Green before Logue got to Boston, called for an enormous amount of residential clearance. The plan stated that out of the Town's 6,476 dwelling units only 2,630 (40 percent) were worth saving and that many of those would require major rehabilitation.[46] It appears that the plan, which represented the best thinking of the pre-Logue era, never got to the Charlestown community.[47] As Green's first contacts with the SHOC people made clear, official planning concepts were geared to a much higher percentage of residential demolition than Townies were willing to tolerate. With the exception of the area locked between Rutherford Avenue and Main Street, the extensive clearance areas delineated by the District Plan were never considered during these discussions. Green's earlier plans for clearance went by the board as he quickly saw the political unreality of such an approach.

As was clear to Green from the start, what SHOC wanted out of renewal was a means of shoring up the residential part of the town, bulwarking it against through traffic, commerce, and industry, and preserving it for the Townies, while making it so enticing with community facilities, public improvements, and new housing that some of those who had left the village would return from suburbia. Renewal was a means, then, of reinforcing and refurbishing an existing life style or, perhaps more realistically, of re-creating "the good old days"—Charlestown as it had been in the past. Other than the "El," which stood as a cause and symbol of all that was wrong with

---

46 Boston City Planning Board, "Charlestown District Study," March 14, 1960, p. 2.
47 The district proposal, while radical in comparison with the plan that eventually emerged from Charlestown's renewal game, is itself a far greater effort at conservation than the recommendation of the 1950 General Plan for Boston, which calls for the redevelopment of all the residential areas in Charlestown other than that represented by the 1,149 units of public housing. (Boston City Planning Board, "Preliminary Report—1950: General Plan for Boston," Boston, December 1950, map facing p. 46.)

Charlestown and was the rallying point of any renewal plan, the specific physical changes which were to be made in the Town—straightening roads and building new schools and shopping facilities—were always seen as being of secondary importance. The underlying goal was to make Charlestown a better community for all residents by providing new housing, making rehabilitation for existing owners and renters an economically viable operation, and ensuring that those who did have to relocate could do so within Charlestown's boundaries.

Renewal was viewed as a tool that could benefit the entire town. As there were no groups in Charlestown seen as "undesirable" by those on the Planning Council, there was no interest in demolition as a means of eliminating some of the Town's residents. Social renewal, an issue that loomed so large in the early days of negotiation in the South End, was never a major factor in the Charlestown situation. The absence of a social welfare interest group and the fact that the Town was not suffering from enormous social disorders kept this aspect of renewal from rising to the surface.

If one were to bet on the outcome of renewal based on the manner in which negotiations were proceeding in the spring of 1961, the odds looked good for a plan being hammered out which would have SHOC's support.

RESTRUCTURING THE TEAMS

The apotheosis of the BRA-SHOC relationship came in the spring of 1961 when Logue and Baldwin both spoke at that yearly reaffirmation of the Townie way of life, the Old Charlestown Schoolboys' Annual Banquet. In his speech, Logue emphasized how much Charlestown had changed in a year and that "the fierce pride shown by Charlestown residents in SHOC had given rise to the thought that SHOC's motto should be 'Don't tread on me.' "[48]

At the time Logue had no idea how prophetic he was being. During that same spring Dick Green was suddenly pulled off the Charlestown project, and with his exit one can say that the first stage of planning came to an abrupt halt. Green was transferred because Logue had decided that it would facilitate planning negotiations in Charlestown to have, as one observer put it, "a nice Irish boy in the Town."[49] This assumption represented a total misreading of the Charlestown community, as Logue is now willing to admit. Later, when the official opposition story of the renewal process in Charlestown was fully constructed, it would be put forth that Green was "zipped to another project because he got too friendly."[50] Such was not the

48 *SHOC Talk*, Vol. IX, June 1961.
49 Author's interview with Gene Hennessey.
50 Author's interview with Mike Mansfield, March 3, 1966.

case, but it was convenient to see Green's removal as just one of a long string of conspiratorial moves on the part of Logue and City Hall to sell Charlestown down the river.

Throughout this exposition, emphasis has been placed on the significance of the Local Planning Agency's "style" and understanding of the sociopolitical dynamics of the local community as factors in the rehabilitation planning game. At no point in any of the projects under study is the change of the BRA's approach to the local community more critical than the transfer from Green to Pat MacCarthy, the new project director for Charlestown. While carrying an Irish name and with, as one Townie commented, "the map of Ireland written all over his face,"[51] MacCarthy would find that both these characteristics worked against him in Charlestown. Being Irish, he was expected to understand how things worked in an Irish town, yet MacCarthy was an outsider and very much a member of the middle class.

Relationships between the Harvard Irishman and SHOC did not run smoothly. The free-swinging SHOC meetings, which "provided an outlet for blowing off steam and acquiring information,"[52] were not to MacCarthy's liking. Moreover, during his tenure in Charlestown, he would negotiate in a manner that rubbed some Townies the wrong way. MacCarthy seemed to convey to many residents the impression of an outsider to be viewed with suspicion.

While the BRA team was radically jarred by the arrival of MacCarthy and the departure of Green, the community team would never again be as clearly defined as at the Old Charlestown Schoolboys' Annual Banquet; for at about the same time as Green's exit, SHOC's right to the renewal mandate for Charlestown was being seriously questioned.

Throughout the first year of its existence, SHOC was a grass-roots organization that fired the imagination of Charlestown people. As one *SHOC Talk* editorial stated in the winter of 1961,

SHOC is growing more powerful every day, and we must be careful that we use our power prudently and morally for the common-spread-out-good of *all* of Charlestown . . . let's keep cool and play it close to the chest—we've really got something here.[53]

Among the many things that SHOC had was an ambitious, articulate leader who dominated the organization with his administrative capacities, imagination, and personality. As a result of his activity with SHOC, Baldwin became a well-known figure not only in Charlestown but in the larger community as well. He was written up in the Boston papers, appeared on television, and spoke at the prestigious Boston College Seminar.

51 Author's interview with Gene Hennessey.
52 Baldwin, *op. cit.*
53 *SHOC Talk*, Vol. VI, January 1961.

There is no question that SHOC enhanced Baldwin's prestige, and many people in Charlestown were not going to support an organization that seemed to serve as the vehicle for another Townie's success. Baldwin had been involved in politics in the early fifties and thus was open to the suspicion that all Townies have of "their own" who are known to have political leanings. Moreover, early in the renewal planning game, other Townies came to wonder if Baldwin might not be too much of a firebrand to handle the delicate art of renewal negotiation. Concluding that SHOC was irresponsible and that Baldwin often acted on his own and precipitously, some of those initially involved in the organization pulled out.

Still other Townies did not become involved in SHOC because they felt it lacked prestige:

SHOC was made up of common people. Not that I have anything against common people. I am not being a snob. I have been a longshoreman. But the real powers in the community were not a part of SHOC. SHOC had a good reputation for cleaning up the streets and holding teen parties, and people were proud of what they had done, but it was not seen as a group that included all the big guns of the town and was not seen as a group that could lead the battle for urban renewal.[54]

The most significant "big guns" that SHOC did not include were members of the Charlestown clergy. While all local churches had warmly backed SHOC at its inception and praised its good work in the community, the clergymen—one Catholic and one Protestant—who had been actively involved in SHOC's initial activity had gradually withdrawn their support.

Thus, for all its success and zeal, SHOC faced some real problems in terms of its relationships to powerful people and organizations in the complex Charlestown community. For, unlike the South End where he who calls himself a leader can step into a position of authority, in Charlestown Baldwin and SHOC faced active competition when they purported to speak for the Town. Important voices that could influence the success of renewal had been cut off from negotiation by the nature of the organization to which the BRA had given the renewal mandate.

In the summer of 1961, the tenuous relationship of SHOC to the other centers of power in Charlestown became apparent to Joe Vilemas, the ABCD representative who was sent into the community to work with Baldwin's organization.[55] Vilemas quickly came to the conclusion that "All you

---

54 Interview March 8, 1966. (The source wishes to remain anonymous.)
55 The report of Vilemas' introduction to the SHOC Executive Board provides an extremely interesting insight into the extent to which fear of political maneuvering was a conditioned reflex of a Townie organization. After some discussion of the role that Vilemas would play —he would "work with SHOC committees on all phases of the operation from small complaints to the business of home mortgages" (SHOC, Executive Board Meeting, Minutes, July 20, 1961)—it was decided to take Vilemas on because he was "from out of state and has no political aspiration, keeping in mind that SHOC was founded and is being carried on by persons who are not politically inclined." (*Ibid.*) SHOC took the ABCD worker on

had to do was talk to fifty people in the fall of 1961 to realize that you did not have a viable instrument for renewal in SHOC."[56] While SHOC saw Vilemas as their hired man, Vilemas viewed his role in the far larger terms of organizing Charlestown to deal with urban renewal and ensuring that those who could say "no" to the process would be brought into the proponents' camp by the day of the public hearing.

Vilemas saw SHOC as an inversion of the usual neighborhood group. Rather than being top-heavy with prestigious residents, as would be the case in Washington Park, SHOC was a freewheeling group of Townies united by zealous leadership and common enthusiasm. Vilemas concluded not only that SHOC lacked the participation of many significant people, among whom the clergy loomed largest but also that its approach to renewal negotiations was such as would jeopardize the possibility of a meaningful program. To Vilemas' mind a different local team was necessary if renewal negotiations were to move forward in Charlestown. His decision can be viewed as the most significant one in the entire Charlestown planning game; as such, it is important to examine the strategic reasons behind the move.

Vilemas' reasoning was that in an Irish-Catholic community the voice of the clergy carries enormous weight. Moreover, the pulpit provides a key position from which to convey information. Given a town in which egalitarianism and political infighting result in a continual toppling of leaders, none of whom is considered above attack, the clergy alone stand beyond the battle line. Not only could the Charlestown clergy provide leadership that would be able to operate above the usual political infighting and thus keep renewal from falling victim to the machinations of Townie politics, but also Logue's renewal program appeared to be ideally suited to the needs of the local parishes. As one Monsignor succinctly put the case,

With the dwindling population, we are depending more and more on the few faithful and elderly people who remain in Charlestown. . . . Salvation is free but religion costs money, and I think we ought to be realistic about it when the poor box goes around on Sunday.[57]

Residential renewal for Charlestown, with its promise of halting the population drain and bringing back those who had left, would help to spread the costs of maintaining three expensive parish operations among a larger, younger, and more affluent population.

Thus, the clergy represented not only a group with enormous influence in the Town, but also one with great self-interest in the success of the re-

---

the condition that the organization could dismiss him "on 24-hour notice" because "we are suspicious even of our own (and with good reason)." (*SHOC Talk*, September 1961.)
56 Author's interview with Joe Vilemas, March 30, 1966.
57 BRA: Charlestown, "Proposed Charlestown Renewal Project: Before BRA Board," Stenographic Transcript, January 7, 1963, pp. 26–27.

newal process. Yet the clergy's unwillingness to be dominated by Baldwin and his organization, coupled with SHOC's refusal to be in any way controlled by the clergy, had resulted in the Church's lack of active participation in the renewal planning game. It was clear to Vilemas that a means had to be found to bring in the clergy.

Believing strongly in a process with structured continuity, Vilemas was troubled by the forum for renewal bargaining offered by SHOC. He reacted to SHOC's wide-open sessions much as MacCarthy did, but perhaps for different reasons. Where MacCarthy was simply uncomfortable dealing with the aggressive Townie manner, Vilemas felt such freewheeling sessions were a luxury Charlestown could not afford. Renewal was a tough and complicated business requiring patient negotiation within a structured framework. While diverse groups in the Town had to be represented, some privacy in which to bargain was also needed. Such an atmosphere was simply impossible in SHOC.

Baldwin's view of Vilemas' community organization concept provides a somewhat different interpretation of the rationale for a highly structured local team.

He [Vilemas] held the belief that power should be vested in the influential few and was of the expressed opinion that the open meeting and free wheeling policy that SHOC practiced was potentially dangerous and might prove difficult to control.[58]

A meeting in November 1961 provides a good example of the way SHOC played the renewal game and of the differing ways of interpreting the organization's role. On November 23 the *Patriot* headlined, "Citizens protest redevelopment delay. Officials deny master plan made for Charlestown. The meeting [was] mixed with angry protests over BRA delays and sober reflection on the complexities of planning."[59] Several Townies who were leading figures in SHOC at the time look back on the occasion with a smile. "It scared the BRA to death, and MacCarthy vowed he would never go to another such meeting; but they shouldn't have worried. It was just the way SHOC operated. We had everything under control."[60] From Vilemas' point of view, the event was typical of SHOC's unstructured shouting matches that would get renewal nowhere. As Vilemas recalls the situation, Baldwin had scheduled an executive meeting of SHOC. When the BRA staff appeared at the Knights of Columbus Hall, they found themselves eyeball to eyeball with four hundred Townies who ended up the evening by shouting, "Yankee go home."[61] BRA staff members, fresh from the sanctity of City Hall, were shaken back on their heels. What to Baldwin and his followers was "real

[58] Baldwin, *op. cit.*, p. 19.
[59] *Charlestown Patriot*, November 23, 1961.
[60] Author's interview with Gene Hennessey, March 12, 1966.
[61] Author's interview with Joe Vilemas.

grass-roots democracy"[62] and nothing more than an expression of Townie "style" was to Vilemas chaos that appreciably retarded the course of renewal planning.

There are many participants in the Charlestown planning game who feel that Vilemas had options other than creating a totally new organization. These individuals maintain that SHOC could have been expanded to include the important Townies not yet involved in the planning game. Diplomatic tactics might have convinced the clergy to enter the negotiations, not as the spearhead for renewal, but simply as an important interest group concerned with rehabilitation planning. As the adherents of this strategy point out, the churches had too much to gain from renewal to oppose it and therefore ultimately—if they wanted any role in the planning whatsoever—would have been forced to recognize the significance of Baldwin's organization and come to terms with it. Convincing Baldwin of the necessity for restraint and instituting a more structured format for renewal meetings were both within the realm of possibility, or so the supporters of this strategy maintain. Indeed, there is much evidence to indicate that SHOC was willing to expand to involve more people, organizations, and points of view. For example, at an October 1961 Executive Board meeting, a long discussion took place over the problems SHOC was having in getting organizations, businessmen, and churches involved in the renewal effort. As a result of the discussion Baldwin reactivated a Community Participation Committee whose job it was to "find ways and means to obtain more active participation by businessmen and organizations of Charlestown."[63]

Vilemas made the judgment that restructuring SHOC was out of the question and that, given the role of formal groups in the life of the Town, a federation of local organizations would be the most effective way of creating a highly structured renewal team in which the clergy could play a major role. In bypassing SHOC, such a federation could start out with a clean slate and avoid the political and social divisions that had already solidified around SHOC's relationship to the rest of Charlestown. Drawn by the prospect of a more peaceful atmosphere in which to negotiate and convinced by Vilemas' analysis of SHOC and the clergy, MacCarthy agreed to go along with the idea of a federation.

The process whereby the renewal mandate was switched from SHOC to the federation is an example of politics in the best Townie tradition. The complexities of the maneuvering do not concern us here, but as one of the many ironies of the Charlestown renewal story it must be noted that Leo

62 Author's interview with Gene Hennessey, March 12, 1966.
63 SHOC, Executive Board, Minutes, October 5, 1961.

Baldwin proposed the creation of a federation at a SHOC Planning Council meeting advertised with the following notice:

We are fast approaching the serious Planning Stages of Urban Renewal in Charlestown. To expedite matters in this regard, it is necessary to have one "Voice" speaking for the people of Charlestown. . . . SHOC is recognized by the Urban Renewal authorities as that "Voice." However, we in SHOC feel that your organization should have representation on the Planning Council of SHOC.[64]

One can conclude from the invitation that the intention of the meeting was to expand the membership of SHOC, not to establish a new organization. At the gathering, however, Baldwin recommended a federation of Charlestown organizations of which SHOC would be only a participating member. Gene Hennessey, who as chairman of the SHOC Planning Council was running the meeting, was as surprised as anyone in the room when Baldwin made his suggestion. It is difficult to decipher Baldwin's motivation for bringing into the open a plan that had been weaving in the background of Charlestown affairs for some months. Whatever Baldwin's motive, the result of his suggestion was the lightninglike transfer of authority from SHOC to the newly conceived Federation of Charlestown Organizations. On January 31 the formation meeting was held, once again under the leadership of the SHOC Planning Council Chairman. Temporary Federation officers were elected. Vilemas left off working with SHOC in order to staff the new organization, and MacCarthy no longer dealt with the SHOC Planning Council. By February 8 the BRA was ready to show "preliminary sketch plans" to the officers of the Federation.[65]

THE POLITICS OF RENEWAL NEGATION:
THE FAILURE OF THE PLANNING GAME

Almost one year to the day after Baldwin's proposal for a federation, the Charlestown renewal game was blown to pieces by a public hearing on the night of January 7, 1963. At that time 85 percent of the 1,000 people present were emphatically opposed to the proposals of the BRA supported by the Charlestown Federation.[66] Rather than facilitating the renewal planning game, the Federation brought about the very thing it had been instituted to prevent, the opposition of those with the capacity to make their presence felt at a public meeting.

The main factor leading to the explosion of January 7 was the incapacity of the Federation to absorb, silence, or pacify all members of the SHOC

64 SHOC, notice of meeting, January 1, 1962.
65 SHOC was so thoroughly cut off from its former close relationship with the BRA that a request by the SHOC Executive Board to see the three sketches was greeted by a "no" from MacCarthy, who said that any such request would have to go through the Federation. Only after much urging did he finally relent on the basis of "all that SHOC has done for me." (Author's interview with Gene Hennessey, February 14, 1966.)
66 The Boston Traveler, January 8, 1963.

leadership group. Throughout the months between the two Januaries one can see SHOC's role changing from that of the loyal opposition to that of a revolutionary faction. Unlike the flexibility provided in the democratic political system whereby one party can transplant the other through the election process, SHOC had no formal means of regaining power; it had divested itself of the authority granted it by the BRA and had no way to recover its role as the mandate agent for Charlestown renewal. When the dust settled following Baldwin's recommendation for a federation, the members of SHOC found themselves just another group in a highly structured organization that was from its inception clearly dominated by the clergy.

The chairman of the newly created Federation was from several points of view a good man for the job. Bobby Lee had been a state senator and was a vice-president of a large Boston insurance company. He knew his way around Washington as well as around the Mayor's office and was a devout Catholic and a booster of Charlestown. However, while important in the world outside the town, Lee had not been involved for years in Charlestown's internal affairs. The very characteristics that made him a powerful force in the larger community cut him off from the inner life of the town. Leo Baldwin may have been caught in the crosscurrent of Townie politics, but at least his reputation had been built in Charlestown. Yet three weeks after the call for a federation, it was Bobby Lee, rather than Leo Baldwin, who led the local renewal team.

Once in operation the Federation provided the SHOC leadership with several sources of discontent. The new organization, dominated by the clergy and chaired by a man who had not been heard from for years, was not the representative body it was touted to be. While democratic in theory, Federation structure was less so in operation. Each member organization was to have one representative on the Board of Directors, and well over fifty groups had been selected from Charlestown's numerous organizations.[67] There is general agreement, however, that many of these groups existed only on paper. It was hard for SHOC leaders to accept the fact that the Boston College Alumni Association in Charlestown (whose membership ranged from one to three alumni) should have the same representation as SHOC. Moreover, the churches seemed overrepresented. Not only did each of the three Catholic and three tiny Protestant congregations have a man on the Board of Directors, but the host of Catholic sodalities were represented as well.

While there was equal representation on the Board, which gave small

[67] The most significant organizations were the American Legion Auxiliary, the Charlestown Community Council, Charlestown High Booster, Charlestown Merchants Association, Daughters of Isabella #1, International Longshoremen's Association, Old Charlestown Schoolboy's Association, Veterans of Foreign Wars Auxiliary, and Kiwanis.

organizations and church groups oversubscription, the Federation annual election of officers was one of proportional representation. As the Catholic parishes were the largest organizations in the Town, they clearly dominated the election proceedings. While people active in church affairs might be tied to the Federation through three or four lines, others, especially the non-Townies, might not be represented at all. The Federation claim that it spoke for "over 18,000 people through their churches, unions, clubs, businesses, and patriot and fraternal groups"[68] was clearly an overstatement.

Adding to the discontent generated by a skewed representation process that was weighted in favor of the churches was the tight control exercised at Federation meetings, where the procedural format was a startling contrast to the loosely structured SHOC gatherings. Bobby Lee would tolerate none of the "blowing off steam" that had characterized Baldwin's gatherings. The interpretation of Lee's approach depended on one's point of view. To some members of the Town who had either avoided the SHOC sessions or been put off by their noisiness, the ex-senator was "a master at running a meeting." To others, used to the freewheeling atmosphere of SHOC, he had a "fast gavel and was a front man for the Church."[69]

While it is impossible to totally isolate planning issues from the structure and personnel involved in the renewal game—indeed, the basic theme of the Charlestown renewal story is the inseparability of the three—there is no question that the Federation's approach to renewal planning was the cause for much of SHOC's antagonism. Within days after the Federation was formed, the BRA announced that it had three sketch plans ready to be shown and that the plans would be presented to the member organizations of the Federation in alphabetical order. One by one, 45 groups met with the BRA and were given a run-through of the three plans. In the process, over 2,500 people in groups of 15 to 125 saw the sketches.[70] SHOC leaders, however, became critical of the process shortly after its innovation. At a Federation meeting in April, Gene Hennessey, the chairman of the SHOC Planning Council, "wanted it known that the BRA is not giving the people the answers and that the Federation was not dealing for the people."[71] At the same meeting Baldwin stated that he did not like the way the sketch plans were being shown, that people were confused as to what renewal was all about, and that the BRA should prepare some educational material on the

[68] *Charlestown Patriot*, December 29, 1962.
[69] Author's interview March 8, 1966. (The source wishes to remain anonymous.)
[70] BRA: Charlestown, "Proposed Charlestown Renewal Project: Before BRA Board," Stenographic Transcript, January 7, 1963, pp. 9–15.
[71] Federation of Charlestown Organizations, Executive Committee Meeting, Minutes, April 11, 1962.

process.[72] It is interesting to note that the complaints were not about the nature of the sketch plans but about the manner in which they were being presented. Unlike the South End, where opposition during the first round of the renewal game was directed at the plan itself, the SHOC discontent had little to do with the specific characteristics of the renewal proposal.

At the series of meetings little negative reaction was recorded against the plans for they reflected quite closely the public position put forward by the SHOC Planning Council in November 1961. That position had urged maximum rehabilitation, assurance that relocatees would find housing in Charlestown, new low- and middle-income housing "in keeping with [Charlestown's] . . . present working-man's character [to] . . . reverse the exodus of the past decade,"[73] and resistance to public housing projects except for the aged.

While three plans were shown, a composite version became the design over which the Federation Renewal Coordinating Committee negotiated during the fall of 1962. The proposal called for the rehabilitation of 81 percent of the Town's dwelling units and the construction of 200 new units of housing for the elderly and 1,200 units of "sales and rental opportunities for the residents of Charlestown at prices they can afford."[74] Plan features included removal of the "El" from Main Street and construction of two elementary schools, shopping facilities, and new recreation areas. If one looks at the proposal in terms of parish lines, it is apparent that each of the Monsignori got some new housing, a community facility or two, and a scattering of commercial buildings. Unlike the District Plan of 1960, the proposal making the rounds in the winter of 1962 was geared to preserving the basic structure of the Charlestown community while adding housing and commercial and community facilities along the three sides of the residential triangle. The clearance percentages of that earlier proposal had clearly been ignored.

While BRA personnel are today quite willing to admit that particular aspects of the plan were fuzzy when the sketches were being shown to the different organizations, they maintain that the general outlines of the plan were clear and that proposals for new housing were in line with the earlier SHOC demands.

During the period in which the Federation was settling down to business and the plans were being shown, efforts were made to placate the old SHOC leaders. Baldwin was a vice-president of the new organization. There was a

72 *Ibid.*
73 *SHOC Talk,* Vol. XIII, November 1961.
74 "Charlestown—A Residential Neighborhood," A map produced by the BRA, January 1, 1963.

solid overlap between SHOC and Federation leaders and little difference in the occupational background of the key people in each group. However, Bobby Lee and the clergymen were not about to let the new organization serve as a vehicle for SHOC and made certain that SHOC leaders did not dominate its committees. Given a situation in which under the best of circumstances SHOC sensibilities would be tender, the relationship between the Federation executives and the SHOC leaders went badly from the start. The failure at this point to convince the SHOC personnel of their importance to the new organization resulted in an estrangement that would never be overcome.

The gap between SHOC and the Federation widened as a result of the SHOC election in the spring of 1962, when Baldwin "declined to run again"[75] and was replaced by James Sweeney, the organization's former vice-president. Sweeney, eventually to become a die-hard foe of renewal, was at this time simply a popular figure in SHOC, with a wife who wanted him to be Federation president. Baldwin's exit, coupled with the Federation's domination of the renewal game, spelled the end of SHOC as a zealous force for community betterment and its emergence as the vehicle for antirenewal feeling. For all his criticism of the Federation's proceedings, Baldwin had made every effort to explain to his SHOC followers the need for the Federation. No such efforts were made once he stepped down.

In the fall of 1962 the gulf between Federation and SHOC leaders widened. A September Federation Directors' meeting resulted in what many considered to be a "fast gavel" on the North Terminal Area Study plans, a project dealing with the transportation network around Charlestown. The study was put to a vote without discussion, a move that resulted in a SHOC public meeting entitled "Are We Being Planned With or For?" MacCarthy and the BRA made their position clear by boycotting the meeting. Mrs. Sweeney ensured that the gathering would be a lively one by inviting a perennial antirenewal city councilman and another councilman who intended to run against Collins in the 1963 mayoralty contest. The Boston papers, for whom renewal was a major source of news under any circumstances, caught wind of the friction generating in Charlestown and headlined events in the community under such banners as "Another Bunker Hill Battle Brewing."[76]

Thus the delicate art of the planning game was escalating well beyond the confines of a structure in which local and BRA teams bargain over the contents of a renewal proposal. For by November 1962 the Charlestown picture was complicated by an organized forum for dissent, the realization on the

---

75 Baldwin, op. cit., p. 23.
76 The Record American, December 7, 1962.

part of Boston politicians that political hay could be made in the Charlestown renewal situation, and the eagle eye of the press seeking out further signs of conflict. At this point the real weakness of the planning team's approach was the inability of either Vilemas or MacCarthy to comprehend the significance of the opposition their negotiating structure was generating. The inevitable scars left by the transfer of power had not healed. The Federation's "fast gavel" and MacCarthy's boycotting of SHOC poured salt into still open wounds. Rather than take time out to determine the extent to which the dissenters could be co-opted by a change of tactics, the steps to a public hearing were taken as though there were no such thing as opposition or as though the opposition could be overpowered by the weight of the Federation's leaders backed by the clergy.

An irony of the Charlestown proceedings is that it was the Federation's Renewal Coordinating Committee insistence on relocation housing (a point on which SHOC had been adamant from the start) that led to the fiasco of January 7, 1963. The Coordinating Committee had been meeting with MacCarthy during October and November, working over the three sketch proposals shown to the member organizations during the previous spring. In their negotiations the Coordinating Committee pursued basically the same goals that SHOC had pursued before them. The major premise of the Committee, like that of SHOC, was that "the residents of Charlestown wish to remain within their district and . . . every provision must be made for this to be assured."[77] To this end 81 percent of the existing housing units were to be rehabilitated, and "a program of careful and suitable relocation of the remaining 19% of the population . . . into new and existing housing within the community"[78] was to be carried out. To ensure this relocation, the Committee

requested the Boston Redevelopment Staff to immediately acquire a large tract of land in the Little Mystic area . . . under Early Land Acquisition; in order that . . . four to five hundred new rental housing units may be constructed in advance of any relocation. . . . In addition we have requested the Boston Redevelopment Authority to consider under Early Land Acquisition three smaller tracts of land within the District, which can be used for development of additional housing units for private sales and for old age housing as well as for a second new elementary school.[79]

The Early Land proposal would have involved the acquisition of 45 acres and the relocation of 87 families.[80]

Bobby Lee stressed, "If you go along with our suggestions, put up the new buildings before relocation, I am sure you will find us responsive. We're

77 Federation of Charlestown Organizations, "Renewal Coordinating Committee," November 1962, p. 2.
78 Ibid.
79 Ibid., pp. 2–3.
80 The Boston Globe, November 28, 1962.

willing to buy this plan."[81] On November 28, with the SHOC representative in opposition, the Federation Board approved the "general site plan for the renewal of Charlestown."[82] Assured by Federation leaders that local support would be forthcoming, Logue asked the BRA board for a public hearing to pass on the Early Land issue.

What from the Federation's point of view was felt to be a piece of hard bargaining with the BRA was viewed by some SHOC leaders as a proposal rammed through the Federation Board of Directors, with little consideration of what was involved in the commitment. By means of Early Land Acquisition, the BRA was being allowed to come into the community without a final plan and without guaranteeing the one thing upon which any renewal plan for Charlestown had been predicated, the removal of the "El" on Main Street.

As BRA staff will now admit, it was true that a final plan for the community had not been completely worked out, and while the dark stories that have grown up as to the BRA's evil intentions have been exaggerated, there is little question that Charlestown's bargaining position would have been diminished by allowing the BRA into the community in any way whatsoever before a final plan had been agreed upon. Moreover, rehabilitation costs had been discussed only vaguely, and there was no real indication that Charlestown homeowners could afford the program.

If SHOC's already tender sensibilities needed any help in viewing the Early Land proposal with suspicion, the BRA itself obliged remarkably well by communicating the whole concept of Early Land with a minimum of clarity. The Authority printed maps with the boundaries of the acquisition areas larger than those of the individual properties to be taken, thus giving the impression that huge pieces of Charlestown's housing were to be cleared. An announcement in the *City Record,* the official journal of City Hall news, discussed "Perimeter Boundaries of Clearance Section Tracts,"[83] which once again encompassed more than the actual properties slated for acquisition. The next week the *Record* was amended to read, "Perimeter Boundaries of Early Land Acquisition Tracts."[84] The damage, however, had been done. Many Townies with long memories of duplicity on the part of the city saw the confusing designation of residential areas as evidence of just one more plot by outsiders to hurt the town for the benefit of Boston as a whole.

During December, Charlestown rumbled with discontent that was noted

81 *Ibid.*
82 *Charlestown Patriot,* December 29, 1962.
83 City of Boston, *City Record,* Vol. LIV, No. 49 (December 8, 1962), p. 1062.
84 *Ibid.,* No. 50 (December 15, 1962), p. 1086.

by the newspapers but evidently not heeded by the BRA. SHOC held a meeting on January 4 at which renewal's foes from outside Charlestown, as well as political opponents of Collins invited by Mrs. Sweeney, added further fuel to an already seething mixture of confusion, resentment, and fear. Over the weekend, SHOC sound trucks made the rounds of Charlestown streets, announcing that if people wanted to "save their homes," they had better get down to the local Clarence Edwards School on Monday night for the public hearing. *The Boston Globe* helped the SHOC cause by reprinting the map showing bold black lines around areas far larger than those slated for acquisition. On January 5 and 6 a flyer was distributed widely in the Town effectively portraying the view that many people in the Town held of the Federation: five men with guns stand halfway up a pyramid with Lee, Logue, and MacCarthy seated at the top. The guards, unnamed and in street clothes, are supposed to be clear to one and all as the clergy. The five are themselves protected by the Federation committee heads,[85] who are keeping residents off the pyramid. The cartoon is captioned, "The residents on the bottom level of the picture are finding it impossible to be heard or to be informed of the future plans for Charlestown. They cannot penetrate the above pyramid unless more residents join the fight."[86] The flyer was enormously effective in conveying the image of a small band of individuals preventing the broad mass of Townies from exercising their natural right to participate in the renewal planning game.

All in all, the SHOC leaders did a masterful job of organizing. As one Boston paper stated, "This old opposition, aware that so many urban renewal meetings of planning with people get stacked by the pros, outmaneuvered the maneuvers."[87] Two years later Logue could look back on that evening and admit, "We were clobbered."[88] And clobbered they were, for SHOC managed to get out somewhere between eight hundred and a thousand Townies to voice opposition to the BRA and Federation-backed request for Early Land.[89]

The culmination of the residential renewal game, the public hearing, resulted in the demolition of the procedure put together by MacCarthy and

---

[85] It is interesting to note that before and during the January hearing criticism of the clergy was rarely articulated in public. The flyer is a perfect example. Those Townies with any awareness of what was going on in the Federation knew the role the church fathers were playing, yet it was not until after the January 7 hearing that open opposition to the clergy's role was heard in the Town.

[86] *SHOC Flyer,* January 5, 1963.

[87] *Boston Sunday Advertiser,* January 13, 1963.

[88] BRA: Charlestown, "Proposed Charlestown Renewal Project: Before BRA Board," *op. cit.,* p. 7.

[89] *The Boston Globe,* January 8, 1963.

Vilemas, and showed the bankruptcy of that system's assumption that a clergy-backed, elitist team would be allowed to speak for the Town as a whole.

Nothing makes clearer the extent to which the BRA-ABCD team was out of touch with reality than the fact that MacCarthy and Vilemas were stunned by the strength of the opposition that completely dominated the hearing. Logue's shock was understandable. He had been assured by his staff and the Federation leaders that all fronts were covered and opposition virtually non-existent. The night of January 7, 1963, demonstrated clearly the fate of a neighborhood renewal team not constituted to co-opt or neutralize all "powerful" voices in the community.

To put through renewal, Vilemas and MacCarthy had relied on the clergy and a highly structured organizational framework led by someone who was basically removed from the life of the Town. SHOC's performance demonstrated that such an approach had cut off far too many Townies from active participation in some aspect of the planning process—the informational aspect if nothing else. The egalitarian, politically astute nature of the Townies who were, or who thought they were, excluded blew apart the formal renewal system. Lack of adequate communications between Federation leaders and the rest of the community kept from many Townies any basis on which to belittle the SHOC cry of "save your homes." The same capacity to take part in community affairs that had filled the Knights of Columbus Hall when Leo Baldwin had first raised the idea of a town betterment effort made equally possible the mobilization of the opposition on January 7.

It would be wrong to say that the opposition reflected the feelings of the entire Charlestown community. The opposition constituted a select group of those who were sufficiently roused to appear at the Edwards School. The Federation and the BRA simply had not made a serious enough effort to rally their supporters. Moreover, the renewal planning process was still so young and the Federation communication network so crude that many in the Town were unaware of what was happening and thus made no effort to appear at the hearing. It was a few SHOC leaders who, out of a combined motive of fear, political competitiveness, and genuine disapproval, led the rally and got out the vote. In the political market place of the urban renewal public hearing, domination of the forum at the moment of decision is the critical necessity. SHOC produced, and the Federation did not.

For all the booing, catcalls, and what some described as complete chaos, the opposition on January 7 was for the most part precise, articulate, and concerned with the substantive issues of plan content and planning procedures. While Boston newspapers put a great deal of emphasis on rabble rousers with political motives who appeared from outside Charlestown,[90] 36 of the 39 speakers in opposition were members of the Charlestown community. Moreover, one aspect of the meeting generally overlooked was a printed form, headed "Compliments of SHOC," which was distributed before the hearing and stated:

> I am for urban renewal in Charlestown without early land acquisition and only after an acceptable comprehensive plan has been submitted to the people of Charlestown directly, and not through any Federation.
> Any acceptable plan must start with:
> 1. removal of the elevated structure
> 2. rehabilitation of the existing housing.[91]

During the course of the evening 580 of these slips were signed and handed to the BRA officials. Thus, the majority of the crowd, loud and rough in classic Townie style, wished not to throw renewal out of Charlestown but to bring about changes in the BRA's approach and in the content of its plan.

Of the 36 Townies who spoke out against the plan, all but one had specific reasons for being in opposition; and nine stated that they were in favor of urban renewal for Charlestown under conditions different from those put to them that evening. The following is a list of all points mentioned and of the number of times each point was raised. As many speakers hit on more than one theme, the total is greater than thirty-five.

1. Criticism of the way the BRA planned in the community — 7
2. Ideological opposition to renewal *per se* — 4
3. General fear of the renewal program — 2
4. Fear that rents will rise with renewal — 6
5. Belief that a referendum is the only fair way to determine the wishes of Charlestown's people — 3
6. Fear of losing their home — 5
7. Opposition to the idea of early land — 10
8. Confusion about what renewal will do — 8
9. Refusal to accept the vote of the Federation as binding on the rest of Charlestown — 11
10. Refusal to approve any plan until the demolition of the "El" is guaranteed[92] — 10

Substantive issues aside, there is no question that political rivalry constituted an integral part of SHOC's opposition, as Leo Baldwin made clear when he split off from his SHOC allies and went on record as supporting Early Land Acquisition:

90 *The Boston Herald*, January 9, 1963.
91 *SHOC Flyer*, January 7, 1963.
92 BRA: Charlestown, "Proposed Charlestown Renewal Project: BRA Board," *op. cit.* (author's summary of points made throughout the course of the hearing).

I am speaking as a private citizen. . . . Do we want a better town? Or do we want to play "who is king of the mountain?" . . . the decision has to be made by the people of Charlestown. . . . There has been bungling here with renewal . . . [SHOC and the Federation] both have good people in them, but they are too concerned with personality conflicts when they should be shoulder to shoulder. . . . You add personality conflicts and lack of communication, and what is the sum total? Confusion.[93]

As the detailed examination of the steps leading to the public hearing makes clear, the SHOC opposition cannot be explained in terms of social class differences. The major challenge of the Charlestown opposition was to the right of one Townie to speak for another Townie. In the words of critics at the hearing, a major issue was the failure of the Charlestown planning team structure to encompass the needs of an egalitarian society.

I am for this town. I belong to organizations in this town, organizations supposed to represent me, but I represent myself.

All the people of Charlestown are sincere, capable, and do live within their means, and when they have something presented to them, I feel they themselves should be the only ones to speak.[94]

The real key to the conflict over renewal can be found in the politics of Charlestown's planning team. The chaos of January 7 is explicable only when one understands the unique character of the Town's people and the manner in which Vilemas and MacCarthy misjudged that character when structuring the local organization to whom they gave the renewal planning mandate. In an egalitarian community, an elitist organization like the Federation did not constitute a viable structure for neutralizing opposition. Failure to assess properly the distribution of power in Charlestown—the capacity to be for or against renewal—resulted in the breakdown of the Town's renewal planning game.

AFTER THE FALL:
REASSESSMENT OF THE CHARLESTOWN PLANNING GAME

As a result of the January 7 events, the Charlestown planning game underwent a radical shift. The very thing that the Federation had been constructed to facilitate, a highly regimented, orderly forum for negotiation, was now further from reality than it had been during the days of Leo Baldwin's freewheeling SHOC meetings. Logue, with far more political astuteness than his subordinates, saw through the smoke of January 7 that negotiations over the substantive elements of the renewal plan could bring many of the opposition leaders into the prorenewal camp. Immediately after the public hearing, Logue talked with most of the SHOC leaders. He asked Gene Hennessey, a leading architect of the revolt, what the BRA had done wrong. Hennessey pointed to the overemphasis on the clergy and to the decision to bring in a

---

[93] *Ibid.*, pp. 86–88.
[94] *Ibid.*, pp. 64, 106.

professional Irishman as critical misjudgments of Townie style. He then outlined a four-point plan that would gain his support and that of his followers in SHOC: the "El's" removal, a comprehensive renewal plan for Charlestown, demonstration of rehabilitation's economic feasibility, and a serious effort to inform all of Charlestown's residents about the renewal plans. Logue agreed to work on all four points, and from that agreement emerged the Moderate Middle party.[95]

While Hennessey and his followers might have been willing to negotiate the substantive issues of renewal, the formal SHOC organization was prepared for no such arrangement. The formal transition of SHOC from the party of honest doubt and political rivalry to that of virulent antirenewal ideology came as a result of the organization's spring election. The issue in that contest was whether the Moderate Middle, led by Hennessey, could beat Jim Sweeney, now clearly at the head of a band ideologically opposed to urban renewal. With Logue's blessings, Hennessey ran at the head of a slate "neither categorically for nor against renewal."[96] The days of the moderates in SHOC were over, however, and in Hennessey's words, "We were buried." With that election SHOC became the home of those "opposed to urban renewal without reservation."[97]

As a result of the election Charlestown was divided into three camps: the Federation, SHOC, and the Moderate Middle. It is important to note that all three were clearly dominated by those whom we have described as Townies. While in no camp was the significance of Project People and non-Townies more than minimal, each camp maintained that its position on renewal was the one which would do the most good for Charlestown as a whole. The split over renewal was not due to conflicting goals for Charlestown: all three factions were willing to admit that Charlestown's physical framework was falling apart at the seams. The conflict arose over how one ought to go about dealing with that problem. The groups were essentially remnants of unsuccessful efforts to build a representative renewal team in the Charlestown community and should be examined in some detail in order to demonstrate that each is the product of events and personal relationships rather than of basic socioeconomic differences within the Town.

THE FEDERATION

Prior to the public hearing, the 45 members of the Federation's Board had been pictured as the renewal negotiating team for all of Charlestown. Covetous of that position, the Board emerged from the January hearing as a

---

[95] Author's interviews with Gene Hennessey, February 14, 1966, and March 12, 1966.
[96] *Charlestown Patriot*, May 2, 1963.
[97] *The Boston Herald*, May 22, 1964.

prorenewal faction that would tolerate no compromise with the enemy, that is, those who had come out against the Early Land proposal. Just as SHOC had been bewildered and resentful at having the renewal mandate taken away from them by the Federation, so were the Federation leaders, especially the clergy, hurt and angered by what they had been forced to endure at the public meeting. For the clergymen to be required to face down an angry mob was an extraordinary and unprecedented experience. They had entered the lists of renewal bargaining in good faith, believing that they were doing the right thing for Charlestown. To have their judgment and intent brought into question hardened them against those who had brought about the Donnybrook. Among nonclerical Federation leaders were those who resented the manner in which the BRA seemed to make most of its overtures after the hearing to those who had yelled the loudest in opposition rather than to those in the Federation who had stood up to be counted for urban renewal. As one Federation member stated in a letter to the *Patriot*, "The BRA threw this organization to the wolves."[98] And to many of the Federation leaders "wolves" were as much the Moderate Middle as the virulent SHOC opposition.

THE MODERATE MIDDLE

Gene Hennessey was the mainstay of those who "were neither categorically for nor against renewal."[99] He, Baldwin, and other leaders of the original SHOC movement constantly tried to bridge the gap between SHOC and the Federation and just as constantly were spurned by both sides. In the words of a SHOC publication, "Having been rebuffed both by the opposition and the proponent organization, these two [Baldwin and Hennessey] are like a couple of old-time vaudeville hoofers, still seeking the spotlight."[100] While the comment fails to do justice to their efforts to make reasoned discussion a possibility, it does describe the way the two were often viewed by the two polar factions. Yet, in all probability, the position taken by the Middle Majority leaders of support for Hennessey's four-point program was backed by a larger percentage of Charlestown's population than was the stance of either other group.

SHOC

The SHOC that emerged from the election following the Early Land hearing solidified into a band of Townies categorically opposed to renewal on any terms. The motivations behind the twenty or so individuals who constituted

98 *Charlestown Patriot*, May 2, 1963.
99 *Ibid.*
100 "The Minuteman," March 27, 1965.

the hardcore of the SHOC active membership of over two hundred are so complex as to require a far more detailed analysis than can be given here. What is important to stress, however, is that SHOC was very much a product of the Charlestown environment of internal grudges, political one-upmanship, and xenophobic fear of outsiders and change that might threaten the Town. It is important to note that the SHOC leaders were all Townies in the sense we have defined. All grew up in Charlestown, and while none were from the "top of the hill," many had known Federation leaders since childhood. Some of those in the Federation would look down their noses and call the SHOC people "nobodies" who now found themselves in the spotlight being interviewed by newspaper reporters and asked to speak on television and radio shows. If Federation representatives derived their status from being members of the renewal team, SHOC members derived theirs from public exposure.

Beyond the whole question of politics and social standing, both very much a part of the SHOC-Federation rivalry, lies the fact, overlooked by those who write SHOC off as consisting of troublemakers and "kooks," that for many people in Charlestown renewal was seen as a fundamental threat to the Townie way of life. As one SHOC leader said to Pat MacCarthy:

You're jealous of me and you want to make me have the same problems you have. You're jealous of my way of life because I'm not trying to live in a fancy house and have fancy parties and friends. You're up to here in debt and always worried about the kind of impression you're making.[101]

While few would be this articulate, many in Charlestown feared that renewal meant that the BRA would impose middle-class standards, values, and costs on a Town that was happy in its working-class ways.

SHOC became an arena for those who had anticlerical leanings and had never found the courage or the platform from which to voice such criticism. SHOC became a vehicle for those who fought zealously in the organization's early days, people who had marched to City Hall to battle for Ed Logue's appointment and who felt betrayed by the transfer of power to the Federation. SHOC became a base for Townies with political aspirations, and the organization became a means whereby personal feuds could be translated into the objective terms of renewal. The fervor of its members and their extraordinary devotion to their cause put the organization very much in the tradition described in Eric Hoffer's *The True Believer*.[102] For SHOC the ends justified the means, and the means employed to convince the people of Charlestown of the evils of urban renewal were often rough. Threatening phone calls, fabricated statistics, and pressure to get prorenewal people fired from jobs were typical of SHOC tactics.

101 Author's interview with John Harrington, March 3, 1966.
102 Eric Hoffer, *The True Believer* (New York: Mentor Books, 1958).

The formal SHOC position, which offered no basis for compromise, can be summed up as follows:

1. SHOC is made up of two groups: those who are opposed to renewal because they fear the process will take their homes or businesses, and those who feel that eminent domain proceedings as employed in urban renewal are unconstitutional and therefore un-American.

2. The Federation is made up of three groups: those who honestly believe that renewal will help Charlestown, those who hope to get something out of the process, and those who support the idea because they are told to by the clergy.

3. Not only is the idea of urban renewal undemocratic and un-American, but the BRA—especially Logue—is untrustworthy, devious, and incapable of giving Charlestown a fair deal. Moreover, the plan that has been proposed is unworkable and badly conceived. Rents will rise. No low-income housing for large families is proposed, and public housing is no solution because Charlestown people do not want to go on the dole. The public interest of Charlestown can be served best by getting Logue and his team of planners out of the community.

4. Urban renewal is an unworkable process. SHOC has looked at projects in New Haven, New York, and several other cities, and nowhere has the effort done anything but shift the slums from one area to another.

5. All of the things that renewal promises—new schools, roads, and public facilities—are Charlestown's due right, and no renewal program is necessary to get them. If the City of Boston had treated Charlestown fairly, the Town would never have gotten into the bad condition in which it now finds itself.

6. The clergy should get back into the churches and stop forcing renewal down people's throats.

7. Only a referendum can tell the true feelings of the people of Charlestown, and Mayor Collins refuses to support one because he is afraid such a move would result in renewal being thrown out of Charlestown.

8. Only SHOC stands between Charlestown and disaster. Despite all the unfair things said by those who would discredit the organization, SHOC will fight to the end for the good of Charlestown.

SHOC constituted formidable opposition. The organization was armed with a willingness to employ any tactical maneuver to turn people against renewal and with an extraordinary amount of information on the renewal process. As a group willing to oppose Logue in particular and renewal in general, it received spiritual, intellectual, and financial aid from antirenewal groups all over the city of Boston. The *condottieri* of SHOC became so familiar with renewal proceedings that Jim Sweeney could say with certainty that "so much study and research has gone into what the people in this organization know about urban renewal that staff members of the Boston Redevelopment Authority have made the comment that we know more about urban renewal than some of their employees."[103]

THE BRA: A CHANGE OF TACTICS

The history of the renewal planning game in Charlestown from the spring of 1963 to the spring of 1965 is one of intricate maneuvering by the BRA in and around the Federation and the Moderate Middle camps, in hopes of picking up enough support to overpower SHOC at the next public hearing. The substance of negotiations was provided by Hennessey's four-point program: demonstration of the feasibility of rehabilitation, increased dissemination of information to the people of Charlestown, detailing of a final comprehensive plan, and guarantee of the "El's" removal. Not until these points had been met would the BRA face the community at a hearing.

In June 1963, a Home Improvement Center was opened in Charlestown by members of the BRA staff. Offering free architectural and construction service, those in the office made every possible effort to disassociate themselves from the BRA, the Federation, and the Charlestown renewal plan, while concentrating on the rehabilitation of at least one house in each of the Town's seven precincts. The Center not only met one of the Moderate Middle demands but also gave the BRA personnel a chance to talk and work with Townies, as they had not done prior to the public hearing. As soon as the houses started to show painted exteriors and new kitchens, the word was spread through the reliable Charlestown grapevine. The rehabilitation office made no overt effort to proselytize renewal, but by showing the possibilities of home improvements won the confidence of many doubters in the Town. By February 1965, the Center had provided service to 139 residents, had completed work on 25 houses, and could estimate that as a result of the Center's efforts, "contagious rehabilitation" had sprung up in Charlestown, and 350 owners had voluntarily made major exterior improvements on their property.[104] A rehabilitation slide program, showing the work done by the Home Improvement Center, was produced in the spring of 1964 and presented more than sixty times at various meetings in the Town. Concentrating on that aspect of renewal which was of prime significance to the 1805 homeowning Townies,[105] the presentation made urban renewal a concrete reality in a way that the Federation meetings over the sketch plans had never done.

---

[103] City of Boston, City Council, "Charlestown Urban Renewal Project: Before Committee on Urban Renewal," *op. cit.*, p. 1247.
[104] Memorandum from Frank Del Vecchio to Edward Logue, BRA Files, February 9, 1965.
[105] BRA, "A Working Paper on Rehabilitation," Winter 1964–1965, p. 4.

The Home Improvement Center was but one example of the manner in which the BRA approach to the community changed after the January hearing. While MacCarthy stayed with the project until the next fall, his replacement at that point constituted another shift in BRA's tactics. Frank Del Vecchio, the new project director, was a young lawyer who had been with the program since the summer of 1962. His reaction to the chaos created by the MacCarthy-Vilemas approach was to shy away from reliance on any group or formal team as a means of negotiating the renewal plan. He had seen the extent of Charlestown's truculent democracy, realized that each person speaks for himself in Charlestown and felt that only an approach based on a door-to-door selling job could gain enough support in the town to withstand a public hearing. The situation in Charlestown made such an approach mandatory. Unlike MacCarthy, who had held his BRA staff in City Hall while he alone negotiated in Charlestown, Del Vecchio encouraged as much interaction as possible between his team and members of the Charlestown community. Willing to talk to anyone, anytime, he soon found himself under pressure from Federation leaders who felt that he was backing down on commitments made by MacCarthy while spending too much time talking to members of the Moderate Middle and even SHOC.

As a result of their disapproval of Del Vecchio's approach to Charlestown renewal planning, Bobby Lee and two members of the clergy went to Mayor Collins and demanded that Logue take over as chief of the Charlestown project and reportedly stated that if the Federation continued to be bypassed, "the leaders were prepared to revise their earlier support and publicly repudiate the BRA in Charlestown."[106] Collins and Logue refused to bow to the wishes of the Federation, realizing that to do so would jeopardize the progress that had been made with the Moderate Middle.

Eventually the Federation was pacified. Bobby Lee's death and the more conciliatory attitude of the new president helped to calm relationships between that organization and the BRA. Joe Vilemas must be given an enormous amount of credit for keeping the Federation and the clergy involved in the renewal process, for increasingly his job was to hold the Federation block in line, while it was left to Del Vecchio to negotiate with the other leaders and groups in Charlestown that might be swung into support of renewal.

To the concreteness of the rehabilitation effort undertaken by the Home Improvement Center, Del Vecchio added a series of block meetings in the spring and summer of 1964 at which blowups of individual streets were on

---

106 *The Boston Traveler,* January 28, 1964.

display, as well as other material relating to the final and comprehensive renewal plan that had been completed late in 1963. These gatherings were for the purposes of explaining the plan, not negotiating it. But the presence of SHOC members at every meeting ensured that the BRA staff had to be on its toes in a manner that was never necessary in the second round of planning in the South End. The Charlestown meetings were to inform individuals, not as members of a club but as residents of an area, about the particular plans for their block. Moving systematically up and down Charlestown's streets, meetings were held three or four times a week for three months, with an estimated total involvement of 4,000 people. SHOC members threw the first gathering into total disorder, but eventually Del Vecchio and his staff learned how to deal with SHOC questions. In fact, as Del Vecchio himself says, "They forced us to sharpen our answers about rehabilitation and the plan until those answers began to satisfy people."[107]

The long delay occasioned by negotiations with the Federal Government over renewal funds for the "El's" removal gave both pro- and antirenewal forces ample time to promote their causes. The number of Townies who knew what was going on at the Early Land hearing may have been a minority, but by the time the second public hearing rolled around, Logue could say with great accuracy, "I think it is about the most published, most publicized urban renewal plan that I know about in the United States."[108] Or as a little lady from Charlestown described the situation:

When the plan first started to come to our town, I didn't take any notice. I thought it was politics, but then everybody started talking about it. It has gotten so in our town you don't even ask how you are any more, you ask about urban renewal. We used to get a rest on Sundays, but it has gotten even now we get it off our altars.[109]

The grim determination with which SHOC, the Federation, the Moderate Middle, and the BRA battled to gain support also ensured that the result of the proselytizing would be a bitterly divided town. As one SHOC leader stated,

It is a five year war of nerves . . . today neighbors and friends aren't speaking over urban renewal . . . whether the plan goes through or not the damage that has been done in Charlestown will take years to heal.[110]

The Politics of Renewal Affirmation

With a guarantee finally obtained from the Urban Renewal Administration

---

107 Author's interview with Frank Del Vecchio.
108 BRA: Charlestown, "Charlestown Renewal Area: Public Hearing Held by BRA," Stenographic Transcript, March 14, 1965, p. 7.
109 City of Boston, City Council, "Charlestown Urban Renewal Project: Before Committee on Urban Renewal," *op. cit.,* p. 1005.
110 *Ibid.,* p. 1080.

for federal funds with which to remove the "El," 5,000 signatures raised by the Federation in support of renewal, and the promise of a new ABCD-backed multiservice center for Charlestown, Logue felt that the moment had come to try again. In the weeks following the announcement of the "El" funds, the entire BRA mobilized to do battle with the SHOC forces. This time around there was no hope of co-opting opposition or stacking the hall only with proponents. SHOC would be there en masse. The question was whether the combined efforts of the Federation and the Moderate Middle, urged on by the BRA and ABCD, could muster enough support to counter whatever voices SHOC could produce.

The Boston newspapers watched with fascination as the lines of battle formed. One story reported that "General Logue takes no chances in the New Battle of Bunker Hill."[111] The BRA strategy during this period was to refuse to recognize any opposition to the plan other than that voiced by SHOC and then to label SHOC irresponsible and filled with "kooks."[112] Thus an individual who might object to some aspect of the BRA proposal had to run the risk of being identified with SHOC, by this time an extremely fanatic organization using every tactic it could imagine to turn people against the renewal plan. SHOC's strategy was to flood the telephones and streets of Charlestown with messages of "save your home" and to try to convince one and all that the BRA plan was a lie and that not one house in the town was safe from the bulldozer that had taken down the West End.

For the first time during the course of the rehabilitation planning game, residents of the Charlestown public housing project were actively courted by both sides in an effort to win their votes for or against the renewal plan.

As the day for the public hearing before the BRA Board drew closer, Logue himself took to the hustings with the announcement that "We'll get the truth going . . . and for every sound truck that goes around spouting lies, we'll match it with three and I'll even man one myself if I have to."[113] At this point a series of house parties were arranged by Hennessey and others of the Moderate Middle; and three or four nights a week for about a month, Logue dropped in on as many as three parties an evening to meet Townies. According to all reports, the Development Administrator charmed the residents with his knowledge of their families and their community. Nothing symbolizes the fusion of planning and politics more completely than Logue's barnstorming campaign before the second Charlestown BRA hearing.

March 14 was set as the hearing date. In a conference session Logue, the Federation, and SHOC set the rules for the occasion: one hour for the pro-

---

111 *The Boston Herald,* March 21, 1965.
112 *Ibid.,* and author's interview with Michael Matt.
113 *The Boston Herald,* February 10, 1965.

ponents, one hour for the opposition, and then alternating half-hours "until all who wish to be heard have been given the opportunity to do so."[114]

Right up to the last minute the proponent ranks were split over the lineup of speakers. The Federation leadership was simply unwilling to let Hennessey and Baldwin be among the first to speak, and the friction that had existed between the two groups since the Early Land hearing threatened to shatter their tenuous alliance. After much maneuvering on the part of the BRA staff, Baldwin and Hennessey were put in the front row and were among the first to voice approval for a renewal program for Charlestown, thus successfully breaking into the string of Federation members and clergy that had dominated the hearing in January 1963.

The gathering of about 2,800 proceeded with amazing calm through the first hour of the proponents' statements. It was during the opposition's hour that the now-famous remark was made by an extremely emotional leader of SHOC, a remark that told the BRA in no uncertain terms what the agency could do with its money: " 'I don't have to do it. I don't have to do it. It's my home and that's what I am fighting for. You can stick the money up your ass.' [boos and applause]"[115] The meeting never recovered its equilibrium. When one of the Charlestown Monsignori, in the words of a SHOC leader, "whipping up the crowd like it was some kind of fascist rally,"[116] called out, "all those in favor of a renewal plan for Charlestown . . . stand . . . stand,"[117] the meeting broke into pandemonium. A vote was called for. Logue was photographed standing on a tabletop, counting hands. Any semblance of an orderly exposition of opinions on the issue of renewal for Charlestown went by the boards. Newspapers varied in their recording of the results of the hand count but general agreement had it that the proponents won a majority of the 2,000 or so people in the hall. The estimates varied from 1,500 to 1,800 for and from 500 to 700 against. As a result of the vote, SHOC was provided with further ammunition for the position that the BRA could not be trusted: SHOC maintained, quite correctly, that the prehearing pact had said nothing about a vote. On the other hand, there were those among the proponents who later argued that SHOC had been prepared to wait it out all night in the Armory where the hearing was being held until the supporters of renewal had worn themselves out and gone home. At that point SHOC would have called for a vote on renewal. Ac-

---

114 BRA: Charlestown, "Public Hearing—Charlestown Urban Renewal Project: Rules for the Conduct of the Public Hearing," March 14, 1965.
115 BRA: Charlestown, "Charlestown Renewal Area: Public Hearing Held by BRA," *op. cit.*, p. 48.
116 Author's interview with John Harrington.
117 BRA: Charlestown, "Charlestown Renewal Area: Public Hearing Held by BRA," *op. cit.*, p. 73.

cording to this argument, the decision to call a vote was forced upon the proponents by the rumored SHOC tactics. If anything, the heat generated by urban renewal in Charlestown was more intense after the March 14 hearing than before.

With what the BRA took to be an affirmative vote in the Armory, the decision was made to go to the City Council hearing. The SHOC forces raised havoc there for days and continued to do so long after those hearings were over. The issue of renewal for Charlestown was essentially decided, however, at the BRA hearing. Collins and Logue could count on a 7 to 2 majority in the City Council and could be assured of City Council support no matter what arguments or tactics SHOC might bring to bear, and SHOC did every thing it could to make the hearings one of the free-for-alls of the century.

The hearing at the Armory was the telling blow. While chaos reigned, the BRA was able to get a majority, as it had been unable to do in 1963. An enormous expenditure of economic and political resources[118] had been made to ensure that at that critical moment, the majority of the people in the hall would stand up for a renewal program for Charlestown.[119]

THE CHARACTER OF THE CHARLESTOWN PLAN

It was a long trip from the low-pressure days of Dick Green's dealings with the original SHOC to the power politics of the months preceding the March 1965 public hearing, months that required the BRA team to pull out all the

---

118 It is impossible to get accurate figures, but one BRA estimate puts the total cost to the BRA of the planning phase in Charlestown at close to $1,000,000. (Author's interview with Frank Del Vecchio.)

119 The extent to which the issues had changed between the two BRA hearings is made clear by a breakdown of opposition reasons voiced at the Armory on March 14, 1965:

1. In opposition to the plan, no reason given	252
2. Critical of the clergy's role	15
3. Can't trust the BRA	13
4. Hostility toward Edward Logue	18
5. Fear of losing home	13
6. Fear rents will rise	2
7. Fear of another West End	3
8. Only a referendum can tell where people stand	6
9. No need for urban renewal in Charlestown; self-help can handle the job	4
10. The plan for Charlestown is a bad one	3
11. Ideological opposition to urban renewal	7
12. Opposition because of the way the hearing is being run	6
13. Opposition to the process of representation used in determining the plan	1

The degree to which negotiation was impossible at this stage is made clear by the number of people who simply wanted to be recorded as being in opposition. Substantive issues, which had dominated the criticisms at the Early Land hearing in January 1963, were replaced by vituperations of Logue, comparing him to Hitler, and of the clergy, calling them "sky-pilots" and "Judases." By March 14, 1965, fear, distrust, and internal dissension in the Town made the basic issues of renewal only marginally relevant to the manner in which people cast their votes.

stops in order to ensure that the frail union of Federation and Moderate Middle forces could overpower a determined and highly organized band of antirenewal zealots.

Despite the turmoil and feuding in Charlestown over the manner in which the renewal game should be played, or over the question of whether it should be played at all, the proposal that emerged at the Armory hearing warranted Logue's saying, "I certainly am not familiar with an urban renewal plan that does less harm in the United States."[120] The combination of a vocal, often scathingly articulate, opposition and of a shaky coalition of proponents, who themselves placed specific demands on the BRA, produced a plan that made a serious effort to preserve the fabric of the entire Charlestown community. The wide-open planning game, which gave the BRA little latitude to make a move without everyone in Charlestown knowing about it by morning, produced results that are the closest of our three studies to that limiting situation having as its goal the preservation of an entire residential community.

The steady decline of residential structures slated for demolition constitutes a major theme running through Charlestown's planning game. The pre-Logue District concept has estimated that only 40 percent of the area's housing was worth saving. In 1962 the MacCarthy sketch proposal cut this estimate drastically and indicated that approximately 4,000 people, or 19 percent of the families in the Town, would have to relocate.[121] The final plan called for the demolition of 11 percent of the Town's residential structures, thereby creating a relocation load of 525 families (about 2,000 people), or 8.8 percent of Charlestown's households.[122]

If one studies the relationship between building conditions in Charlestown and areas slated for acquisition by the BRA, it is clear that to a large extent spot clearance and vacant lots were utilized in the BRA pattern of land taking. Most buildings, and, therefore, most of the housing in "C" and "D" condition (that is, in need of extensive or major repair), were left standing. With the exception of the belt between Rutherford Avenue and Main Street, there were no extensive demolition areas. Since much of the belt is occupied by commercial and warehousing facilities, it is fair to say that there was no major tract of residential clearance proposed in the Charlestown plan. However, the low level of clearance was not the result of

120 City of Boston, City Council, "Charlestown Urban Renewal Project: Before Committee on Urban Renewal," *op. cit.*, p. 406.
121 *The Boston Globe*, March 1, 1962.
122 Given the characteristics of the BRA figures for Charlestown, "households" here includes persons living alone. Relocation figures are taken from BRA: Charlestown, "Application for Loan and Grant Part I: Final Project Report Charlestown Urban Renewal Area," February 25, 1965, R-223.

superior structural conditions: the BRA exterior building survey estimated that 47 percent of Charlestown's residential structure were in "C" condition and 17 percent in "D".[123] The low level of clearance was the direct result of the manner in which the rehabilitation game had to be structured in order to gain the maximum amount of political support that could be squeezed out of a town where almost every resident had the capacity to be "for or against" urban renewal.

While almost two thirds of the 525 families to be relocated are eligible for public housing, a BRA survey found that only 25 percent of those eligible desired to move into such accommodations. The BRA estimates that the "majority of families who will relocate into public housing are elderly persons,"[124] of whom there are 122 in the relocation load. Relocation is to take place over a four-year period, which means that the average number of moves per year will be about 130. As a BRA statement points out, "apart from Urban Renewal, Charlestown has been losing about 600 people a year, so that the relocation indicated . . . is much less than what has been happening under present conditions."[125]

As the Federation and SHOC before them insisted, the BRA predicated its relocation placements on the assumption that all relocatees could be provided with accommodation in Charlestown.[126] Table 4.2 indicates the ways in which the BRA planned to carry out this goal.[127]

Although these figures are both static and optimistic, they represent a detailed and serious effort on the part of the BRA staff to find a place for all the relocatees in the renewed Charlestown and to relate housing needs to housing costs. On the assumption that building and relocation schedules bear some relationship to each other, the goal of rehousing 525 families in Charlestown falls within the realm of reason.

In view of the distinction we have drawn between Townies and those who moved to Charlestown during the last decade or so to take advantage of low rents, it is interesting to note that the relocation load is characterized by a high percentage of families who must clearly be considered Townies. Close to 90 percent of the relocatees expressed a desire to remain in Charlestown.[128] While one might argue that the reason for wanting to stay is simply a ques-

123 *Ibid.*, R-221.
124 BRA: Charlestown, "Urban Renewal Plan: Charlestown Urban Renewal Area," February 25, 1965, p. 11.
125 BRA: Charlestown, "Analytical Summary of the Public Hearing Before the Boston City Council Regarding the Charlestown Urban Renewal Project," Spring 1965, p. 7.
126 *Ibid.*, p. 5.
127 BRA: Charlestown, "Urban Renewal Plan: Charlestown Urban Renewal Area," February 25, 1965, p. 13.
128 BRA: Charlestown, "Application for Loan and Grant Part I: Final Project Report Charlestown Urban Renewal Area," *op. cit.*, R-223.

TABLE 4.2 RELOCATION DEMAND AND SUPPLY ON A TWELVE-MONTH BASIS (to run 4 years)

	No. Units Required by Charlestown Relocatees	Available in Charlestown*
Elderly	22	50
Low income	10	60
Rehabilitation demonstration	15	25
Private rentals	50	90
Private sales	34	30

* BRA: Charlestown, "Urban Renewal Plan: Charlestown Urban Renewal Area," February 25, 1965, p. 13. The following are the bases for these numerical calculations: (1) Two hundred units of housing for the elderly are part of the renewal package—averaging fifty a year. (2) Given a 10 percent annual turnover in the 1,149 unit Charlestown housing project, the BRA assumes it could capture, if necessary, one half of that turnover. (3) The BRA can rehabilitate up to 100 units of demonstration housing, which can then be turned over to Charlestown residents. (4) Twelve hundred units of 221 d3 housing will be constructed, and over 100 units of single family "sales" housing will be built. (Much of the spot clearance of individual lots and purchase of open lots will be devoted to sales units.)

tion of rents, the results of a careful survey of the first group scheduled for relocation portrays a picture of attachment to Charlestown beyond that motivated wholly by concern for cheap housing. In a group of 84 households, BRA relocation workers found 54 "deeply committed" to Charlestown, 20 "indifferent," and 10 "positively" wanting to leave the Town. Thus well over half of the sample can be considered Townies on the basis of their attitude toward the district. Almost three quarters of the same group have lived in Charlestown for more than fifteen years, making a large majority of the relocatees more than recent arrivals, if not necessarily Charlestown born and bred. Thus while non-Townies were not a particularly significant element during planning negotiations, they would not be disproportionately affected by residential dislocation.

In a project in which only 11 percent of the residential stock is to be bulldozed, enormous weight is put on the rehabilitation process. Three considerations are important here: the owners' desire to rehabilitate, their financial capacity to do so, and tenants' ability to pay the higher rents resulting from rehabilitation costs. As a result of the demand at the January 7, 1963, hearing that rehabilitation be tested, the BRA staff was able to go into the public hearing in March 1965 with the following statistics:

Under its voluntary program of technical assistance to Charlestown homeowners, the BRA has drawn up plans for the conservation and rehabilitation of 76 buildings containing 144 dwelling units. About half of these buildings are single family homes and most of the remaining are two and three family homes. These homes are located in every part of Charlestown. . . . The BRA's analysis for these homes showed that about 65% of them had violations of the safety and health codes and that an average expenditure of $467.02 for each dwelling unit was needed to correct these violations. In many cases such corrections would cost from $100 to $300. In a number of cases, however, some extensive structural work was required, and there are several instances of code work costing from $2000 to $4000. Apart from correcting code violations, the BRA found that the homeowner really desired to do much more. In fact for all 144 units, the average total cost per dwelling unit was $1,427.70.[129]

Of the three projects under study only in Charlestown were rehabilitation costs widely quantified by actual experience at the time of the public hearing. That Charlestown homeowners spent more than three times as much on their homes as necessary to bring them to the level of code indicates that for those 76 owners housing was no longer an inferior good but a middle-class value worthy of investment.

BRA surveys estimate that 75 percent of all residential structures have an owner on the premises and that fewer than 10 percent of all the houses in the Town are owned by individuals not living in Charlestown.[130] It is impossible to indicate how many of Charlestown's 1,800 resident homeowners are in a position to carry the economic demands of rehabilitation. However, on the basis of an estimated nonpublic housing project average income of more than $6,000, Charlestown's relatively low average housing expenditure, and the estimated expenditure necessary to bring buildings to code, the BRA concludes that "Charlestown has the highest potential for conservation and rehabilitation."[131] Moreover, estimates of rental increases due to rehabilitation are minimal:

Based upon the analysis of the average cost of rehabilitating residential structures in Charlestown the monthly cost of the new debt service will not amount to more than six dollars per month per unit. However because more liberal financing in terms of longer amortization periods than lending institutions have allowed in the area will be available to property owners, it is estimated that monthly debt service costs will decrease for the majority of properties and remain about the same for others.[132]

As with all rehabilitation feasibility estimates, this assumption of rent stability is undoubtedly overoptimistic. However, whatever the rise in rents, Charlestown tenants can absorb the rise more readily than practically any other group in Boston. As has been pointed out, the current low rent in Charlestown produces a relative slack in the district's rental structure. The point here is not that a rise in rents is viewed as desirable but that such a rise would not put intolerable strain on a large majority of Charlestown tenants.

While the characteristics of demolition, relocation, and rehabilitation are

129 BRA: Charlestown, "Analytical Summary of the Public Hearing Before the Boston City Council Regarding the Charlestown Urban Renewal Project," *op. cit.*, p. 10.
130 Author's interview with Frank Del Vecchio.
131 BRA: Charlestown, "Analytical Summary of the Public Hearing Before the Boston City Council Regarding the Charlestown Urban Renewal Project," *op. cit.*, p. 11.
132 BRA, "Application for Loan and Grant Part I: Final Project Report Charlestown Urban Renewal Area," *op. cit.*, Section R-221, p. 2.

the most critical elements to consider in the results of the rehabilitation planning game, one can also get a sense of the bargaining power of the district by the extent to which public resources are expended to gain the support of the local rehabilitation team. Charlestown has its share of typical renewal game public expenditures. Three new elementary schools, one in each parish, are proposed to replace the three ancient buildings that grandparents of today's Charlestown youngsters "may have attended a century ago."[133] Open space, which Charlestown sorely lacks, is a major element in the plan. With a new major recreation center and expanded school playfields, the district's sports-minded population at last has facilities on which to perform. Two new fire stations are included in the plan, as is a radical transformation of the local road pattern in order to route traffic out of Charlestown's heartland. The lack of shopping facilities, which drove 85 percent of Townie commercial dollars to neighboring communities, will be remedied by a large shopping center.

Beyond what might be called routine physical changes, three specific elements of the Charlestown plan indicate the extent to which the BRA team was willing to expend resources to gain support in the community. Removal of the "El" constitutes $12,000,000 of the estimated net project cost of $38,000,000. The BRA invested enormous quantities of time and money lobbying the Urban Renewal Administration to convince it that removal of the "El" represented a valid expenditure of federal renewal funds. In no other situation in the projects under study was such an effort made. Charlestown, however, could not be moved to accept renewal without the guarantee that the "El" would come down, thus not until Logue and Del Vecchio had finally secured URA funds would the BRA even consider another public hearing. With renewal funds for "El" removal, the BRA had fulfilled one of the major requirements of the Moderate Middle and could argue that only with an urban renewal program could Charlestown be sure that the "El" would be eliminated.

The Massachusetts Bay Community College, a two-year state-supported school, will provide "high quality, low cost education for qualified high school graduates within easy commuting distance of home."[134] While many areas in and around Boston battled to get the college, it ended up in Charlestown in an area earmarked for industry under MacCarthy's proposal. SHOC maintained that the college would be better suited elsewhere than on the fifty acres of prime industrial territory offered in Charlestown, and without question land that could be valuable for industry is being turned over to the college. The college, however, has enormous sales appeal to many of Charles-

---

133 BRA, "Charlestown, A Residential Neighborhood," Winter 1965.
134 Ibid.

town's residents, who see in it a real educational opportunity for Charlestown's young people. Just as getting rid of the "El" was universally considered a "good thing" for the Town, convincing the Community College to locate in Charlestown became a key rallying point for many Townies. When the college did finally decide to take the location, the move was viewed as an enormous triumph for the Town and made the renewal plan that much more appealing, because only within the context of a renewal plan could the site be turned over to the educational institution.

The Community College and the "El" are significant in that they represent more than a routine resource expenditure by the BRA. Getting rid of the "El" required enormous effort on the BRA's part; yet it was effort that was demanded by the political situation in Charlestown. In a setting in which opposition had a solid organizational base and the representative renewal team was broken wide open to include every individual in the Town, the BRA team was forced to "up its ante" to ensure local support.

The amendment clause in the Charlestown plan further demonstrates the extent to which the BRA had to expend resources in order to achieve a politically successful program. In both the South End and Washington Park, the BRA has the leeway to change elements of the proposal negotiated in the planning game if such becomes necessary during the course of the execution period. Amending the plan, and thus going through the complex approval procedures of the original proposal, is necessary only when the changes proposed "in the opinion of the Authority, substantially . . . alter . . . the Plan."[135] This leeway allowed the BRA in the other two projects is not permitted in Charlestown, where the amendment clause states that "any addition to the properties to be acquired under the Urban Renewal Plan as shown on the Treatment Areas Map shall be considered to be an amendment to a basic element of the Urban Renewal Plan."[136] In Charlestown the BRA is locked into the plan approved on March 14, 1965. While such a clause may be unrealistic and perhaps ultimately as harmful to the local community as to the BRA, its presence demonstrates the extent to which the BRA was willing to bend to the demands of the wide range of people confronting it in Charlestown and to guarantee that the renewal plan would be executed as presented at the public hearing.

Charlestown is a city planner's dream. Problems clearly soluble by a restructuring of the physical environment combine with enormous social attachment to the particular geographic area. It would be unrealistic and naïve to assume that rents will not rise in Charlestown as a result of renewal.

[135] BRA, "South End Urban Renewal Plan," Summer 1965, p. 39.
[136] BRA: Charlestown, "Urban Renewal Plan: Charlestown Urban Renewal Area," op. cit., p. 50.

Some renters and owners will obviously be priced out of the local housing market; but under the blanket statement that more people will feel the financial pinch of rehabilitation than BRA figures would anticipate, Charlestown, of the three projects under study, imposes the least severe penalties directly, in terms of demolition and relocation, or indirectly, in terms of rehabilitation. In Charlestown the politics of renewal affirmation went as far as would seem possible under current techniques to preserve the fabric of the urban village. For all the Byzantine politics, internal feuds, and protracted negotiations, the emerging plan is a model of preservation of a town and its residents, who may differ in incomes and attitudes toward the BRA, but who basically share the same goals for Charlestown. In the Town, egalitarian representation and internal conflict ensured a plan as benign as could be conceived within the renewal process as it existed at the moment of plan approval.

5

Washington Park

Part One

THE PEOPLE, HISTORY AND GEOGRAPHY OF WASHINGTON PARK:
AN OVERVIEW

Nine years ago "Washington Park," to those for whom the expression had any meaning at all, referred to a large grassy plot of land in the middle of Boston's Roxbury district. Today Washington Park as a residential community of 502 acres exists by planning fiat. Nine years as a renewal project have given the area some sense of identity apart from the Roxbury district to which it belongs.

The Washington Park project is a triangle, defined on two sides by radial streets leading outward from the center of Boston and bulwarked on the south by the open spaces of Franklin Park. Orientation of the project along, rather than across, radial lines has, in this particular case, meant that Washington Park cuts through two areas, each of which has independent identity in the history of Boston's residential neighborhoods. (See Figure 5.1.)

To simplify a description that is of constant debate among local residents,

GNRP✱ AREA
RENEWAL AREA

BOUNDARY

✱GENERAL NEIGHBORHOOD RENEWAL PLAN

0   1/4   1/2   3/4   1
MILES

FIGURE 5.1 WASHINGTON PARK URBAN RENEWAL AREA

the district from which Washington Park is carved can be divided into Middle and Upper Roxbury, divisions that, with Lower Roxbury, indicate both social status and geographic contours.[1] Washington Park just misses Lower Roxbury, which has historically been a low-income residential section between the clearly identifiable bowfronts of the South End and the two-family frame houses of Middle and Upper Roxbury.[2]

At the moment of renewal's entry into the area, Washington Park physically was a mixture, the well-kept streets next to Franklin Park standing in stark contrast to the desolate area along the Lower Roxbury fringe, where shabby three-deckers, small frame houses bursting with apartments, abandoned buildings, and empty lots dominated the scene.

While Washington Park remained undeveloped until the 1830's, Roxbury itself is an ancient town dating back to 1630.[3] When in 1868 the village gave up its independent status to join Boston, Yankee-populated Upper Roxbury dominated the affairs of the community.[4] Unlike the South End, which has been a City Wilderness for decades, or Charlestown, which has withstood waves of ethnic diversity, Washington Park, a cross section of Roxbury, has served as a way station between the inner city and the suburbs. Thus the history of Washington Park from the last quarter of the nineteenth century to the present is a study in successive invasions of ethnic, economic, and racial groups moving from the north, the center of Boston, to the south, the suburban communities.

During the 1870's and 1880's the Irish swept through on their way to Dorchester and the suburbs. In the 1890's the Jews and Canadians replaced the Irish as the district's dominant group.[5] By the mid-1920's a few Negroes began to move into Upper Roxbury.[6] In 1960 the most important social, physical, and economic fact about the area designated Washington Park was that the preceding decade had witnessed another in-migration from the north; for during the ten-year period, the area completely reversed its racial composition from 70 percent white to 70 percent nonwhite.[7]

1 See Sam B. Warner, Jr., *Streetcar Suburbs* (Cambridge: Harvard University Press and The M.I.T. Press, 1962), for a careful analysis of development patterns in Roxbury during the last half of the nineteenth century, also for another view of the boundaries of Upper and Lower Roxbury.

2 Forty years ago Robert Woods wrote, "Especially from the points of view of recreation, vocation, and morality does Lower Roxbury have its most serious and obvious shortcomings. In fact the distinction for the largest number of arrests for juvenile offenders comes to this part of the city." Robert A. Woods and Albert J. Kennedy, *The Zone of Emergence*, abridged and edited with a preface by Sam B. Warner, Jr. (Cambridge: Joint Center for Urban Studies, Harvard University Press, 1962), p. 93.

3 Boston Redevelopment Authority: Washington Park, Chester Rapkin, "The Washington Park Urban Renewal Area," December 1961, p. 15 (referred to hereafter as Rapkin, Report I).

4 Warner, *Streetcar Suburbs, op. cit.,* p. 111.

5 *Ibid.,* p. 65.

6 Rapkin, Report I, p. 15.

7 For all intents and purposes one can read "Negro" for "nonwhite"; the two categories will be used synonymously in the discussion of the Washington Park planning game.

Table 5.1 shows the aggregate characteristics of Washington Park around 1960. A comparison at the census tract level of income, occupation, and educational differences between the Washington Park population of 1950 and 1960 gives some indication of the extent to which socioeconomic transition accompanied racial change. In percentage terms the loss of professional workers was about three times as high as the net population loss. Conversely, in 1960 unskilled workers stood high above their proportion of Washington Park's 1950 work force. In terms of income, the 1950 census tracts for Washington Park range from slightly lower to much higher than the Boston average. Educationally the area held its own with the city. By 1960 this symmetry had radically changed, and both income and education levels were well below those of the Boston median. Table 5.1 gives an idea of the social problems that accompanied Washington Park's decade of social, economic, and racial transformation.

INTEREST GROUPS

Only a detailed examination of the interest groups represented by these statistics can bring out the significance for urban renewal of this residential transformation in the geographic area arbitrarily carved out by the Washington Park boundaries. The usual way to characterize the people of Washington Park is expressed in an *Architectural Forum* report.

The 502 acre Washington Park project is the heart of Boston's Negro ghetto. . . . The Washington Park section of Roxbury is really two neighborhoods. The northernmost one comprises 186 acres. Some 25 percent of the existing housing is unsalvageable, and all but one percent of the rest needs rehabilitation. The area was two-thirds white in 1950 and now is almost entirely Negro. Average family income is $4,000 and 40% of the families earn less than $3,000 a year. From Townsend Street to Franklin Park lies Boston's equivalent of Harlem's "Sugar Hill," where almost all of Boston's upper-income Negro families live. . . . The wealthier families have little to do with the lower-income families to the north. Most of the latter are newcomers to Boston, which adds to their isolation. In the upper-income area there are sturdy community organizations, while to the north there is growing disorganization.[8]

This image of two Negro communities, one rich, the other poor, is acceptable as an extremely general statement. In fact, however, Upper and Middle Roxbury not only are internally more complex but also have a more significant relationship to each other than the *Forum* description would allow. As the nature of the urban renewal planning game and its outcome are to a large degree dependent on the social complexities of the Washington Park community, it is worth looking at that community in detail.

If we think again in terms of socioeconomic groups with various interests in the residential rehabilitation game, four significant categories emerge in

8 *Architectural Forum*, Special Issue: "Boston," Vol. 120, No. 6 (June, 1964), p. 103.

TABLE 5.1   AREA CHARACTERISTICS

	Washington Park	City of Boston
ECONOMIC CHARACTERISTICS		
% Unemployed—1960	6.2%*	5.0%
Median family income—1960	$5,023	$5,757
% of families with incomes under $3,000—1960	29%	16.7%
% of families with incomes over $10,000—1960	8%	13.6%
HEALTH CHARACTERISTICS		
Death rate of infants per 1,000 under one year old—1961	36	26.1
% of Boston cases of pulmonary tuberculosis—1961	8.5%*	100.0%
HOUSING CHARACTERISTICS		
% units owner occupied—1960	18%	27.7%
Population per household—1960	2.8	2.9
% sound dwelling units—1960	63%	73.3%
Median gross monthly rent—1960	$80.00	$78.00
POPULATION CHARACTERISTICS		
Total population—1960	25,922	697,197
% decline from 1950 population	20%	12.5%
% population nonwhite	71%	9.8%
% numerical increase of 1960 nonwhite population over 1950 nonwhite population	126%	60.0%
% of 1960 population under 18	34.2%	28.7%
% of 1960 population 65 and over	11%	12.3%
Families (2 persons or more) as a % of all households	79%	73%
Families (2 persons or more) with children	63%	63%
WELFARE CHARACTERISTICS		
Population as a % of total city population—1964	4%	100.0%
% of city welfare cases in area—1964	7%*	100.0%
% of city Old Age Assistance cases in area—1964	4%*	100.0%
% of city AFDC families living in area—1964	12.4%	100.0%
% of city General Relief cases in area—1964	10%*	100.0%
YOUTH CHARACTERISTICS		
% of Boston's youths 7–17 living in area—1960	4.5%*	100.0%
Youth court appearances 1959–1961 as a % of Boston's total	8%*	100.0%

* Figures followed by asterisks are derived from statistics for the Roxbury–North Dorchester General Neighborhood Renewal Plan (GNRP) as a whole. The 1960 population of Washington Park represented about 31 percent of the total GNRP. In figuring Washington Park percentages, then, a flat 31 percent of the total GNRP figure has been used. This is a rough estimate at best and tends to understate the Washington Park figures, which certainly are proportionally higher than the GNRP as a whole in welfare characteristics. *Sources:* Statistics compiled by Anti-Poverty Planning Unit, ABCD, Winter 1964–1965, and "Social Facts by Census Tracts—1960," data compiled by United Community Services.

Washington Park: (1) the Whites, (2) the Negro Elite, (3) the Blue-Collar Negroes, and (4) the Black Proletariat.

THE WHITES

Reaction to the size of Washington Park's white population depends on one's point of view. One can focus on the rapid reversal of percentages of white and Negro between 1950 and 1960 and thus on the extent to which Negroes have taken over the district; but if one thinks of Washington Park as Boston's Black Ghetto, as does *Forum*, with all the implications of white exclusion contained in that expression, one's view of the monolithic character of the Ghetto is checked by the fact that almost 30 percent of the district's population was white in 1960.

That white population shares the almost universal characteristic of those who are left behind when an area is abandoned by one ethnic group to another. The whites are for the most part old, and their socioeconomic status follows the contours of the rest of Washington Park in that the poorest of the residents live close to the Lower Roxbury line, where they "share with the low-income Negroes a fairly high incidence of social problems."[9] In Upper Roxbury the remnants of the area's previous ethnic majority, the Jewish colony, which moved out en masse during the 1950's, make up 80 percent of the white residents.[10] In the solid medium- to high-rent apartment buildings that line the street facing Franklin Park, middle-class Jewish tenants constitute nearly 50 percent of the population.[11] Yet here, too, it is the elderly who have hung on. While Upper Roxbury's white community numbers less than a quarter of the area's residents, its members account for more than two thirds of the area's over sixty-five population.[12]

During the period of racial transition there was little overt hostility between the Jewish apartment dwellers and the in-migrant Negro population. In fact, there was little communication between the two groups. As Chester Rapkin points out:

This in part stems from the fact that those Jews that have remained are not the out going community type. . . . There are no Jewish block associations . . . with little sense of future, there is not much incentive for neighborhood renewal. There is a desire for city projects for the elderly . . . and for better city services . . . but probably little contribution to a self-help rehabilitation program could be expected.[13]

Beyond this Jewish population, the renewal area also maintains a scattering of Poles, Greeks, and some Irish groups that, for the most part, are also made up of old or poor people.

---

9 Rapkin, Report I, p. 28.
10 BRA: Washington Park, Chester Rapkin, "The Seaver-Townsend Urban Renewal Area," January 1962, p. 19 (referred to hereafter as Rapkin, Report II).
11 *Ibid.* Census tract U-6B, which includes many of these apartment buildings, has a median gross monthly rental of $91, the highest of any of the census tracts in the areas under study.
12 *Ibid.*, p. 22.
13 *Ibid.*, p. 40.

Thus, while the appellation of Boston's Negro Ghetto is a convenient title to pin on Washington Park, one must bear in mind the extent to which white residents constituted a significant interest group at the time that renewal was being planned for the area. As we shall see when discussing the extent of horizontal integration in Washington Park as a social system, individual whites took an active part in community affairs. While the bulk of the white population may have been elderly, poor, or both (and for either reason unlikely to become involved in the renewal game), some long-time residents of Washington Park were deeply concerned with the future of their area and able to translate that concern into participation on the local residential renewal team. As it was scattered throughout the Washington Park project area, however, the white community as an interest group would appear to offer little in the way of positive or negative involvement in the renewal game.

THE NEGRO COMMUNITY[14]

As *Architectural Forum* points out, Washington Park cuts through the heart of Boston's Negro Ghetto. The traditional socioeconomic stratification from Lower to Upper Roxbury, in existence long before Negroes became the dominant ethnic group in the community, combined with the unique functional characteristics of the Negro community, has produced in Washington Park a vivid cross section of the Negro class system. St. Clair Drake's general description of that system summarizes beautifully the social groupings of the 18,000 Negroes who live in Washington Park.

---

[14] With no effort at all, one can become hopelessly embroiled in a scholastic argument about the "significant" class differences in the Negro Ghetto. For example, where Drake talks about upper, middle and lower class in Negro life (St. Clair Drake, "The Social and Economic Status of the Negro in the United States," *Daedalus*, Vol. 94, No. 4 [Fall 1965], pp. 771–814), Rubin concentrates on middle, Blue-Collar and lower (Morton Rubin, "Resident Response to Urban Rehabilitation in a Negro Working-Class Neighborhood," in Arthur Shostak and William Gomberg, eds., *Blue Collar World* [Englewood Cliffs, N.J.: Prentice-Hall, 1964], pp. 248–256), and Watts focuses on economic factors to determine the contours of social groupings in Washington Park (Lewis Watts *et al.*, *The Middle Income Negro Family Faces Urban Renewal*, Massachusetts Department of Commerce and Development, 1964). My purpose is not to dispute any of these distinctions but to focus on the social divisions in the Washington Park Negro community which are of significance for the rehabilitation planning game.

In the renewal game context, the critical dividing line in the Negro community is between middle- and lower-class "life styles" (see Drake, *op. cit.*, p. 779, for a solid discussion of "life style"). What we have termed the Negro Elite and Blue-Collar Negro can both be said to partake of a "middle class life style," which Drake describes as "placing heavy emphasis upon decorous public behavior and general respectability, insisting that their children 'get an education' and 'make something out of themselves'" (*ibid.*). As both partake of the "middle class life style," one might argue that the Negro Elite and the Blue-Collar Negro are one and the same interest group. But for purposes of the renewal game, the Negro Elite provides a leadership potential that is worth examining in and of itself.

Negro class structure is "pyramidal" with a large lower class, a somewhat smaller middle class, and a tiny upper class (made up of people whose income and occupation would make them only middle class in white society). White class profiles tend to be "diamond shaped," with smaller lower and upper classes and a large middle class.[15]

In order to understand the reaction to renewal in Boston's Negro community, one has first to understand the particular contours of Negro class structure in Washington Park.

THE UPPER CLASS: THE NEGRO ELITE

The small Negro upper class . . . is a group in the professions, along with well-to-do businessmen who have had some education. . . . Within this group are individuals who maintain some type of contact . . . with members of the local white power elite.[16]

"There are more Black brains between Seaver and Townsend Street than anywhere else in Massachusetts" was the way one member of the BRA Washington Park staff described the composition of the Negro community in Upper Roxbury.[17] Rapkin calls the location a "prestige area for long-established Negroes."[18] It is a fact of overwhelming importance for renewal in Washington Park that Boston's Negro Elite is located in the project area.

While the significance of Upper Roxbury as the Negro status community cannot be overemphasized, one should not have the impression conveyed by *Architectural Forum*'s statement that Upper Roxbury is composed solely of rich Negro professionals. As Drake points out, "wealthier" and "upper income" mean something different in a Negro community than in white society. The fact that 13.6 percent of the families in Boston earn over $10,000 and that only one of the several Upper Roxbury census tracts meets this average indicates that the area is not "wealthy" by the standards of white America. Moreover, the percentage of professionals and level of education in Upper Roxbury are, at the census tract level, well below the city average.

While the number of professional high-income Negroes is relatively small even in the prestige areas of the Negro community, one could expect the established elite to play a significant role in any renewal game.

The Negro Elite is, for the most part, made up of families who bought or rented in Washington Park when the area was predominantly a middle-income Jewish neighborhood.[19] Some have lived in the area since the 1930's and constitute the Negro equivalent of the "Old Boston" families. These people have invested a good deal of money in their properties, as a glance

15 Drake, *op. cit.*, p. 785.
16 *Ibid.*, p. 781.
17 Author's interview with Walter Smart, March 15, 1966.
18 Rapkin, Report II, p. 19.
19 Census Tract U-5, running through the heart of Upper Roxbury, held a population more than 50 percent Negro in 1950.

in 1960 at the residences lining the streets of Upper Roxbury would indicate. As Rapkin says of the Negro Elite:

They want to prevent the area from becoming a colored Ghetto; they want to protect the value of their property and they want to preserve the prestige position that [Upper] Roxbury . . . enjoys among Negroes. It is among this group also that there is the most community cohesiveness, a good deal of concerned leadership, and useful neighborhood associations.[20]

The presence of an established elite in Upper Roxbury is a function of the Negro's situation in Boston and in American life. The high-status aspirations as well as achievements of Washington Park's Negro establishment would have resulted in the flight to suburbia that has characterized the white middle classes in the period following World War II were it not for racial barriers that have prohibited or made extremely difficult the assimilation of the Negro into suburban life. With rare exceptions, the siren song of suburbia that lured Charlestown's upwardly mobile population was not for the ears of Washington Park's successful Negro families during the 1950's. Thus the Washington Park area held a phenomenon unique to the Negro ghetto, an articulate elite concerned with the very thing that physical renewal guaranteed to produce—better community facilities and services and removal of neighborhood blighting influences.

It is important to remember that renewal came to Washington Park before expressions like *de facto* segregation or Black Power had become part of the language. As will be seen when discussing the actual planning game in Washington Park, the questions of integration and segregation were far less a factor in decision making than they would have been three years later. In 1960, urban renewal was seen by members of the Negro Elite as a means of preserving a racially mixed neighborhood by holding on to members of the rapidly diminishing white community.[21]

THE MIDDLE CLASS: THE BLUE-COLLAR NEGRO

What sociologists call the Negro middle class is merely a collection of people who have similar life styles and aspirations, whose basic goals are "living well," being respectable. . . . Middle-class Negroes, by and large, are not concerned about mobility into the Negro upper class or integration with whites.[22]

Architectural Forum's image of a rich Upper Roxbury trying to isolate itself from the blighting influence of Middle Roxbury fails to take into account the presence in both areas of what Morton Rubin has called "Blue Collar Negroes,"[23] a group that falls within Drake's description of the middle class. In a careful analysis of one street in Middle Roxbury (predominantly Negro since World War II), Rubin describes a group of Negroes the

[20] Rapkin, Report II, p. 37.
[21] Author's interview with Genevieve Kealey, March 29, 1966.
[22] Drake, *op. cit.*, p. 782.
[23] See Rubin, *op. cit.*

vast majority of whom constitute "a collection of people who have similar life styles." The area holds small property owners and stable families with steady income. The kind of worker that Rubin talks of can be found throughout Washington Park, for as Rapkin points out many of the Negro families in Upper Roxbury are established blue-collar workers.[24] What is of concern here is not the income level of these workers, which may vary from almost poverty level to well over five thousand dollars a year, but their shared attitudes toward work, education, and property—aspects of a "middle class life style."

Having a deep desire for quality services and a concern for maintaining a good neighborhood, the loose collection of Washington Park Negroes, not members of the elite but sharing Drake's middle-class life style, would constitute a broad base of support for any effort to improve the neighborhood through the tools of renewal. Combining the leadership and organizational skills of an upper-class elite with the basically sympathetic views of a broad spectrum of less affluent, less articulate residents, would most likely produce a solid prorenewal coalition.

THE LOWER CLASS: THE BLACK PROLETARIAT

With 60 percent of America's Negro families earning less than $4000.00 a year, social strata emerge between the upper and lower boundaries of "no earned income" and $4000.00. Some families live a "middle-class style of life" . . .

Within the same income range, and not always at the lower margin of it, other families live a "lower-class life-style" being part of the "organized" lower class, while at the lowest income levels an "unorganized" lower class exists whose members tend always to become *dis*organized.[25]

The most significant aspect of Washington Park's racial transformation during the 1950's is the large percentage of in-migrants that are low-income Negroes "with all the social problems which customarily attend migration and low economic status."[26] As Drake makes clear, there is no necessary correlation between income and "lower class life style," but given the number of low-income Negroes that overwhelmed Middle Roxbury and filtered into Upper Roxbury after 1950, one is assured of a sizable number of residents for whom the middle-class values of work, education, "social respectability," and "living well" are not central.

In this host of newcomers, many from the South, it is the disorganized lower-class element and the multiproblem families that Rapkin sees as "responsible for the rise in social problems in the area, including a mounting number of unwed teenage mothers and antisocial teenage gangs."[27] As a

24 Rapkin, Report II, p. 26.
25 Drake, *op. cit.*, p. 779.
26 Rapkin, Report I, p. 3.
27 Rapkin, Report II, p. 41.

glance at the aggregate social statistics on Washington Park will indicate, the area is far above the city average in juvenile delinquency and welfare assistance; and while the in-migration of lower-class Negroes has been felt in all parts of Washington Park, Middle Roxbury has borne the brunt of the influx.

In terms of what urban renewal could or could not do for the Black Proletariat, it must be kept in mind that most of these newcomers settled in Washington Park during the 1950's for one reason: there were rental opportunities available to Negro families of low income.[28] If renewal could provide better housing at equal or lower rents, the process would benefit the Black Proletariat. If, on the other hand, renewal cut back on the supply of low-cost housing within the Negro community, the rehabilitation game would exacerbate the problems of a group already well provided with troubles.

In describing the lower-class Negro, Drake makes a clear distinction between the antisocial multiproblem household and the stable lower-class family that, while not sharing in many of the norms of the middle-class life style, has nonetheless some form of social organization.[29] To try to differentiate between the organized and disorganized newcomers in Washington Park would be extremely difficult. Probably the Negro Elite and Blue-Collar Negroes have far overestimated the percentage constituting the real antisocial element. Whatever the actual breakdown numerically, it is safe to say that a large majority of the in-migrant Negroes earning less than $3,000 annually are part of the culture of poverty, which combines alienation from social institutions, except perhaps a store-front church, with a day-to-day struggle for survival so time and energy consuming as to preclude concern for or involvement in the demands of the rehabilitation planning game.

If one can assume that there is some correlation between income and life style, the extent of Middle Roxbury's lower-class families is apparent from the statistics in Table 5.2.

While Upper Roxbury has many people earning below $3,000 (more than the Boston average), Middle Roxbury is overwhelmed by low-income families.

---

[28] During the 1950's Charlestown with its rapidly declining population, large apartments, and low rents offered an attractive economic alternative to low-income Negroes in search of cheap housing; but social barriers in white Irish Charlestown were such as to preclude Negro Elite, Blue-Collar, or Proletariat from getting near the opportunities offered there. That even Middle Roxbury did not offer the low-income Negro much of a deal on housing is made clear by the BRA figures, which estimate that a quarter of the area's houses were in such bad condition as to preclude economic rehabilitation, while another quarter had serious structural problems (Rapkin, Report I, p. 4). Yet in 1961 68 percent of the Middle Roxbury residents spent more than 25 percent of their monthly income on gross rent (Rapkin, Report I, p. 28).

[29] Drake, *op. cit.*, p. 780.

TABLE 5.2 PERCENTAGE OF WASHINGTON PARK FAMILIES BY INCOME CATEGORY—1961–1962

Gross Family Income	Upper Roxbury*	Middle Roxbury†
Below $3,000	21	42
$3,000–4,500	28	33
$4,500–7,500	36	22
$7,500 +	15	3

* Rapkin, Report II, p. 32.
† Rapkin, Report I, p. 29.

To assess the potential role of the Black Proletariat in the renewal game, one has to examine also the relationship of these newcomers to the rest of the Negro community. The single most important fact about that relationship is the apprehension with which not only the White but also the Blue-Collar and Negro Elite groups watched the in-migration of low-income Negroes during the 1950's. In Middle Roxbury Rapkin found that:

Several of the Negro respondents in this group [the middle class] were at least as critical of the newcomers as were most of the whites. They expressed resentment and asserted that the recent in-migrants hurt the area and caused white hostility to rebound against all Negroes regardless of attainment or behavior. The area around Washington Park, formerly viewed as one of high status for Negroes, has now declined to the point that many middle income Negroes have left or are seeking to move to other areas.[30]

WASHINGTON PARK AS A COMMUNITY

The population transformation of the 1950's shattered the image that the Blue-Collar Negroes and the few Negro Elite in Middle Roxbury had held of their neighborhood as an integrated middle-class environment. By 1960 most of the middle-income white population had departed, leaving only the poor and elderly behind. Low-income, low-status Negroes had engulfed Middle Roxbury and threatened the tree-lined streets of Upper Roxbury as well. While an enormous social gap existed in 1960 between the Black Proletariat and the established Negro families, the physical distance was all too slight for those in Middle Roxbury who saw themselves surrounded by newcomers from the South and those in Upper Roxbury who felt that their area would not hold out long as the prestige Negro community in Massachusetts.

HORIZONTAL INTEGRATION

As has been pointed out, Washington Park emerged as a distinct residential district at the stroke of the planners' pen rather than through the logic of history or natural boundaries. Thus when designated as a renewal project, the district had virtually no formal or informal institutions geared to link

[30] Rapkin, Report I, p. 34.

together the four residential interest groups found within the project boundaries.

When one considers the district's rapid population turnover during the 1950's, the conflict between "life styles" in the Negro community, the isolation of the large majority of the white population from public affairs, and the social distance between Middle and Upper Roxbury, the absence of community-wide organizations drawing together the area's disparate groups is totally explicable. When one adds the project area's lack of geographic and historical identity to the list of causes for fragmentation, the absence of horizontal integration seems totally assured.

While one cannot find organizations specifically geared to the area called Washington Park, during the 1950's two organizations, Freedom House and the Roxbury Community Council, did focus attention on the problems of communication and stability in the rapidly changing Roxbury district.

Freedom House originated in 1949 when two members of the Upper Roxbury Negro Elite, Muriel and Otto Snowden, called together some friends and neighbors "to talk about ways of keeping Roxbury from becoming another slum."[31] Out of that discussion and many others like it emerged a unique civic organization, eventually located in a building called Freedom House. Its goals, "somewhat fuzzy and nebulous at first,"[32] ultimately became the conservation and improvement of Upper Roxbury while providing opportunities for greater interracial contact "both within the community itself and between its residents and those of Greater Boston."[33]

Even in 1951 the Snowdens were worried about Upper Roxbury's future as a racially integrated, middle-income community. Disturbed by the number of "responsible Jews and Negroes" who were moving from the area, Freedom House made great efforts persuading families to remain to "conserve what we have . . . to have people pitch in and help each other."[34] The Snowdens' own roots in Upper Roxbury ran deep, and unlike many of their Negro and Jewish friends, they were unwilling to abandon the area to the wave of newcomers pushing in from Lower Roxbury. Because of its emphasis on stabilizing Upper Roxbury's interracial community, Freedom House drew its support not only from the Negro Elite in Upper Roxbury but also from Jews who still lived or had once lived in the area. The Snowdens are energetic and able administrators with a vast range of contacts not only in Roxbury but in the Metropolitan Boston area as well, and the Freedom

31 Otto and Muriel Snowden, "Citizen Participation," *Journal of Housing*, No. 8 (September 1963), p. 435.
32 *Ibid.*
33 *Ibid.*, p. 436.
34 Freedom House, "Prospectus," 1951, p. 3.

House Board includes some of the most influential Jewish and Negro leaders in Massachusetts.

The story of Freedom House's activities during the 1950's is well known.[35] The Snowdens tried in a variety of ways to keep Roxbury "from becoming another slum."[36] They helped to establish block organizations to deal with neighborhood problems and in 1956 set up the Freedom House Neighborhood Improvement Association, an umbrella organization of block groups While constituted to cover what was to become the Washington Park project area, the groups were for the most part active only in the streets of Upper Roxbury.

Another organization making efforts during the 1950's to stabilize the rapidly changing Washington Park district was the Roxbury Community Council (RCC), which emerged in 1954, as its by-laws state, "to provide an opportunity for its members to consider together matters of community interest and arrange for appropriate action."[37] In the late fifties a report on citizen organization in Greater Boston commented:

> The Roxbury Community Council has been . . . the group in this district which has been directly concerned with, among other problems, the problems of urban blight through local or city aided programs . . . including urban renewal.[38]

From its start, the Council was a broadly inclusive, loosely structured body with representation from 65 Roxbury-based organizations. Represented were local stores, schools, churches, Roxbury's multitude of welfare organizations, and several neighborhood groups. During the first three years of its existence, the Council had no executive director and was staffed by the part-time service of leaders from four of Roxbury's major social welfare operations.

Washington Park, like Roxbury in general, has many churches, but during the 1950's the churches felt the rapid population turnover. In Lower Roxbury the Catholic parish diminished during the transition, and of the four major Protestant organizations, by 1960 two were integrated, while a third was predominantly Negro.[39] Store-front churches grew in number during the 1950's and served as one of the few social contacts for many of the recently arrived Black Proletariat. While several of the Protestant churches had community service programs, their funds were limited, their clientele was changing, and their inability to reach the low-income newcomers was

[35] See Otto and Muriel Snowden, op. cit., p. 435.
[36] Ibid.
[37] William Loring, Frank Sweetser, and Frank Ernst, Community Organization for Citizen Participation in Urban Renewal, prepared by the Housing Association of Metropolitan Boston for the Massachusetts Department of Commerce (Cambridge: Cambridge Press, 1957), p. 58.
[38] Ibid.
[39] Rapkin, Report I, p. 11.

apparent.[40] At the same time, they recognized the tremendous need for programs to serve the latest and poorest of Washington Park's residents.

Despite the problems the churches faced, the clergymen in Washington Park and the surrounding areas of Roxbury constituted an extremely important agent of communication among the disparate residential groups in the renewal area.

When investigating the extent of horizontal linking agents in the Washington Park area, it is important to bear in mind that the project has been arbitrarily carved out of the larger Roxbury community. Thus many of the integrating forces in Roxbury, such as the RCC, were geared to the larger district of which Washington Park is only a part. Moreover, other organizations, for example, the Warren Street Neighborhood Association set up in 1956 by the RCC, were cut in two by the boundaries of the Washington Park project. If one matches integrative organizations against the area defined by the renewal boundary lines, the lack of fit is apparent. This gap between established geographic lines of "turf" for different organizations and the boundaries of the renewal district would be an opportunity for some and a liability for others during the renewal planning period.

Roxbury itself is jammed with social welfare organizations, as the membership of the RCC indicates. Yet for all the social service in the district, during its period of racial transition Washington Park remained an island served exclusively by no organizations other than Freedom House and St. Mark's Social Center, a facility that was at that time viewed by observers as small and inadequate.

VERTICAL INTEGRATION

To discuss the linkages between Washington Park and the rest of Boston is to consider the traditional relationship of Boston's Negro community to the city at large. As Robert Coard stated in 1961,

Generally and traditionally the attitude of the larger community has been one of paternalistic liberalism. . . . The absence of explosive racial incidents and tensions in Boston up to now has tended to encourage factionalism and indifference.[41]

In Boston politics, Washington Park carried little weight during the 1950's. The at-large election of the nine-man City Council ensured that there was no representative from the Negro minority, which carried at best 12 percent of Boston's voting strength.[42]

---

40 Rapkin, Report I, p. 38.
41 ABCD, Rheable Edwards, Laura Morris, and Robert Coard, "The Negro in Boston," Boston, 1961, p. 13D.
42 This lack of representation was ended in 1967 when Thomas Atkins, a Negro, was elected to the City Council.

Washington Park is for the most part within Ward 12, which generally elects two Negro representatives to the State House. Ward 9, cutting through the top of the project, also sends a Negro to the state General Court. Thus Washington Park's political power is in one sense stronger at the state level than within the city itself.

Throughout the 1950's the attitude of the Washington Park leadership was not one of hostility toward City Hall, as was the case in Charlestown, but rather annoyance that the city had done little by way of public improvements and services to help the community during an extremely trying period. The RCC and Freedom House were continually urging Downtown to lend more of a helping hand in coping with the enormous problems accompanying Roxbury's socioeconomic transformation. While many of the leaders in Washington Park had a "pipeline" to City Hall, such linkages were based on individual connections rather than on group relationships.

WASHINGTON PARK AS A PATTERN OF POWER

There are two critical points to consider in an appraisal of the potential for involvement in Washington Park's planning game. The first is the socioeconomic structure peculiar to the Negro ghetto. The second is the rapid socioeconomic transformation that had engulfed the area during the 1950's. In combination these two factors produced a situation in which articulate and organized members of the Negro Elite were actively involved in efforts to revitalize their prestigious area and preserve it from invasion from the North, while an aged and insular White minority and a young, disorganized, Black Proletariat passively looked on.

The existence of a highly organized and capable Negro Elite, backed by a sympathetic Blue-Collar interest, produced a distribution of power, by which I mean the estimated capacity to mobilize for the renewal game, which was heavily loaded toward Upper Roxbury but which had strong support in Middle Roxbury as well. Of all the communities under study, Washington Park had the most articulate and sympathetic group of prorenewalites before the advent of the rehabilitation planning game.

5
Part Two

THE ADVENT OF RENEWAL: PRE-LOGUE NEGOTIATIONS

In Charlestown and the South End, renewal planning had basically similar origins. Ed Logue came to Boston, defined the project area, and granted the mandate to an organization within the district. In Washington Park, however, work to bring renewal to the area started in the early 1950's. The definition of the project area was the subject of debate before Logue himself revised the boundaries, and the renewal chief arrived in Boston at a time when local leadership for the Washington Park program was being contested between Freedom House and the Roxbury Community Council.

One cannot appreciate the nature of Logue's success in Washington Park without a solid understanding of events in Roxbury during the years prior to his arrival. What is fundamental to this understanding is the realization that many influential citizens in Roxbury—white and Negro—had been trying since the passage of the federal Housing Act of 1954 to use the program offered by that act as a means of dealing with their area's mounting problems. For these long-time residents of Washington Park and the surrounding Roxbury area, renewal was seen as a way of halting the exodus of middle-class whites and Negroes and of establishing the area as a fine residential community.

The Roxbury Community Council had been created in 1954 primarily as a district organization that could deal with issues of renewal and rehabilitation.[43] In an effort to drum up support in Roxbury and to convince the then less-than-dynamic BRA that the community was serious about renewal, the RCC helped create a pilot neighborhood association as a test area for rehabilitation and community organization techniques, with the hopes of "future expansion of the program to other rehabilitable neighborhoods."[44] Throughout 1955 the Community Council kept pressuring the Mayor's office to consider the Roxbury area for rehabilitation. However, the newness of the renewal program and the BRA's general lack of enthusiasm for getting involved in the external and internal building surveys requested by the RCC led to a stalemate. In 1955 the Community Council once again wrote Mayor Hynes, requesting that "high priority in the selection of areas for rehabilitation"[45] be given the Warren Street neighborhood.

Thus during this period it was local neighborhood leaders rather than the BRA that made overtures for renewal's entry into the Roxbury area. And it seemed as though the city had very little interest in designating Roxbury for rehabilitation.[46]

In 1958 the president of the RCC, a lawyer and member of the Upper Roxbury Negro Elite, wrote to Community Council members,

> Your RCC has been working since December 1955 to urge the City of Boston to bring a concrete program of urban renewal to Roxbury. . . . In order to qualify for Federal funds a municipality . . . must give evidence that the citizens of the area support an urban renewal project. . . . [Therefore] communicate your organization or agency's endorsement of urban renewal in Roxbury.[47]

During the period that the Community Council was negotiating with a reluctant City Hall for some kind of renewal program for the entire Roxbury area, Freedom House was involved in setting up block organizations in Upper Roxbury. In 1959 eleven neighborhood associations were affiliated with the Snowdens' operation, all but one of them in Upper Roxbury.[48] While some triumphs were recorded by these groups in their efforts to halt the neighborhood decline, the general conclusion drawn from the experience was one of pessimism as to the effectiveness of citizen efforts alone to

43 Loring, Sweetzer, and Ernst, *op. cit.,* p. 58.
44 *Ibid.,* p. 65.
45 *Ibid.,* p. 79.
46 Loring, Sweetzer, and Ernst, *op. cit.,* devote a great deal of attention to the activities of the RCC from 1954 to 1956, focusing on the efforts made by the Community Council to convince the BRA and the Mayor's office of Roxbury's need for renewal.
47 Memorandum from RCC President Herbert Tucker to Roxbury residents, August 5, 1958.
48 Memorandum from Freedom House to the Boston City Council, April 16, 1959.

turn the tide. As Mrs. Snowden puts it, "We had by this time recognized that clean-up campaigns, property improvement projects, petitions for street paving and the like had little success potential without being related to some kind of over-all planning.[49]

Moreover, in 1958 parts of Roxbury became "red line" insurance areas. Residents around Washington Park could not get fire insurance, and banks became increasingly reluctant to grant mortgage financing.[50] As one long-time community leader remembers, "You'd open up the mail and here would be your cancelled insurance. Without renewal we knew we couldn't do anything about this sort of business."[51] Thus, when it became apparent in 1958 that City Hall might finally promote renewal for the district, there were many Roxbury organizations and individuals who saw some kind of "roll back the blight" campaign as the only way to save their neighborhoods from complete physical decline.[52]

In February, 1959, the BRA approved two survey and planning applications for Roxbury, one a 1,000 acre plot encompassing the entire Roxbury district, the other 186 acres that would eventually be the Middle Roxbury section of the current Washington Park project. The rationale for the two project areas, the smaller included within the larger, was simply the availability of federal funds. At that time, money for 186 acres was assured, but there was less certainty for the 1,000. In any case the BRA planners agreed it best to submit both applications together as renewal in the smaller area was felt to be meaningful only within the context of the larger operation.[53]

The BRA reasons for selecting the Middle Roxbury end of Washington Park as the priority renewal area are extremely interesting in light of the later justifications for changing the smaller project's boundaries.

The Washington Park Renewal Area [the 186 acre project] is the most logical starting point for rehabilitation action in the city's "roll back the blight" campaign.

The proposed renewal area was selected for its rehabilitation potential. With the exception of a few scattered blocks where spot clearance and redevelopment will be required, most of the existing housing will need rehabilitation. . . .[54]

The Washington Park area is centrally located in one of the principal residential sections of the city. It is part of a larger zone of transition between conditions of more extreme deterioration to the north and more stable well maintained neighborhoods to the south. . . .

---

49 Otto and Muriel Snowden, *op. cit.*, p. 437.
50 Walter McQuade, "Boston: What Can a Sick City Do?" *Fortune*, Vol. LXIX, No. 6 (June 1964), p. 164.
51 Author's interview with James Ballard, April 19, 1966.
52 One must bear in mind that throughout the fifties, physical renewal in the form of rehabilitation and clearance was the sole concern of the Freedom House and RCC pressure for governmental action. Social renewal, until Logue arrived, was not considered one of the tools that could be employed to help a neighborhood suffering from blight.
53 City of Boston, City Council, "Proceedings of City Council," March 2, 1959, p. 118.
54 At the time this statement was made, BRA planners thought that 5 percent clearance of residential structures would be all the demolition necessary to shore up Washington Park.

. . . The Washington Park renewal area is neither the best nor the worst of Boston's areas, but one of the most rapidly declining and one which needs immediate and prompt attention. . . . It is an area which could serve to deter the spread of blight.[55]

Unlike the South End and Charlestown, the resurrections of which were viewed as ends in themselves, Washington Park started out as a pawn in a much larger concept, the vanguard in an effort to stabilize the Roxbury community, and to prevent blight from creeping out to Boston neighborhoods beyond Roxbury. Blight was viewed as a marching, conquering army, and Roxbury was where the defenders of the city were to take a stand. Considerations were never raised as to the socioeconomic capacity of the Washington Park area to endure the rigors of planning and executing a rehabilitation project. The critical factor was that Washington Park constituted the middle ground between the solid residential neighborhood of Upper Roxbury and the clearly deteriorated streets of Lower Roxbury. If blight could be rolled out of Middle Roxbury, the residential areas to the south would be preserved. The strategy of warring against physical decay dictated the terms defining the rehabilitation area.

In April 1959 the Boston City Council held a public hearing on the two renewal proposals before a "large number[56] of well-informed interested citizens from the proposed Roxbury Renewal Area . . . [a turnout] which greatly encouraged" the members of the City Council who felt such participation "bodes well for the eventual success of the project."[57]

The citizens' forces at the meeting were led by the president of the RCC, who "presented to the committee for statements, many persons prominent in the proposed project area."[58] No one at the hearing came forward in opposition to the proposal, and the City Council voted unanimously that application be made for survey and planning funds.[59] While it was the RCC that led the delegation at the City Council hearing, Freedom House, too, had been active in rounding up support for the meeting, and in a memo sent to the City Council on the day prior to the hearing the Snowdens made clear their interest in the renewal program:

In the past two years with the aid of a foundation grant added to citizen financial support, Freedom House as a civic center association has been able to accelerate its progress in organizing and developing citizen participation *specifically* for urban

[55] City of Boston, City Council, "Proceedings of City Council," March 2, 1959, p. 119.
[56] A Freedom House memorandum states that 1,000 Roxbury residents turned out for the hearing. (Freedom House, "Progress Report," April 1959.)
[57] City of Boston, City Council, "Proceedings of City Council," April 17, 1959, p. 182.
[58] *Ibid.*
[59] The survey and planning application filed by the BRA with the City Council in April 1959 is a masterpiece of understatement. Describing an area that was in the throes of rapid socioeconomic and racial transition, the sole comment in the entire application on the phenomenon is that "an increase in the non-white population has been noticeable since 1950." (City of Boston, City Council, "Proceedings of City Council," March 2, 1959, p. 121.)

renewal through the formation of block associations. . . . We shall continue to offer through Freedom House programs an exciting example of real citizen interest, support, and participation in urban renewal.[60]

In 1959 rehabilitation was felt to be a magic wand that, if properly waved, could undo the disruptive forces of ten years of violent population transition. The desire for some kind of renewal program, so evident among the white and Negro leaders of the Roxbury community in the fifties, did not diminish in the years after the initial City Council approval of "rolling back the blight" in the Washington Park area.

WHO SPEAKS FOR ROXBURY?
THE ISSUE OF THE PLANNING MANDATE

While reports of the April City Council hearings give one the impression that solid community support had been lined up behind the banner of the RCC, the issue of leadership in the emerging renewal forum was anything but settled, for the Snowdens were very unhappy at the role that Freedom House was being asked to play in the process.

In a memo written just before the April public hearing, Muriel Snowden outlined her objections to the RCC handling of the renewal leadership role. She pointed out that the original intention had been to make the RCC a delegate body

chiefly representing organized groups, rather than an organization of individuals. It was assumed that any matter coming to the Council's attention and requiring action would be referred to the organization or agency capable of handling it.[61]

It was on the issue of referral that Mrs. Snowden felt the greatest misunderstanding existed between Freedom House and the Council. "For some reason or other the Council has never been willing to accept Freedom House as an organization with community conservation and improvement as its specific local program."[62] Moreover, when the Council had set up a series of block demonstrations in the Freedom House area, it had not consulted the Snowdens and their board about the move. Not only was the Council ignoring the efforts that Freedom House had made in Upper Roxbury but in renewal proceedings before the BRA and the City Council was representing itself as the sole voice of Roxbury. From Mrs. Snowden's point of view, the small group of people controlling the Council, "by not mentioning Freedom House but by talking about Block Associations . . . have used us in making their case before the Authority."[63] She felt that the RCC should bring to the atten-

[60] Freedom House, Memorandum from Freedom House to the Boston City Council, April 16, 1959.
[61] Freedom House, Muriel Snowden, Memorandum on Relationship of Freedom House and Roxbury Community Council, March, 1959.
[62] *Ibid.*
[63] *Ibid.*

tion of the proper city authorities "the specific role of Freedom House as the most effective urban renewal resource in Upper Roxbury . . . and the [Roxbury Community] Council should refer urban renewal matters in this area to Freedom House."[64] Ultimately, Mrs. Snowden did not think that the Council was the proper agency to negotiate renewal for Roxbury. She felt that the Council was weak, controlled by a small "ruling clique," and loaded down with the wrong kind of professional people—social case workers rather than community organizers. What was needed was an over-all Roxbury renewal committee on which Freedom House would serve "as the largest citizen organization in the South Roxbury area."[65] If there were to be urban renewal in Washington Park, Freedom House wanted a major role in the process, even if that meant taking over the Community Council or openly contesting the organization's leadership. From the way events were proceeding in the spring of 1959, it looked as though Freedom House and the Snowdens would have to take a back seat to the Council in renewal affairs.

The position Community Council members took toward the conflict between their organization and the Snowdens' was that Freedom House was basically concerned with keeping itself in the limelight and simply resented the Council stealing some of its luster. These people felt that if the Snowdens cared about the Roxbury community as much as they cared about their own publicity, they would not have created such a fuss and would have realized that there was room in the renewal game for both organizations without one necessarily stepping on the other.

It is important to point out that the antagonism between Freedom House and the RCC was not over the issue of renewal goals for Roxbury. The question was not "Should Roxbury have urban renewal?" but "Who will lead the local team during the planning process?" Both groups were equally anxious to get BRA help as quickly as possible, and both shared the concept of a middle-income community in Roxbury. There was no class cleavage between the two groups. Several key figures on the Council, the "ruling clique" that Mrs. Snowden mentioned, were the social peers of the Freedom House leaders within the ranks of the Upper Roxbury Negro Elite. The jockeying for the leadership position in negotiations prior to Logue's arrival is significant in view of the later moves in the planning game which resulted in Freedom House becoming the undisputed spokesman for the Washington Park renewal area.

The period between City Council approval of the two Roxbury applications and the winter of 1961, when Logue's presence began to be felt in the district, was primarily one of "waiting for the Feds," to use Logue's term. In

64 *Ibid.*
65 *Ibid.*

the summer of 1961 federal approval was forthcoming only for the smaller of the two projects. Washington Park alone had funds with which to begin planning, and the grand concept of rehabilitating the entire Roxbury district was temporarily shelved.

Throughout this period an uneasy truce existed between Freedom House and the RCC. But that the Community Council was still considered the basis for citizen participation in renewal even in the smaller Washington Park project is made clear by a comment in early 1960 in Roxbury's leading newspaper:

> The Redevelopment Authority is looking to the RCC to help them formulate and carry out its program . . . communication of the needs and desires of the residents of Washington Park to the Authority will be one of the tasks of the Council. The Authority looks to the Council to strengthen the Washington Park neighborhood associations so that they will have a definite part in planning the rehabilitation of their area.[66]

The city planner who maintained continuity in Washington Park from the pre-Logue era well into Logue's regime was Lloyd Sinclair, who had been involved in one way or another in the Roxbury community since the early 1950's. Working first for the old Boston City Planning Board and then for the BRA, he had taken a major role in the formulation of the two plans for Roxbury approved by the City Council in the spring of 1959. While drawing up the proposals, Sinclair had come to know the leaders of the four Roxbury settlement houses, as well as members of the Community Council and the Snowdens. While, as he himself admits, he did not get down to "the grass roots of the district,"[67] Sinclair's years in the Roxbury area prior to Logue's arrival not only had given him a solid understanding of the area's problems but also had convinced the settlement house people and neighborhood leaders working with him that he was a sincere person who would try to do the very best by Roxbury and Washington Park. He always had made every effort to include both Freedom House and the Community Council leadership in any and all discussions about the future of the area. As he saw it, the basic split between the two groups was not over the goals of renewal but over whether those goals could best be reached by utilizing the leadership of a big, cumbersome organization concerned with all of Roxbury or a small tight "elitist" operation that was ready and able to move incisively in the Washington Park area. Believing that both were necessary, Sinclair was unwilling to choose one over the other. He felt that Washington Park was simply a pilot effort that would yield good experience that could be utilized when the over-all Roxbury project was tackled. While Freedom House might be geared to operate effectively in the Washington Park area, the remaining

66 *Roxbury Citizen*, March 10, 1960.
67 Author's interview with Lloyd Sinclair, March 17, 1966.

residential expanses of Roxbury could be involved only with the help of the settlement houses, neighborhood groups, and leaders with connections in those areas, the very people who were represented on the Community Council.

In a sense one can say that all the events in Roxbury prior to the winter of 1961 were prologue to the planning drive that was instituted once Logue was firmly established as Development Administrator. But those events were of enormous significance in establishing a leadership group geared not only to accept but positively to seek renewal and in creating a solid relationship between the BRA (as represented by Lloyd Sinclair) and Roxbury's important organizations and leaders.

ORIGINS OF THE REHABILITATION PLANNING TEAM: FREEDOM HOUSE TAKES CHARGE

When Logue came to town, he found himself with an already approved rehabilitation project in the middle of Roxbury, a local Community Council that had been able to muster 1,000 Roxbury residents for a public hearing, and federal survey and planning funds waiting in the BRA coffers. Unlike the other two areas we have studied, Washington Park as a renewal game situation was at the time of Logue's arrival a *fait accompli*. Cut away from its surroundings by the failure of the federal government to approve the entire Roxbury district as a renewal project, the 186 acres of Middle Roxbury stood as the forerunner of the district-wide programs that Logue would put together for Charlestown and the South End.

Washington Park assumed top priority in the early days of the Logue regime not so much because it was felt to be an ideal area in which to begin but because the funds were there, the neighborhood leaders were anxious to move, and, as one former employee of the BRA put it, "Logue had made an application for ten GNRP's [General Neighborhood Renewal Plans] and the feeling in Washington was that what the hell chance did he have with that handful if he couldn't make a go in Washintgon Park."[68] Logue himself would have preferred not starting in Washington Park. The national uproar over the impact of urban renewal on Negroes was beginning to be heard; and he would have liked to avoid dealing with Negro problems. But the momentum of the project gave him no room to back off. Logue therefore revived the concept, recently rejected by the federal government, of the Washington Park project within the larger Roxbury district and pointed out that the smaller area "can be an attractive project if it is part of an over-all area program . . . [but that only the rehabilitation of the over-all

[68] Author's interview with Robert Roland, April 5, 1966.

Roxbury district would ensure] the success of Boston's first effort at urban renewal."[69] It is important to realize that throughout all the remaining negotiations over the size, shape, and content of the Washington Park renewal plan it was assumed, as it had been prior to Logue's arrival, that the project was only the first step in the more ambitious job of rehabilitating all of Roxbury.

As soon as Logue took over as Development Administrator, he put on pressure to get the Washington Park project into the planning and execution stage and to begin organizing for the larger Roxbury GNRP. In response Sinclair looked about him for the basis on which to construct a local team with whom to negotiate a renewal plan. Throughout his years in the community, he had never relied on any one group as his "contact" but, following the advice of those who said that Roxbury was a complex of small factions incapable of being brought together, had constantly made the rounds of the settlement houses, the Community Council, Freedom House, and many other social welfare agencies in the area. Now with the suggestion of the Snowdens reinforcing his own conclusion, Sinclair decided to set up a small group of professional advisors: the directors of the four Roxbury settlement houses, the executive director and president of the Community Council, the Snowdens, and several social workers from Roxbury. The gathering, to be called the Community Organization Steering Committee, represented the organized and professional elite of Roxbury and was, as Sinclair stated,

to give the BRA Project Director counsel for and direct assistance in the preparation and execution of community organization and to assist the Authority in obtaining a maximum degree of citizen understanding and involvement in the renewal of their community.[70]

Members had been chosen on the basis of their knowledge of community organization, of the Roxbury area, and of the urban renewal process. Their organizational base indicated not only the extent to which the Washington Park project was seen in the context of the Roxbury district but also the extent to which the professional welfare community constituted the first link in any effort to establish a local area renewal team. Under Sinclair's leadership the small group seems to have been an effective mechanism for funneling information in and out of Roxbury as well as for neutralizing rivalry between Freedom House and the Community Council.

The general approach to community organization agreed upon at an early meeting was one in which each settlement house would assume responsibility

[69] City of Boston, "The 90 Million Dollar Development Program for Boston," reprinted from the *City Record*, September 24, 1960, p. 10.
[70] Community Organization Steering Committee: Roxbury–North Dorchester GNRP, Minutes, March 15, 1961.

for that section of the Roxbury GNRP in which it was geographically located.[71] The fact that none of the groups represented in the Community Organization Steering Committee was based in the Washington Park project meant that such an approach failed to provide a logical recipient for the job of organization in that 186-acre area. But the mandate for lining up a renewal team in Washington Park did not go undelegated. With Logue's urging, the torch quickly passed to Freedom House.

The Snowdens and Logue had gotten on well from the start. They had supported him in his battle with the Redevelopment Authority and had cheered his victory. In February 1961 a new Freedom House headquarters had been dedicated on Crawford Street in Upper Roxbury, and the Snowdens had used the occasion to introduce Logue to members of the Negro Elite. There seems never to have been any question in Logue's mind, after having talked with and watched the Snowdens in operation, that they were the ones who could mobilize a local renewal team. Sinclair, following Logue's decision, asked Freedom House to assume the responsibility of community organization for Washington Park. With the blessings of the BRA and funds from the fledgling ABCD, Mrs. Snowden announced at an early Steering Committee meeting that Freedom House would take on the task.[72]

Given the Steering Committee's approach of letting each settlement house do the organizational work in its own area, Freedom House, despite its orientation toward Upper Roxbury, was well located and structured to mobilize a citizen team in the 186-acre Washington Park project. While many residents in Middle Roxbury thought of Freedom House as "up there," looking down its nose on the people located around Washington Park,[73] the Snowdens did have long-standing relationships with several organizations and numerous individuals in the renewal project area.

Moreover, the fact that the Washington Park project was seen as merely the first step in the huge Roxbury renewal program assured the other members of the Steering Committee, all of whom were important figures on the Roxbury Community Council, that their individual organizations would receive a share of the renewal package as soon as planning began for the larger district. Anticipation of the job to come canceled out the challenge that might have arisen if Washington Park had been seen as the total end product of renewal in Roxbury.

---

[71] *Ibid.*, March 29, 1961.
[72] The minutes of the Community Organization Steering Committee record one last sparring match between the Community Council and Freedom House as the Council Executive Director asked Mrs. Snowden if she planned to hire "a professional person" to do the community organization (*ibid.*, April 18, 1962), the point being that neither of the Snowdens had a social work degree in community organization.
[73] Author's interview with James Ballard.

Thus, when Muriel Snowden announced Freedom House's willingness to take on the job, the general reaction of the Steering Committee (despite some private mutterings among the RCC leaders) was one of pleasure.[74]

The transfer to Freedom House of all community organization responsibility in Washington Park was a step on which Sinclair took issue with Logue. From his point of view, the Snowdens were highly capable as spokesmen and organizers but elitist in their orientation and basically concerned with preserving the Upper Roxbury area as an integrated middle-class bastion. Sinclair held them in great respect but felt it unwise to put in their hands the entire mandate for pulling together a local team. While Sinclair continued to work with the members of the Community Council and himself always considered the Council an important element in Washington Park negotiations, with Freedom House's assumption of the local "mandate" the die was cast. Neither the Community Council nor any other Roxbury organization would ever again be in a position to contest the Snowdens for the right to pull together a local renewal planning team.

There are some interesting parallels between the transfer of power from the RCC to Freedom House and the switch from SHOC to the Federation in Charlestown. In each case the move was from a loosely structured organization to a more highly controlled and organized base of operation. Yet the differences between the character of the two organizations are more significant than their similarities. For while an observer of the Charlestown renewal scene might have predicted dire consequences resulting from Logue's decision to transfer the mandate to the Snowdens, in Washington Park such a step was a well-calculated political decision that ensured a successful outcome to the renewal planning game. Unlike SHOC, which was a neighborhood organization made up of working-class residents, the Community Council, as a BRA planner put it, "was a focal point for leadership and professional people, not for citizen participation."[75] Made up of representatives of many independent organizations, each jealously guarding its role in the life of the Roxbury community, the RCC was unable to mobilize for rapid action.[76] Unlike SHOC's egalitarian Irish, the Council's middle-class leaders were not prepared either by motivation or by political capability to challenge Freedom House for the Washington Park planning mandate.

The structure of events, organizations, and individuals involved in Washington Park in the spring of 1961 made the transfer of the renewal mandate far from the jarring event such a tactic produced in Charlestown. However,

74 Community Organization Steering Committee: Roxbury–North Dorchester GNRP, Minutes, April 26, 1961.
75 Author's interview with Robert Roland.
76 Author's interviews with Les Houston, April 5, 1966, and Genevieve Kealey, March 29, 1966.

in view of Mrs. Snowden's determination to prevent the RCC from controlling renewal negotiations as it had in 1959, it is interesting to contemplate what would have happened in Washington Park if the transfer had not been made. Certainly the district's renewal game would have been far more charged with political infighting than was to be the case.

WASHINGTON PARK PLANS FOR RENEWAL:
ROUND ONE

Once given responsibility, the Snowdens moved with characteristic speed. The BRA schedule called for the Washington Park planning phase to be completed by the end of June and project execution to begin by October.[77] From Logue's point of view, planning for Washington Park was as good as over, and the project was to be quickly gotten under way so that attention could be turned to the rest of the complex Boston renewal program.

The Snowdens' approach to generation of a local team had two aspects: first they planned to establish a committee of about 25 leaders from the Washington Park area "to come together as individuals rather than as representatives of groups."[78] Second, they wanted to develop a "citizens council [to be named CURE] which would have one representative on every block in the entire Washington Park area."[79] The leadership role of Freedom House was spelled out in no uncertain terms with Mrs. Snowden's statement that "Freedom House as a temporary center for renewal information would be able to coordinate and centralize the entire renewal operation."[80]

The first Committee meeting, held on May 1, 1961, assembled a group chosen from five categories: Freedom House Board members living in the project area or with "special interest" in the renewal operation, clergy, educators, neighborhood association leaders, and "others," which included representatives from the YMCA and St. Mark's social center. The group, soon expanded to include more neighborhood representatives from Washington Park, met weekly at first and then somewhat more irregularly until December 1961.[81]

The "original" Washington Park Steering Committee, as the group put together by the Snowdens came to be known, has been the subject of much debate among observers of Boston's renewal program. The critics maintain that the members were "handpicked" by the Snowdens and represented

---

[77] Washington Park Steering Committee, Minutes, May 1, 1961.
[78] *Ibid.*
[79] *Ibid.*
[80] *Ibid.*
[81] It is important to note that several of the members of the Committee were white. While the president of the Roxbury Community Council was not on the original list drawn up by the Snowdens, she was soon added to the group.

nothing more than the voice of the remaining middle-class white and Negro elite in the Middle Roxbury section of Washington Park. Mrs. Snowden asserts that if an election had been held in Washington Park to designate 25 key people for renewal negotiations, practically the same group would have emerged, for, she maintains, the Steering Committee represented, insofar as any group could, the real leaders in the area.[82]

Certainly some of the residents on the Committee were, in the words of a participant in those meetings, "creatures of Freedom House."[83] On the other hand, there were representatives from block organizations that were not products of the Snowdens' organizational efforts during the fifties as well as individuals whose loyalties lay with the Roxbury Community Council. While there is no question that many members of the Washington Park Steering Committee were anything but pawns in the hands of Freedom House, the group was made up of members of the white community and Negro Elite, with some representation of the Blue-Collar Negro community. As one of the Committee recalls, "We were people who were old-time Washington Park residents."[84] The two groups that Sinclair was aware were not represented on the Committee were the newcomers and the "store-front church people"[85]—in other words, the Black Proletariat.

The sense of urgency during the first two and one-half months of the Washington Park Steering Committee's life precluded leisurely discussion of the kind indulged in by the South End Urban Renewal Committee during the first year of its operation. Under enormous pressure to produce a plan, Sinclair viewed the Washington Park Steering Committee not as the basis for grass-roots involvement in the planning process but rather as a means whereby leaders in Washington Park could come to understand the potential and limitations of urban renewal. Thus, education of a small team of local leaders, rather than bargaining or negotiating with a broad-based citizen organization, was the basic format of the Steering Committee–BRA team relationship.

While the Steering Committee met throughout the summer of 1961, officers were not elected until the middle of October. Summer weather and vacations were perhaps responsible for cutting back attendance. On August 14, for example, only six representatives from the area were present at a meeting with a wide range of Freedom House and BRA personnel.[86]

It would be difficult to argue that these sessions posed two teams, that of the neighborhood and the BRA, in a negotiating game over the future of

82 Author's interview with Muriel Snowden, March 28, 1966.
83 Author's interview with Morton Rubin, June 8, 1966.
84 Author's interview with Genevieve Kealey.
85 Author's interview with Lloyd Sinclair.
86 Washington Park Steering Committee, Minutes, August 14, 1961.

Washington Park. Freedom House certainly was not playing against the BRA, and the rest of the people assembled were for the most part not bargaining but simply finding out about the urban renewal process and what it meant for Washington Park. Despite the absence of hard negotiation, however, there was a great deal of interchange between the Committee and Sinclair's staff on various components of an urban renewal plan: schools, playground standards, mass transit and highway patterns, shopping centers, libraries, and fire stations. There was considerable agreement between Committee recommendations and BRA proposals for school and playground locations.

In general, relations between the Committee and the BRA remained cordial throughout the sessions, with the exception of one meeting when several members complained about the "lack of information this committee was receiving about plans."[87] So much confidence was expressed in the planners that Muriel Snowden's suggestion that each member of the Committee draw a map of the ideal Washington Park met with some objections from those who felt that such procedures could well be left to the professional BRA staff.

While various physical components of the plan were considered at length during this period, there does not seem to have been any discussion of relocation housing or the process of relocation itself. Nor was the place of public housing in the renewed Washington Park a topic of much conversation. At an early meeting of the Steering Committee, Sinclair had stated that there was a definite need for public housing of some sort in Washington Park as "most people with low incomes cannot locate homes at rents they can afford to pay."[88] But the topic was not pursued. As one member of the "original" Washington Park Steering Committee recalls, "Public housing was a hot issue all the way along the line. People would fight it the minute the subject came up at a meeting so the reaction of the BRA was not to let it come up. Public housing was the one thing that could not be talked about."[89]

Throughout these summer meetings the exact responsibility of Steering Committee members to the community at large was never entirely clear. The BRA, focusing on the task of educating a small group of Washington Park leaders in the complexities of urban planning, passed out a great deal of information, most of which never got back to the neighborhood level. The fact that there were only two neighborhood associations actually functioning in the Washington Park project area meant there was no systematic way whereby the Steering Committee could convey what they had learned

87 *Ibid.*, June 12, 1961.
88 C.O. Steering Committee: Roxbury–North Dorchester GNRP, Minutes, June 21, 1961.
89 Author's interview with James Ballard.

to a wider audience. However, while there was a definite lack of communication between the Steering Committee and the large majority of Washington Park residents, the absence of open criticism of the group reveals the extent to which those with the capacity to object were in accord with the direction that renewal planning was taking.

The second part of the Snowdens' approach to community participation, the larger group of representatives from each block, never really got off the ground. While there were several larger meetings during the months in which the Steering Committee was in session, the block groups did not come together regularly, and rather than being organized around representatives from particular streets, as the Snowdens had originally envisaged, the meetings were open to the public at large. As Mrs. Snowden points out,[90] the meetings did serve to get information back to the neighborhood level, a function not being fulfilled by the Steering Committee.

The drive to be in execution by autumn, which had been the assumption under which the BRA, Freedom House, and the community leaders had been operating, was brought to a halt in July by Sinclair's announcement that the project area would be expanded to include the area of Upper Roxbury between Seaver and Townsend Streets, the home of the Negro Elite. The need to develop renewal proposals for the new area meant that the amount of time devoted to planning could be increased and the rush to get into execution abated.

Freedom House had always fought to have the Upper Roxbury area included in the Washington Park project and thus was delighted. The Negro Elite, many of whom during the 1950's had spearheaded the drive for a Roxbury renewal program under RCC auspices, were far from displeased.

Doubling the size of the Washington Park project is the one instance in our three case studies where a radical change was made in the boundaries of the renewal area during the course of the planning period. Originally emerging from the planner's brush strokes as a triangle of land in the middle of Roxbury with no unique history or identity, Washington Park's expansion did no violence to the geographic or social integrity of the original area, which had acquired neither during its short life as a renewal project. At the City Council hearing to seek approval for the expansion of the boundaries, one of the Councilors made the point that the original boundaries had been determined by the availability of federal funds and "were never defended by the Urban Renewal Administration, nor, so far as I am aware, by the BRA, as the logical boundary area."[91]

---

[90] Author's interview with Muriel Snowden.
[91] City of Boston, City Council, "Before Committee on Urban Redevelopment, Rehabilitation, and Renewal," Stenographic Transcript, March 6, 1962, p. 79.

The reasons for the expansion have been a constant source of argument and debate. The publicly stated BRA rationale can be summed up in four points: (1) it made sense to back the project against the firm boundary of Franklin Park rather than the indeterminate line of Townsend Street; (2) relocation from the smaller project area into the Upper Roxbury section might cause "confusion and instability and lack of confidence in the area,"[92] and therefore it was necessary to plan both areas at once; (3) Upper Roxbury provided the project area with solid leadership; and (4) the administrative changes made possible by expanding the project area produced more federal funds for the BRA.

The unstated reasons for the expansion were related to the amount of clearance that would be necessary in the original Washington Park project. Recent BRA surveys, including a pessimistic study by Chester Rapkin on rehabilitation feasibility and housing conditions, indicated that the area's housing stock had declined enormously since Sinclair had investigated the area in 1958. Where he had thought in terms of 5 percent clearance,[93] it was apparent in 1961 that close to 55 percent of the dwelling units would have to come down. That much clearance was simply intolerable to Logue, given his views on the political limits of demolition percentages. Moreover, Washington Park was to be Boston's first residential rehabilitation project. To start off that campaign by bulldozing better than 50 percent of the project's homes would not be particularly fortuitous. Upper Roxbury, with its many streets of sound housing that required little if any demolition, would not only soften the over-all percentages of clearance but also make far more palatable rehabilitation's economic feasibility.[94] Rapkin estimated that in the Upper Roxbury section of Washington Park, 74 percent of the units were in sound condition[95] and that only 7 percent were substandard, while in the original project area of Middle Roxbury about 78 percent of the stock either would have to be demolished or would need major repair.[96]

Thus the criticism leveled at Logue that the move from the original project to the larger area was "simply a numbers game"[97] was in a sense true. The inclusion of the basically sound Upper Roxbury area buried the unpleasant facts of clearance and the difficulties of rehabilitation associated with the original project area. Logue changed the setting and thus the character of the planning game.

---

[92] *Ibid.*, p. 80.
[93] Author's interviews with Robert Roland and Lloyd Sinclair.
[94] *Ibid.*
[95] Rapkin, Report II, p. 49.
[96] Rapkin, Report I, pp. 3–4.
[97] City of Boston, City Council, "Before Committee on Urban Redevelopment, Rehabilitation, and Renewal," Stenographic Transcript, March 28, 1962, p. 304.

Yet another rationale offered for the expansion argues that to ensure the success of the first part of the Roxbury project, the bets had to be somewhat hedged. If including the Negro Elite in Upper Roxbury would help to get Washington Park airborne, in view of the long-range goal of a rehabilitated Roxbury, the juggling was necessary. As Mrs. Snowden put it, "We wanted to lead with our best foot to show what could be done with renewal so that people would sit up and take notice in the rest of Roxbury."[98] This justification once again presupposed that Washington Park was the first and, therefore, the most critical effort in the long job of rehabilitating the entire Roxbury district.

While project extension plans were announced in July, no efforts were made to add people from the Seaver-Townsend area to the Steering Committee until well after October, when plans for the enlarged Washington Park area were unveiled by the BRA.

THE NEIGHBORHOOD TEAM'S RENEWAL GOALS

Looking over the minutes of Steering Committee meetings in the spring and summer of 1961, one gets little sense of what the group saw as goals for a renewed Washington Park. So much time was spent scotching false or misleading "renewal stories" or discussing specific components of the urban renewal plan—schools, roads, shopping centers—that scant time was left for more generalized considerations of what kind of community Washington Park would be as a result of the renewal process. The first really clear insight into the Committee's point of view was revealed as the BRA was unveiling its proposals for the area in late October. In the usual Logue style, three plans of low, medium, and high clearance were presented. Much to Logue's dismay the Committee was favorably impressed by the option that showed 60 percent relocation of residents. When the BRA at the next meeting dutifully produced a plan that included all the same community facilities but only 40 percent relocation of residents, the Committee's reaction was strong, as the minutes record.

It was stated that this plan showed very little renewal at all. It was felt and expressed that the problem of relocation under the 60% plan was feared by the BRA hence the change to 40% relocation. The committee felt this plan represented a "glorified ghetto." . . . It was felt that this was the last chance for Roxbury—if the area doesn't get full scale treatment now, we will be back where we are now in three years. . . . The Committee was very positive in stating that they did not want all low income housing in the project area and it was hoped that the area would be integrated. The group felt this could be accomplished if the housing, both private and public, as well as the neighborhood itself, was attractive to people in out-lying communities.
. . . Mr. Sinclair's statement that rehabilitation was most important to the community and that property owners should be given a chance to fix their property

98 Author's interview with Muriel Snowden.

was met with a great deal of opposition. It was generally felt that the areas which were originally slated for extensive renewal and now were to be left as is constituted, in the most part, dwellings which were beyond repair and would cost too much to put into good condition. It was also felt that the owners of these homes were generally low income families who would find it economically impossible to borrow large sums of money to bring their property up to standard.

... It was brought out that we were originally promised three plans from which to work and the group felt generally that we have nothing to work with now. It was also felt that the philosophy expressed over the past six months by representatives of the BRA had changed concerning the amount of renewal that was absolutely necessary to preserving the community as well as Roxbury as a whole.[99]

As expressed in this statement, renewal was a means of re-establishing a Washington Park that would be, as it had been in the past, an integrated middle-class community. What the Elevated was to Charlestown and the liquor establishments to the South End, the low-income invaders were to the members of the Washington Park Steering Committee—the community's blighting element that could be removed by urban renewal. The sense of urgency with which the Steering Committee viewed the need for action in Washington Park was expressed at an earlier meeting when the statement was made that "it was generally felt that unless some action takes place very soon in both Washington Park and Washington Park Extended there will be even fewer economically stable families left."[100] The group wanted to move fast, and it wanted to move in wide swaths through the Middle Roxbury streets filled with newcomers.

Critics of the Washington Park planning process have often maintained that it was Upper Roxbury that led the battle to clean out the Black Proletariat in Middle Roxbury in order to protect itself against an invasion from the North. In light of this line of criticism it is extremely important to bear in mind that the members of the Steering Committee who articulated the views expressed in the earlier quotation were, with one or two exceptions, not from Upper Roxbury but rather from the Middle Roxbury section of Washington Park, the vestige of a stable residential area striving to beat back the invasion of its neighborhood.

When one considers the respective roles that the local team and the BRA were playing, the situation in Washington Park in the fall of 1961 appears extraordinary. In a series of fall meetings BRA planners were forced to justify their proposals for cutting back clearance, promoting rehabilitation, and lessening the relocation load. In neither of our other studies do we find a similar situation—the mandate group itself seeking a greater amount of relocation and clearance from its district. Yet given the socioeconomic dynamics of Washington Park and the latitude which had been granted the Snowdens in determining members of the Steering Committee, the position

99 Washington Park Steering Committee, Minutes, November 13, 1961.
100 Ibid., September 11, 1961.

is quite explicable. Logue's reaction to the demands of the Committee for a return to the higher clearance proposals was to refuse consideration of what he felt to be an "irresponsible and foolish decision,"[101] and therefore the 60 percent relocation plan was never again presented as an alternative for Washington Park. While the Committee was obviously unhappy over the smaller percentage of clearance, which at that point was reduced to about 30 percent of the area's residential structures, it reluctantly went along with the decision.

The debate on renewal goals for Washington Park, expressed in the argument over percentages of relocation, was the major but not the only point of difference between the BRA staff and the Steering Committee during the late fall and early winter of 1961. In a sense, the series of meetings held to discuss the BRA proposals for renewal was the clearest instance of bargaining in the Washington Park renewal negotiations. Team lines were clearly drawn between the Steering Committee and the BRA project staff.

The Committee successfully blocked the inclusion in Washington Park of a welfare institution for women but had little impact on a BRA proposal that called for a cross-town highway to cut through the heart of the Middle Roxbury section of the project.[102] There was much opposition to the road from the owners of the solid housing that stood in its proposed path—owners who, as long-time Washington Park residents, were well represented on the Steering Committee. While the question was raised, "What price are we paying for this renewal and is it prohibitive?"[103] in the last analysis the cost was not felt by the Committee to be too high. The road stayed.

The preliminary location of a Junior High School in the center of Washington Park was questioned by members of the Steering Committee who felt that the location would inevitably lead to a segregated school population. A committee established to investigate further the implications of the location decision presented solid reasons for the relocation of the building to the periphery of the project where a greater degree of integration could be guaranteed, a recommendation that the BRA accepted.

RESTRUCTURING THE PLANNING GAME

A superficial look at the planning game at the end of 1961 would lead one to believe that both the local team and the BRA were changing their organizations and personnel in order to bargain more effectively with one another.

---

101 Author's interview with Robert Roland.
102 Bower Street, for example, was viewed as one of Washington Park's worst streets both physically and socially. It was filled with members of the Black Proletariat. There were no regrets when the cross-town boulevard was scheduled to take out the entire street. (Author's interview with Morton Rubin.)
103 Washington Park Steering Committee, Minutes, November 6, 1961.

For at this time Lloyd Sinclair left the project, and the neighborhood team was restructured. Yet Sinclair's exit had nothing to do with his failure to come to terms with the community. The reason most often advanced for his departure is that technical rather than political complexities in Washington Park were mounting, and Sinclair was not putting the pieces together fast enough to suit Logue.

Lloyd Sinclair, in what was described by one member of the staff as the "slow burn period,"[104] had been in and around Washington Park for seven years. Throughout most of that period there had been little pressure to get a project under way. He had found time to become acquainted with the civic and social welfare leaders and had established a base of confidence as well as lines of communication that were flourishing when he left the community in 1961. Sinclair had disproved the axiom of city officials, stated when he first went to Roxbury, that "no one speaks for the Negro community." He had put together a system of voices that would speak without public challenge. With his exit the "slow burn period" was over, and the project moved ahead with inexorable precision. An election for mayor was coming up in the fall of 1963, and it would help John Collins no end to have the Washington Park project well under way by that time.

The new project director, who would see the plan through to its final hearing, was Bob Rowland, an individual with a reputation as the "best renewal technician in the business."[105] The staff that Sinclair left behind was acknowledged to be the "smoothest in the BRA."[106] With community organizational talent and a city planner who was reputed to be without peer in working with local residents, the BRA project team presented a formidable array of talent.

For Freedom House the period was one of scrambling to expand the "original" Washington Park Steering Committee. As has been pointed out, the negotiations over the BRA plan for the entire Washington Park project had to this point taken place with a Committee that did not have representatives from Upper Roxbury. The first month of the new year was spent frantically pulling in people from that area to acquaint them with the BRA plans. After a rapid series of gatherings with residents and businessmen, a meeting was held including people from the entire expanded Washington Park Project, where it was decided that, "The consensus of this group is that we accept the general concept of this plan as presented tonight and that the group recommends that the BRA proceed with the yellow light."[107] The

---

104 Author's interview with Richard Bolan, March 31, 1966.
105 *Ibid.*
106 *Ibid.*
107 Washington Park, Urban Renewal Area Meeting, Minutes, January 29, 1962.

results of this meeting represent a good indication of the basic espousal of urban renewal in Upper Roxbury. Anticipating only a small amount of clearance, the area had little to lose and much to gain from a residential rehabilitation project.

THE REVISED WASHINGTON PARK NEIGHBORHOOD TEAM

From March 1962 until January 1963 the Washington Park project held four public hearings—hearings for which support had to be mobilized and which exposed the project to the possibility of criticism and opposition. Voices of opposition, though present, were few and scattered. The machine put together by ABCD, Freedom House, and the BRA, combined with the positive response of Washington Park's powerful people, ground out an almost unanimous verdict for the project on each occasion. Two thousand residents went to a City Council hearing on March 13 to support the expansion of the original 186 acres to include Upper Roxbury. An Early Land Acquisition hearing on June 25 brought 1,100 people before the BRA board. During the dog days of summer, Washington Park residents packed the City Council halls to demonstrate their backing of Early Land proceedings, and on January 13, 1963 the final comprehensive plan for Washington Park was supported by a crowd of 1,300 (or, as one newspaper reported it, 1,200 for and 3 against).[108]

While it is important to emphasize the precision with which the year's events proceeded, the strength of the team that the BRA was able to field and the capable leadership of Freedom House, one should not underestimate the complexities of the steps taken by BRA, Freedom House, and ABCD to ensure continued political support in the community. While the creative planning phase was to all intents and purposes over with the "yellow light" given by the hastily assembled meeting of representatives from the entire project area, several organizational steps were taken to ensure a solid prorenewal turnout, to co-opt the potential opposition of a small group of clergymen, and to nullify the voices of those few souls who spoke out in public opposition to the proposal.

The most significant step taken to inform local residents of the renewal plans for their area was the establishment in the spring of 1962 of Citizens Urban Renewal Action Committee (CURAC). Emerging out of discussions among BRA, Freedom House, ABCD, and the expanded Washington Park Steering Committee, CURAC was envisaged as an organization of 100 to 200 "delegates from virtually every organization suitable for representation . . . [whose function it would be] to consider the proposals for renewal, to

108 *The Boston Globe*, January 15, 1963.

interpret them to the community and to formulate a definite citizens' position reflecting both majority and minority viewpoints."[109] Delegates to CURAC were chosen from among those attending the individual block meetings being held at Freedom House to explain the renewal plan. Despite the enthusiasm with which it was launched, CURAC never got off the ground as an independent organization in the period prior to final approval of the BRA plan. While the organization met throughout the year of the public hearings, it did so as an open forum rather than a structured decision-making group such as the South End Urban Renewal Committee. It was not until well after the January 1963 hearing that CURAC set up by-laws and elected officers.

In addition to block meetings and general CURAC assemblies throughout the spring, summer, and fall, were gatherings of the clergy, which represented another important component in the local coalition producing prorenewal turnouts at the public hearings. Just before the City Council hearing on expansion of the original project, 22 clergymen from Roxbury met with representatives of ABCD, BRA, and Freedom House. The clergy were urged to attend the CURAC meeting and to bring with them those in their congregations interested in supporting urban renewal.[110]

Organized as a result of that meeting into a Roxbury Clergy Committee on Renewal, the clergymen were an extremely important factor in rounding up support for the hearings. In exchange, the BRA and ABCD were forced to make clear that far more attention would be given the clergy in the future than had been in the past. Project Director Rowland was careful to point out to the clergymen that while Freedom House was a point of departure for community organizations, the churches represented a very significant base around which to mobilize the community.[111] As mentioned earlier, Washington Park was seen as the beginning of a much larger project. While the clergy might feel that they had been bypassed in the early planning stages, they, like the Community Council organizations, could be assuaged by the thought that they would have important roles when the Roxbury GNRP became a project area. The GNRP that surrounded Washington Park on all sides constituted a great sponge that could absorb whatever rivalries, frustrations, and criticism emerged from the Washington Park renewal game.[112]

109 Washington Park, Meeting of Freedom House, BRA, and ABCD, Minutes, March 21, 1962.

110 The representative from City Hall at the meeting also "warned against having those present who were anti-renewal." (Washington Park, Meeting with clergy, Minutes, March 9, 1962.)

111 Washington Park, Meeting with clergy, Minutes, March 16, 1962.

112 As events worked out, it was five years before anything happened in the larger area. After many false starts and reversals of strategy, the GNRP with some territorial additions

This move to organize the clergy for renewal was important not only as a mechanism for "getting out the vote" but also for neutralizing criticism of the direction renewal was taking in Washington Park. Several of the churchmen objected to the hard sell being given the plan by Freedom House, the absence of low-income relocation housing, the lack of new low-income housing in the proposal, and the paucity of grass-roots participation during the actual planning period.[113] Throughout the year of critical hearings, however, the combined efforts of ABCD and BRA staff were able to keep such criticism from breaking out into the open; and at the public hearings the clergy were lined up in support of the plan. Thus what could have been a clog in the Washington Park renewal machinery was avoided by the holding action of the BRA and ABCD.

The organization of the clergy can be taken as an indication of the fact that the structure of the urban renewal game was becoming increasingly complex. While Logue was absolutely committed to Freedom House as the group that could produce results in Washington Park, the BRA project staff was not happy with the Snowdens' tight grip on the neighborhood renewal team. The agitation felt by some of the ministers was also expressed by members of the BRA Washington Park staff and ABCD representatives. As the year wore on, one of the fears of the BRA project staff was that Freedom House could not be counted on to turn out a representative crowd at the public hearings; and increasingly efforts were made, such as with the clergy, to expand the scale of involvement to neutralize negative voices in the Washington Park community. But, unlike the South End where USES could be bypassed during the second round of planning, Freedom House was the official organizer of the local team in Washington Park. Not only was Freedom House the generator of community support for renewal but also the Snowdens' efforts were to a large degree financed by funds from the BRA, a situation without parallel in either Charlestown or the South End.

THE PLANNING RUSH

During the rash of hearings the main link between the proposed plan and the residents of Washington Park was the series of block meetings held at Freedom House in the spring and fall of 1962 to discuss the plan proposal given the "yellow light" by the expanded Washington Park Steering Committee. Street by street, block by block, the Snowdens mailed out to each resident of the project area invitations to come to Freedom House and hear about urban renewal. Between March and the end of June there were 28

---

became Boston's Model Cities neighborhood and thereby entered upon a serious and intensive planning effort in the fall of 1967.
[113] ABCD Memorandum from Vincent Chiampa to Joseph Slavet, November 9, 1962.

block meetings held with a combined attendance of about 1,400 people.[114] Gatherings ranged in size from well over 100 to as few as 13 residents. Using basically the same format at each session, the Snowdens explained the features of the renewal plan, pointed out its benefits to Washington Park, reassured those who were fearful of relocation that they would be treated fairly, and in general tried to allay people's fears while answering their inquiries.

There is no question but that during these sessions the Snowdens were selling renewal and selling it hard. These were not game situations in which a local team and a BRA team hammer away at the format of renewal. The Snowdens were telling people what was going to happen and the ways in which Freedom House, the BRA, and ABCD would help in such areas of concern as relocation, rehabilitation, and "people renewal," as the issue of social programs came to be known.

For there was great hope that ABCD's efforts would make deep inroads into "people renewal." And the real significance of that agency during the renewal planning period lay in its role as the organization addressing itself to the problems that physical renewal could not hope to solve: juvenile delinquency, unemployment, and the like. Since its introduction to the Washington Park community early in 1961, ABCD had been concerned with formulating a "social plan" to match the efforts of the physical renewal program. The maneuvers of the various committees that ABCD established to deal with its over-all plan were complex and resulted in few concrete proposals during the life of the renewal planning game. Yet the need for such social programming was apparent and recognized on all sides. As Muriel Snowden pointed out in a report to the BRA during the summer of 1962, "At the block meetings there has been real emphasis on 'people renewal.' Some means should be found for follow up on this apparent readiness for citizen participation in social planning."[115] Or, as Otto Snowden stated when asked what will happen when the BRA job is completed, "We will do our job including people renewal. Planning is being started now. ABCD is doing the ground work for social renewal. Freedom House has through the years stressed this in the community."[116] ABCD's capacity to match in the social area the vast changes BRA was capable of in the physical realm could not be measured until well after the final public hearing for physical renewal, but anticipation in Washington Park ran high as to what the agency might do.

114 Otto and Muriel Snowden, "Quarterly Summary and Critical Evaluation Community Organization Work Program Activities," July 5, 1962.
115 Ibid.
116 Washington Park, Urban Renewal Meeting at Freedom House, Minutes, November 15, 1962.

While there were charges throughout this period that Freedom House had been "bought and paid for by the Redevelopment Authority"[117] and scattered references to the planning period as "sixteen months of brainwashing,"[118] to any veteran of the first-round frenzy of neighborhood hearings in the South End or the activities of SHOC in Charlestown, the most outstanding characteristics of the block meetings were their general orderliness and the absence of negative comment from the large majority of areas slated for demolition. The prevailing mood of the block gatherings was one in which renewal was felt either to be inevitable or to be so beneficial for Washington Park that personal sacrifices were justified. The Cliff Street neighborhood, for example, was to be 90 percent bulldozed. One half of the 180 residents to whom notices had been sent came to the meeting. Rather than raise a storm of protest about the clearance, they seemed to accept their displacement and devoted most of their time to asking about the rents they would have to pay when moved. Otto Snowden quieted their fears by stating that "housing in all price ranges will be available in various sections of the area."[119] One might question the veracity of the statement but not the success it had in calming the fears of those at the meeting.

The passivity of those about to be bulldozed offers a striking contrast to the kind of response that such a proposal would have drawn forth in Charlestown. Moreover, with the rise of Black militancy in the middle 1960's it is doubtful that such a clearance proposal could be made today without evoking either massive resistance or the demand for much firmer guarantees of relocation housing than those offered by Otto Snowden. Yet in 1962 the traditional passivity of Boston's Negro population, combined with the assurances given by the Negro Elite that the renewal plan was in the best interest of the Black community, the absence of significant dissenting leadership, and the promises of housing opportunities in the renewed Washington Park all served to neutralize opposition to clearance proposals.

Critics of the Snowdens and the renewal planning process in Washington Park would point out that the Black Proletariat were not apt to respond to the Snowden's letters, nor were they likely to feel comfortable going "up there" to Freedom House, which was known as a bastion of middle-class respectability.[120] This is not to say that none of the Black Proletariat ap-

---

117 Otto and Muriel Snowden, "Quarterly Summary . . . ," *op. cit.*
118 Washington Park, Bambridge Block Meeting, Minutes, Spring 1962.
119 Washington Park, Block Meeting, Minutes, April 24, 1962.
120 During a gathering of Washington Park leaders to discuss the format of the block meeting, there was much debate over whether or not all the sessions should be held in Freedom House. Mrs. Snowden felt that "for various reasons the initial meeting should be held in Freedom House and after that the groups could decide on where they wanted to meet." Her position carried the day. (Washington Park, Meeting of Officers of Block Associations, Minutes, April 12, 1962). While the reasons weren't stated, the desire to

peared at the block meetings. According to several observers, they attended meetings, and though they did not come regularly or say much, they accepted renewal's reality and wished only to find out what was happening to their homes. One must remember that the Black Proletariat were relative newcomers to the area. Many of them had few roots and little commitment in the Washington Park area. Without leadership or a sense of cohesion, their major concern was that there be a place for them to go if they were forced to move. One of the roles of the block meetings at Freedom House was to provide such assurances.

In view of the middle-class–lower-class dichotomy advanced by James Wilson and Constance Williams as the basic framework around which to structure attitudes and involvement in the renewal game, it is extremely important to recognize that both Blue-Collar Negroes and the Negro Elite from Upper Roxbury were present at these meetings and voiced strong approval for the renewal process. In a survey taken in 1963 among Blue-Collar Negroes living on one Washington Park street, Rubin found a two-to-one feeling of optimism about what urban renewal would do for the neighborhood.[121]

If the economics of rehabilitation and new construction rentals were to preclude members of the Negro Blue-Collar group from remaining in Washington Park after project execution got under way, that preclusion would be neither the desire nor the intention of the Negro Elite leadership when in the process of negotiating a renewal plan.

OPPOSITION

The only organized group opposition within the context of the block meetings was that provided by those whose solid homes were located in the path of the proposed cross-town highway. Their opposition was countered by appeals to the public interest, by which it was maintained that "the overall concern of changes and planning is for the good of the majority of the residents."[122] With the exception of this group, whose situation was felt to be unfortunate and their opposition therefore understandable, little tolerance was granted to criticism of the plan or planning process. As one Washington Park resident said, "These people had become convinced of renewal. They had been talking about it since 1954 and they were not going to let 'trouble-makers' keep them from having it."[123]

---

maintain and strengthen the role of Freedom House in the renewal planning process was probably of paramount concern.
[121] Rubin, *op. cit.,* p. 253.
[122] Washington Park, Bambridge Area Meeting, Minutes, November 1962.
[123] Author's interview with Morton Rubin.

The state of mind that saw those with critical comments as "trouble-makers" is expressed in this excerpt from the minutes of a block meeting at which the local minister stood to warn people of what they were doing:

Residents should be adamant for more specific data and information . . . [he said] when will families be uprooted [?] . . . will [they] receive enough money to purchase another home to start life over[?] . . . Following a minute or two of booing, shouting of "sit down" . . . [the] chairman . . . regained control of the order of business.[124]

One topic upon which local residents dwelled at length was the timing of project execution. Again and again statements were made urging the BRA to speed up its procedures. As one resident whose own home was to be cleared stated, "Ninety percent in this community are in favor of the plan. The only question is when."[125]

A perfect example of Rubin's Blue-Collar Negro, this resident represents those in Washington Park who welcomed renewal and fought for it though they lost their own homes in the process. He had lived for many years in the Middle Roxbury section of Washington Park, which was overwhelmed after 1950 by members of the Black Proletariat. Owning one side of a two-family home, he had watched the other unit fall into total disrepair. From his point of view, renewal was not only a blessing for the neighborhood but also for him personally as it enabled him to get out of an intolerable housing situation. As Rubin points out in his own study, "Renewal is causing a small dispersal of owners, dislocated but compensated at fair appraisal values. Several such persons feel that renewal is an opportunity for them to leave an undesirable situation. There is no bereavement for a lost home."[126]

THE WASHINGTON PARK PLAN

The sketch plans for Washington Park that prompted all of these negotiations were changed three times before final approval in January 1963. While some shifts after January 1962 were made as a result of pressure from the local residential team, for the most part the changes were based on planning considerations internal to the BRA, the changing alignment of a major highway or the difficulty of utilizing a proposed site without further adjustment of its size or shape. Thus we can discuss the characteristics of the plan approved at the public hearing in January 1963, for that plan is basically the same as that of January 1962.

However, it is important to discuss one major change in the clearance pattern made between the two Januaries. The plan that appeared in the fall of 1961 proposed clearance for about 25 percent of the residential structures

124 Washington Park, Dale Area Meeting, Minutes, November 1962.
125 Washington Park, CURAC Meeting, Minutes, November 1962.
126 Rubin, op. cit., p. 254.

in the area. In the fall of 1962 the Washington Park BRA staff came to the conclusion that a greater amount of cleared land was necessary to provide adequate sites for several of the new housing developments in the plan. After much agonizing over whether or not to raise the amount of residential demolition, the staff decided the move was absolutely necessary but that it might be better not to raise the issue with either Logue or Washington Park residents. Moreover, the BRA remembered that the "original" Washington Park Steering Committee had itself pushed for 60 percent clearance. Therefore, while a great deal of explaining was necessary at gatherings of Washington Park residents in the fall of 1962, the clearance change drew no significant opposition from residents at these meetings.

The greatest amount of clearance occurs in the original 186-acre section of the project. The area above Townsend Street, with a few exceptions, is slated for rehabilitation. The final plan calls for the rehabilitation of some 6,500 dwelling units as well as the construction of over 1,500 units of 221 d3 rental housing, in which rents would run from $75 a month for one-bedroom to $105 for four-bedroom apartments. The two ends of the project area are to be unified by the new housing, and community facilities and a shopping center were to be strung along a cross-town highway cutting through the middle of the district. Other new physical elements in the plan are three elementary schools and a civic center that combines municipal field offices, police station, courthouse, branch library, Roxbury Boys' Club, and YMCA.

The percentage of residential structures to be cleared in order to carry out the Washington Park plan is higher than in the South End or Charlestown. Thirty-five percent of existing houses are slated for demolition; and there is a high correlation between the clearance pattern and building conditions in Washington Park; if one matches the needs of those to be relocated (27 percent of the individuals and families in the project area) against the existing and proposed Washington Park supply of low-cost housing, the gap is considerable. While 75 percent of the 1,275 families and 54 percent of the 563 individuals to be relocated were eligible for public housing,[127] prior to renewal there was no public housing whatsoever in Washington Park. However, the plan proposes construction of only 200 units of housing for the elderly. The implications of this lack of fit are fairly clear and consistent with the goals of the "original" Washington Park Steering Commit-

---

127 BRA: Washington Park, "Washington Park Urban Renewal Area: Application for Loan and Grant Part I: Final Project Report," January 25, 1963, Section on Relocation.
   It is freely admitted that many of these people would not want to move into public housing even if it were available and that some of them might be able to find standard housing on the private market that they could afford. Yet the public housing eligibility figure is a good index of probable difficulty in finding private relocation housing, as well as of the economic characteristics of those being forced to move.

tee. Washington Park as an integrated, middle-income community could not survive with low-income families. The renewal plan was structured accordingly.

Washington Park is the one project under study in which the BRA did not formally espouse the goal or demonstrate the means of rehousing all of the residential relocatees within the project boundaries or provide an annual breakdown of the average relocation load. The BRA's approach to the housing needs of the 1,275 families eligible for public housing is as follows:

Based on information from the Boston Housing Authority, it is estimated that accommodations will be available . . . to families displaced from the Washington Park Urban Renewal Area as follows during the forty-eight month project relocation period.

Number [of units] available   Number [of units] required
         5,720   1,275

. . . The computations made in this section about the availability of sufficient public housing accommodations are based on cumulative availability during this period.[128]

The BRA has assumed that the anticipated four-year turnover in Boston's public housing will solve the problem of relocation for Washington Park's low-income families. The assumption that Washington Park relocatees can pick up almost one quarter of the city's annual public housing turnover is hyperoptimistic; and the expectation that all of Boston's public housing can serve as a supply for Washington Park neglects to consider locational preferences or problems facing low-income, large-family, Negro households.

For the Steering Committee to equate public housing with residential units that will service the Black Proletariat is an oversimplification of the relationship between socioeconomic groups and housing needs. As I have pointed out, what distinguishes the Blue-Collar Negro from the Black Proletariat is not so much income as life style. Many of those families to be relocated as a result of the clearance in Washington Park were Blue-Collar Negroes, whose presence posed no threat to the Negro Elite of Upper Roxbury. However, it is certain that the rental level of the housing built in the renewed Washington Park kept many relocated Blue-Collar families from remaining in Washington Park.

In his study of the original 186-acre Washington Park project, Chester Rapkin came to some interesting conclusions about the capacity of the Negro community in general to absorb private housing at the rent levels of 221 d3. Rapkin based his demand schedule for new rental units on the assumption that "Because of the social composition of the area, it is not likely that more than a token number of new units will be occupied by white families, and virtually all of the demand, therefore, will come from

128 BRA: Washington Park, "Urban Renewal Plan for the Washington Park Urban Renewal Area," January 14, 1963, p. 11.

the nonwhite sector of the population."[129] After a detailed examination of annual Negro demand for rental housing in the entire Boston metropolitan area, Rapkin concluded that "over four-fifths of the 1,105 renters will require units under $80 a month and only seven percent will fall in the $100 and over rental category."[130]

Without even considering the fact that the size of a household will influence the number of rooms to be demanded, it is obvious that only a small percentage of the entire Negro population in Boston can afford the 221 d3 units. If one assumes that Rapkin's figures for the Negro community as a whole accurately describe the rental capacities of Negroes displaced from the extended Washington Park project, it is apparent that more than just the Black Proletariat are being excluded from the renewed community. Thus, one must bear in mind that the sheer economics of the proposed Washington Park plan imposes burdens on groups that there was a desire to keep in the project area. While an enormously significant aspect of Washington Park's planning game dynamics, class conflict cannot, then, be viewed as the sole causal factor in the expulsion of lower-income families from the district.

WASHINGTON PARK: AN OVERVIEW

In Washington Park a fortuitous combination of attitudes, individuals, and events produced a renewal game that, of the three areas under study, proceeded with the least overt friction and readjustment between the BRA project staff and the local citizens' team. Washington Park was ripe for renewal. As one observer said, "The BRA would have had to work hard to mess things up in that set-up."[131] The particular character of the Negro Ghetto guaranteed a strong core of articulate residents who were willing to risk the costs of rehabilitation in order to get some help for their neighborhood. The alternative residential locations open to the Negro Elite and Blue-Collar Workers in 1960 were minimal. Washington Park's powerful constituted in large measure a captive audience and thus provided the BRA with a perfect social setting for a rehabilitation planning game.

Added to a social situation in which articulate people demanded physical renewal was the presence on both BRA and neighborhood teams of people admirably suited for the renewal game. For the BRA, Sinclair was enormously adept at establishing lines of communication and confidence. During the "slow burn" period he set the framework for the renewal planning game. When technical *expertise* was required, Rowland was brought in to put

129 Rapkin, Report I, p. 92.
130 *Ibid.*, p. 102.
131 Author's interview with Daniel Broderick, February 21, 1966.

together the pieces of the project. Sinclair assembled a talented staff that arrived at its real capacity under his successor. On the community side, the Snowdens provided dynamic and single-minded leadership. Maintaining their mandate throughout the entire planning period, they were able to move from the "original" Steering Committee to the block meetings to CURAC and never lose command of the situation. Unlike USES, which surrendered its organizing role in the South End, the Snowdens hung on to the reins through the last public hearing and beyond.

Events broke at the right time for Washington Park. The Civil Rights Movement had not gotten under way when the planning period started. *De facto* segregation had not become an issue in Boston politics. Leaders of the NAACP and other Negro organizations saw Washington Park renewal as a great opportunity offering nothing but hope,[132] rather than as a move to stabilize the Negro Ghetto, an accusation that rang out from some circles in later years. The Poverty Program had not yet come into existence. "Maximum feasible involvement of the poor" was not yet a phrase to be reckoned with.

The structure of events avoided certain areas that could have caused flare-ups in the Washington Park game. Unlike SHOC's reaction to the Federation in Charlestown, the Roxbury Community Council was neither willing nor eager to contest Freedom House for the local renewal mandate in Washington Park. Logue was able to shift that mandate from the slow-moving Council to the elitist-oriented Freedom House without repercussion. While the rivalry between the two organizations during the fifties indicated that conflict between them was possible, the existence of the Roxbury GNRP, the arena in which the RCC could dominate the scene, mitigated the struggle that might have arisen had Washington Park been the sole locale of renewal in Roxbury.

Given a socioeconomic setting that guaranteed a solid group in support of renewal and little capacity to be for or against renewal on the part of those most affected by it, the structuring of the renewal game in Washington Park was exceedingly well handled. Yet there were moments, for example when the clergy was close to revolt, when even the most politically successful of the BRA's renewal games could have gone astray. That it did not was due to the individuals involved as well as to the setting that made a relatively placid renewal game almost a foregone conclusion.

Yet the politically successful game imposed certain penalties on those interest groups not taking part in the contest. As relocation figures indicate, a large number of low-income white and Negro families for whom there was scant provision in the existing or proposed housing stock in Washington Park were displaced. Relative to the other two projects, Washington Park has a high ratio of clearance to deteriorated residential structures.

From a political point of view, there was little chance that the Black Proletariat could be included in the renewal game. Their presence was to a large degree the causal factor behind the enthusiasm of the Negro Elite, the Blue-Collar Negroes, and those whites involved in the renewal process. The incompatibility of social classes kept the Black Proletariat from being represented in the renewal game, as their own alienation from organizations and their everyday struggle for existence prevented their personal participation.

The relationship between interest groups in Washington Park in the early 1960's was such as to make the displacement of one of those residential groups, through the removal of their housing, a requirement of the renewal game. Had the BRA team tried to expand the role of the Black Proletariat in the renewal negotiations or in the resulting plan, the BRA would have incurred violent opposition from the groups with which it was planning and upon whose support it depended. In Washington Park the socioeconomic characteristics of the area precluded a local team with direct or representative involvement of "the poor."

6

The Diversity of Neighborhood: A Comparative Analysis

The South End, Charlestown, and Washington Park all produced "successful" planning games. In each district a renewal proposal found sufficient support in the community to withstand a public hearing; yet as is clear from the preceding chapters, the socioeconomic setting, the range and relationship of interest groups, and the dynamic response to the process of renewal planning varied widely among the three.

It is, however, important to emphasize that the variations in process and product among the three districts occurred in basically the same structural framework, for an underlying unity was provided by the demands of rehabilitation planning and by the highly refined strategy developed by Logue for undertaking that planning. What is significant at this point is to consider the variations among the communities in the critical elements of that planning approach to determine how the diversity of neighborhood shaped the style of the planning game, the role and character of the participants, and the final product emerging from the bargaining process.

NEIGHBORHOOD DYNAMICS AT THE MOMENT OF RENEWAL'S ARRIVAL: INITIAL ATTITUDE TOWARD CHANGE

The socioeconomic and political dynamics of each neighborhood at the start of the planning game established not only the number of interest groups and relationships among them but also the character and distribution of "powerful" people and their probable attitude toward the rehabilitation planning game.

While all three of the areas under study lost population more rapidly during the decade of the fifties than did the city of Boston as a whole, the characteristics of those population movements were critically diverse. As our study of census tract shifts by socioeconomic characteristics indicated, the South End was as depressed relative to the Boston average in 1950 as in 1960. Low incomes, bad housing, racial ghettos, and old age were no strangers to that City Wilderness. At the end of the fifties the significant, uncharacteristic population movement in the South End was the barely perceptible in-migration of middle-income professionals taking advantage of the area's town houses and cosmopolitan atmosphere.

Other than a critical loss of young couples, Charlestown during the same decade had not witnessed any startling transformation in the socioeconomic characteristics of its population. While some non-Townies had moved into the houses left empty by suburban-bound Townies, the basic character of the district's residents remained the same.

In Washington Park, however, the 1950's witnessed a dramatic shift in the area's socioeconomic characteristics as population movements produced a reversal from a white to a Negro majority and an increasing clash of life styles. As Figure 6.1 demonstrates, during the 1950's Washington Park's income and employment characteristics moved against those of the city, whereas Charlestown and the South End either moved with the city or were relatively steady.

While Townies generally paid little heed to the decline of their village until Leo Baldwin brought the fact to their attention, most Washington Park leaders worried about the problem for a decade. Townies bristled when they heard Charlestown referred to as a "blighted" area, while Washington Park leaders from 1954 to 1958 were desperately trying to get that adjective applied to their neighborhood in order to bring in urban renewal.

In the South End, however, the process of fighting blight, drink, and poverty had become so institutionalized that talk of solutions to the South End's problems went on in the same ritualized fashion in the fifties as it had during every decade since Robert Woods's day. Where major social problems were new to Middle and Upper Roxbury and a terrifying prospect to middle-

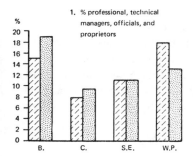

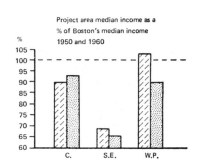

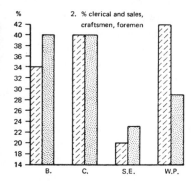

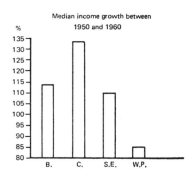

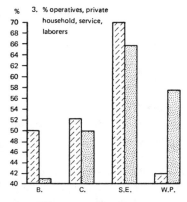

FIGURE 6.1 OCCUPATIONS OF EMPLOYED LABOR FORCE: A COMPARISON BETWEEN 1950 AND 1960

income white and Negro families living there, they constituted a much berated but familiar aspect of life in the City Wilderness.

There can be little question but that the population dynamics within the borders of the three districts under study had a significant impact on the manner in which the residential rehabilitation game proceeded. The urgency with which leaders in Washington Park were able to frame the issue of renewal was simply not possible in Charlestown and the South End, where the relative changes in the areas' physical and social conditions were not as dramatic and the threat to a way of life not as boldly visible as in Washington Park.

THE POWERFUL

At the start of renewal planning, distribution and motivation of the "powerful" in each district was directly related to the number and character of interest groups, their capacity to mobilize for renewal planning, and the degree of compatibility existing among them. Washington Park was a neighborhood in which the majority of Blue-Collar Negroes and Negro Elite saw residential rehabilitation as a "good thing." While in 1960 the Black Proletariat who would be affected by any renewal program constituted a significant interest group in the community, they did not have the capacity to mobilize and demand a place in the planning game. Thus in Washington Park those interests that had to be convinced of rehabilitation renewal before it could be politically sanctioned were already highly motivated and definitely convinced of the appropriateness of the action at the moment of renewal's entry into the community.

In 1960 Charlestown was experiencing none of the socioeconomic turbulence that characterized Washington Park. The great bulk of the population that would be affected by rehabilitation planning constituted a single vocal interest group that maintained an attitude close to what Meyerson and Banfield have called "a communalist unitary conception"[1] of the public interest. Residents might vie with one another for prestige and have radically different incomes and occupations, but when the chips were down, they were all Townies united together against outsiders threatening their urban village—that is, until the issue of renewal split their community into warring factions.

In 1960 the South End sheltered a multiplicity of groups whose interests in the neighborhood were certainly diverse and often conflicting. Lacking the strongly motivated and sizable leadership group of Washington Park and the dominant interest group of Charlestown, the "powerful" in the South

---

[1] Martin Meyerson and Edward C. Banfield, *Politics, Planning, and the Public Interest* (New York: The Free Press of Glencoe, 1955), p. 323.

End were scattered, in both geographic and socioeconomic terms, across the face of the City Wilderness.

In none of the districts under study was there a direct equation between the powerful interests and middle-class status. Working-class groups were involved in varying degrees in each area. While Gans's Urban Villagers may not have had the organizational capacity to defend themselves, the Charlestown working-class Urban Villagers were able not only to mount opposition but also to drive the hardest and, from the point of view of their own self-interest, the "best" bargain with Ed Logue and City Hall. In the South End the protests of the Syrian Urban Villagers constituted one basic reason for the change in the clearance patterns along Shawmut Avenue. In Washington Park many Negro Blue-Collar Workers, while not a vocal force in the planning game, nonetheless actively followed the lead of the Negro Elite in promoting renewal for their district.

Moreover, one must consider that the particular characteristics of each project area structured in different ways the relationships among lower-, working-, and middle-class categories. Charlestown's overwhelmingly working-class population includes individuals who on the basis of their education, income, and occupation have to be considered middle-class. Moreover, some Townies, if judged by their occupation, attitudes, and "problems," fall into Gans's lower-class category. The nature of the Charlestown community, however, renders these objective differences far less significant than similar divisions in Washington Park, where there are no unifying factors of history, geography, and marriage and where conflicting life styles are more significant than racial ties.

In the South End the potential conflict between the middle-class white Urbanites and the working-class lodging house owners was mitigated by the very character of those middle-income whites who sought, for whatever motive, the social heterogeneity offered by the area. In the South End, moreover, long-standing experience with real poverty made tolerable certain lower-class behavior patterns that would not have been accepted by Washington Park's Negro Elite.

The inclusion in the rehabilitation game of a broader spectrum of interests than the middle class brings into question the validity of earlier appraisals of the Washington Park, Charlestown, and South End planning games. As was pointed out in Chapter 2, James Q. Wilson and Constance Williams, in evaluating the success of Washington Park and the explosion at the first Charlestown hearing, arrived at different but equally questionable conclusions. The rigid dichotomy of both analytic frameworks obscures the complex realities of the communities with which they are dealing. Miss Williams falls into the trap implied by Wilson's "public regarding" and "private regarding" categories, which tend to equate approval of rehabilitation with middle-class values and opposition with lower-class values. In order to account for the Charlestown situation, she posits that the opposition must have been made up of working-class people, while those who favored renewal must have been middle-class. As we have demonstrated, a main theme of the Charlestown story is the inability to sort out the community's reaction to renewal in terms of class. Only by considering the complex social and political setting in which the conflict occurs do the lines of battle make any sense at all.

While Miss Williams makes an effort to explain the presence of diverse attitudes toward renewal in both Washington Park and Charlestown, Wilson flattens all internal dissension to demonstrate that Washington Park constitutes an example of a "public regarding" middle-class neighborhood accepting rehabilitation, while Charlestown represents the anticipated lower-class "private regarding" rejection of the same process. The complexity of the planning games in each of these neighborhoods indicates that Dr. Wilson has bent reality to fit his analytic structure.

THE POINT OF INTERVENTION: THE
DIVERSE MECHANISMS FOR BUILDING
A LOCAL TEAM

Logue's neighborhood planning system demanded an organization inside the boundaries of the project area that could be counted on to reach out and absorb into its structure the neighborhood's "powerful." When an existing organization was lacking, it was necessary to find an agent that could *create* a mandate group. The socioeconomic and political dynamics within each community under study determined not only the quality and quantity of local power but also the particular mechanisms through which the mandate group would be organized.

In each neighborhood the organization given the task of building a local planning team constituted the most logical point of intervention for legitimizing the rehabilitation planning game. However, the form and relationship of organization to neighborhood are strikingly different in the three cases and indicative of the districts' structural variations.

Charlestown's SHOC was a broadly based, loosely organized citizens' group that emerged out of the local desire to revitalize the Urban Village physically and socially. In the South End USES was a traditional settlement house that had been trying to bring order to the City Wilderness for over half a century. Where a unitary neighborhood made SHOC possible, USES was committed, not by fact but by ideology, to a similar point of view and was thus determined to build a mandate group with the broadest possible representation.

Rather than a spontaneous expression of a unitary community or an organization with ideological commitment to the entire spectrum of interest groups living in its area of operation, Washington Park's Freedom House had been organized for the express purpose of holding on to the integrated middle-class Upper Roxbury community, the equilibrium of which had been shattered by an invasion of lower-class Negroes and the exodus of middle- and working-class whites.

It is important to note that while both USES and Freedom House were given mandates to create neighborhood teams that would be the legitimatized bargaining agents for the neighborhoods, SHOC constituted both the point of intervention into the community and the mandate group. Unlike Washington Park, which had a tradition of professionalized welfare institutions, Charlestown had no organizers who might intervene between the BRA and the local group brought together to negotiate a renewal plan.

THE FORM AND CONTENT OF THE
REHABILITATION PLANNING GAME

The form and content of each planning game was determined by the goals of the group tapped by the BRA to build a neighborhood team as well as by that group's capacity to absorb the powerful into the formal planning process. As a result of a diversity of goals and capacity there is a variation among the neighborhoods in the degree to which rehabilitation planning emerges as a game situation.

In Washington Park the degree of unanimity between the BRA and Freedom House, coupled with the massive underlying support by the area's articulate people for a renewal program, kept the elements of contest and competition to a minimum. Yet it is important not to overlook the maneuvering that did go on during a negotiation period punctuated by five public hearings.

The South End presented a situation in which the lines between the BRA and neighborhood were sharply drawn. Bargaining could be clearly and consistently identified, as could the change of BRA style, to fit the demands of the local team.

In Charlestown the planning game concept provides a means of structuring the complex events in that project's renewal history. Moreover, the Town's final round of negotiation can best be understood if seen as the result of the breakdown of an organized game situation (where the teams are clear as to the rules of the contest) and as the introduction instead of guerrilla tactics to which rules and ordered negotiation have little relevance.

Despite the similarity of initial BRA strategy in each neighborhood, only the Washington Park project went strictly according to the format of Logue's planning system. Once having received the mandate for organizing Washington Park, Freedom House pulled together a select group of citizens who negotiated and legitimatized a renewal plan for their area. The group expanded, and CURAC replaced the "original" Washington Park Steering Committee. Ministers were brought more into the picture toward the end of the planning process, and a large number of people were exposed to the plan during the block reviews. Yet the Snowdens held the reins at the end of the planning game as they had at the beginning, and local organizations seem to have had little existence apart from the impetus given them by Freedom House.

In the South End, USES started out as the organizing force behind the Urban Renewal Committee and was itself the single most powerful factor on the Committee during the first round of renewal planning; by the time the game drew to a conclusion, USES was just another interest group represented on the URC. The South End's renewal planning structure was maintained despite some real threats to its existence. As USES declined in importance, the neighborhood associations rose in significance, and, in weathering several internal conflicts, the local team acquired a solid legitimacy in carrying out the renewal game.

In Charlestown the mandate was transferred from SHOC to the Federation; but with the negative January 7, 1963, hearing the BRA found itself in a wide-open political battle in which it was necessary to placate the Federation at the same time that the Moderate Middle leaders were brought into the picture and that efforts were made, first to neutralize SHOC, and then to polarize the organization. Charlestown, the most homogeneous of the areas, was unable to maintain any semblance of a closed system in which the mandate group could act as the legitimatized decision-making body for the neighborhood as a whole.

In a sense the form of the renewal games dictated the manner in which particular planning issues would be discussed. The "Original" Washington Park Steering Committee was concerned with particular location decisions on items in the renewal package. Yet the activity never filtered to the neighborhood level as it did in the South End, where much of the negotiation during the second round was concerned with particular decisions on future land use within the confines of the individual neighborhood associations. In Charlestown, without question the area with the greatest exposure of the renewal plan to the local public, there was little negotiation over particular location decisions once the original work of the SHOC Planning Council and Federation Urban Renewal Coordinating Committee had been completed. Less concerned with the location of public facilities than the feasibility of rehabilitation and the minimization of residential demolition, Townies continually evaluated renewal in terms of its impact on the community as a whole. Because Charlestown had no tradition of neighborhoods, Charlestown's planning could not be disaggregated into small bargaining units. The wealth of local organizations for the most part formed on a functional rather than territorial basis had seemed to provide a mechanism for subdistrict negotiation, but the January 7, 1963, hearing proved the bankruptcy of that approach.

Despite the absence of social renewal resources comparable to those of physical renewal, in both the South End and Washington Park great efforts were made to ensure that social programs would accompany physical change. None were more conscious of the need for nonphysical change than the Snowdens, who continually emphasized the vital role that would have to be played by ABCD. Yet, in Washington Park when the Roxbury Community Organization Steering Committee drew up a social equivalent of the renewal plan, the results foundered on the internal relationships of the Roxbury welfare community.

In the South End the format of the URC indicated the extent to which social issues were considered as important as physical change. Despite the emergence of a South End Community Action Program, there was the feeling among many in the community that the success of neighborhood groups in getting changes in the physical plans for their areas drained energy from the more critical areas of social policy.

As is clear from the aggregate statistics measuring welfare case load, delinquency, and health standards, Washington Park and the South End dramatically outdistance Charlestown and the city average. One might argue that, therefore, the social planning game had far greater relevance for two of the projects than for the third. Social planning was never really an issue during the Charlestown renewal planning contest, and yet immediately before the final BRA hearing a Charlestown multiservice center opened to serve the needs of Charlestown's people. Washington Park had no such objective symbol to show for its social planning at the time of final renewal project approval, and while a Community Action Program had been funded in the South End by the time of that area's public hearing, it had no impact on the renewal planning game.

THE PLANNING GAME AND THE MANAGEMENT OF DISSENT

The neutralization of neighborhood opposition and conflict within the framework of the local team is necessary for a successful planning game. Dissent must not be allowed to grow to the point that counterorganizations are set up to operate outside the negotiations of the mandate group. Organized opposition never got off the ground in Washington Park, where, under the firm direction of the Snowdens and a strong and perceptive BRA staff, the few negative public flutters that did emerge were quickly put to rest. The potential revolt of the clergy and of ABCD was neutralized. Once the Snowdens took charge, there was relatively little public struggle over the organizational means with which to organize the community and negotiate a renewal plan.

Unlike Washington Park, the South End planning game contained moments of serious disequilibrium. Yet the structure of the renewal game in that area was the most successful of the neighborhoods under study in arbitrating the goals of different interest groups. The rooming house operators and the Urbanites may have had divergent views on many subjects, but they were willing to abide by the majority decision determined within the framework of the neighborhood associations and the URC. The genius of the South End planning framework was that it provided a mechanism for including those who could be for or against a renewal plan as well as for providing some representation for those, like USES, who would champion the lower-class residents of the South End.

In Charlestown the failure of the structured renewal game to provide a meaningful outlet for differing opinions led to the breakdown of an organized local team and the evolution of an articulate and organized opposition. The planning game as a representative bargaining system was unable to survive the demands of a community in which a high percentage of residents maintained the right to take part personally in that bargaining process.

A question that one must ask is: Given the different impact of residential rehabilitation on diverse neighborhood interest groups, to what extent were opposition and conflict inevitable in Charlestown and to what degree was their absence predictable in Washington Park?

One might argue that conflict was equally possible in Washington Park and that only the perceptions and actions of the BRA staff neutralized such latent opposition before it could be seriously mobilized. It is certainly true that, of the three BRA teams under study, Washington Park constituted the largest and most experienced staff and that the BRA forces in Charlestown represented probably the weakest team. Yet one must bear in mind that in 1960 the goals of the rehabilitation process and those of the Washington Park powerful were one and the same. In Washington Park the BRA staff was dealing with a local team that had become committed to renewal as the salvation of their neighborhood and their way of life long before Logue came to Boston. The urgent demand for a renewal program was unique to Washington Park. In many ways the BRA was lucky. The Black Proletariat was unorganized in 1960 and had few champions among those who could speak out at public hearings. It is extremely unlikely that the kind of plan that sailed through five public hearings in 1962 and 1963 could be passed today. The socioeconomic and political dynamics of Washington Park have changed; the Black Proletariat is now an interest group that has sufficient representation among the powerful to insist that its needs be heeded. But the relevant issue is that at the time and place at which renewal was interjected into the community it was reasonable to assume that the Black Proletariat would not require vocal representation at the bargaining table.

In the South End efforts to mobilize an opposition group met with very limited success. While many South End leaders judge that there was the capacity for strong opposition in their district, they are also quick to admit that after the rumbles over the first plan the BRA became extremely sensitive to the demands of the complex interests making up the South End. Furthermore, the paucity of leadership and the wide range of interests represented in the community meant that there were few dissenters who could mobilize a significant number of followers. A multiplicity of interest groups would tend to neutralize or cancel each other out and prohibit the kind of polarization that emerged in Charlestown. The kind of massive and sustained opposition that SHOC was able to mount required a community with a high degree of political sophistication, well-developed patterns of internal communication, and a relatively homogeneous population—none of which characterized the South End.

It is unquestionably true that each rehabilitation planning game in Boston carried within itself seeds of discontent and the possibility of generating opposition. Yet events in the three projects under study give clear indication that while the BRA team strategy was enormously important either in containing and neutralizing opposition or, in Charlestown, in generating and exacerbating opposition, the likelihood of opposition rising to sufficient strength to disrupt the planning game was to a large degree dependent upon the unique political and socioeconomic characteristics of each project area.

THE ROLE OF THE PLANNER

In Chapter 1 we pointed out the problems posed by the rehabilitation game for the planner who has somehow to reconcile the demands of his professional standards, the city-wide goals of the renewal agency, and the pressures generated at the neighborhood level as he goes about the task of working out a plan for the rehabilitation of a residential area. In a setting such as Boston, where local political approval is the key to the rehabilitation planning system, the nature of each renewal game determines the extent to which there may be conflict among these three demands. The BRA planner's role is that of negotiating plan approval at the local level within the opportunity area afforded by city-wide political and planning constraints, and yet that role imposed different demands upon the planners in each of the projects studied.

In Chapter 1 we also discussed the spectrum of possible planner roles from that of Jane Jacob's middle-class bureaucrat to the advocate planner who is basically a mobilizer of public opinion. There is little question that BRA planners are closer to the second role than to the first. Out in the individual neighborhoods and on the political firing line, the planners' scope of action is determined not only by housing, health, or design standards but also by the political realities of city life at the district level. Yet given this general location of BRA planning on an "objective-advocate" spectrum, the three projects under study assume different positions along that spectrum.

Washington Park constitutes a situation in which the BRA staff was viewed by the local planning team as a group of experts who could help the local community realize its goal of neighborhood restoration. Bob Rowland's work is symbolic of the role open to a planner in Washington Park after Lloyd Sinclair's careful ground work had been done. Rowland, the seasoned professional who could grind through the masses of detail involved in designing an urban renewal program, is very much a technician with definite views as to professional planning standards. In Washington Park, Rowland had the political leeway to carry out "objective planning principles." For example, the change in the clearance percentages for Washington Park came about because Rowland felt it was professionally irresponsible not to make such changes, not because the neighborhood demanded such an alteration.

In the South End the role the planner was able to play was less the objective technician than the mobilizer of public support. Caught in a more complex political situation than Washington Park with far less of the unified mandate for physical change, Dick Green had to build his political base slowly, with negotiation at many points of possible conflict. Greatly conscious of the ultimate necessity of local approval, he changed his basic principles whenever neighborhood pressure so dictated and fought those in the BRA central office who would hamper his flexibility at the district level. When it became apparent that rigid adherence to the design would cause political flare-ups, the "concept" was quickly violated, much to the distress of the urban designers in the BRA's downtown office. But Green had learned from the conflict generated by the first round of planning that failure to adapt the plan to neighborhood demands would jeopardize the success of the planning game. Green was not so much a technical expert as a patient negotiator, bending the concept of "good planning principles" to suit the needs of the individual neighborhood associations with which he was dealing.

In Charlestown the cross fire in which the BRA found itself as a result of the January 7, 1963, hearing turned the planning process into a contest of political strength. Professional criteria came to mean very little. To Townies the planners and the BRA were just another group of politicians, though nonelected, selling a program; the question was whether or not to buy what that program offered. Frank Del Vecchio became a salesman for what he considered a good product. While making an effort to meet all the demands of the Moderate Middle, he rang almost every doorbell in the Town to promote his wares—a multimillion-dollar renewal program. The goals of the Charlestown project staff became the goals of the entire BRA operation, as Logue pulled out all the stops to ensure support of the renewal plan.

Thus the role of the planner was different in each of the projects under study. The more politically charged the situation, the less the leeway to emerge as the expert or objective planner. The Negro Elite, given its middle-class values, was far more willing to listen to experts than was working-class Charlestown, with its disregard for the expertise of anyone from City Hall.

It must be recognized, however, that a planning game may generate conflict and opposition and political tension because of the inability of the Local Planning Agency to assess the distribution of neighborhood power and the failure to ensure that the framework for negotiation is structured to take account of that distribution. We have emphasized the importance of neighborhood dynamics in determining the extent to which the planner can base his decisions on physical criteria alone; yet even in the most benign neighborhood atmosphere the planner's grasp of political realities goes a long way toward dampening potential opposition. Washington Park was not so intent on urban renewal that the BRA could have done absolutely anything in the community; and Rowland was no novice at understanding the nature of power in that district. Had the BRA decided to put a large public housing project into Upper Roxbury, it is not difficult to imagine the instant and total opposition that would have been generated.

Thus the role that the planner was able to play in the Boston projects was determined by the political climate in which he was operating and by his own understanding of the nature of that climate. Charlestown became a hotbed of dissent and conflict because of certain characteristics in the dynamics of the community which were exacerbated by the BRA's and ABCD's failure to understand the nature and distribution of local power.

THE DIVERSITY OF THE PLANNING GAME'S PRODUCT

While the local teams in all three areas were concerned with such issues as rehabilitation feasibility, provision for relocation housing, and the nature and extent of public investment that would be made in their area, each project had one issue around which the local team could consistently be mobilized and on which all its members could agree. In Charlestown the "El" running the length of Main Street became the symbol of the community's problems. All shades of Townie faction could be united under the banner of "get rid of the 'El.' " In the South End each interest group participating in the negotiations heartily affirmed the removal of many of the liquor licenses in the City Wilderness. Even USES and the rest of the professional welfare community that continually supported efforts to deal with the plight of Skid Row were in favor of any move that would eliminate bars and package stores. In Washington Park there was a clear though not explicitly stated position that unless many of the Black Proletariat were removed, there was no hope of preserving what little middle-class integrated community remained and certainly no hope of enticing more whites into the community.

The symbol of renewal in Charlestown was a physical object, the demolition of which would benefit everyone living in the Town. The symbol in the South End was indirectly related to the removal of an interest group in the district—"If you get rid of the bars you get rid of the bums." The symbol in Washington Park was a combination of physical and social objects—the removal of blighted houses and of the people living in them. Nothing indicates more clearly the degree of latitude within each project area for residential demolition than these diverse symbols around which neighborhood support could be mobilized.

Thus the planning solutions that emerge from renewal negotiations are as much a function of the local team's character as of the structure and style of the renewal game itself. The diverse goals pursued by the local teams in the projects under study can be seen in the manner in which the final product of the renewal game deals with such characteristics of the project area as the relationship between deteriorated housing and clearance, the provision of housing for low-income relocatees, and the costs of rehabilitation to those renters and owners whose homes are to be preserved.

CLEARANCE

As has been pointed out, the residential rehabilitation game is based on the assumption that some of the housing in the project area is deteriorated or dilapidated and must be removed in order to insure the future well-being of the surrounding neighborhood. The real bargaining between the LPA and the local team is over the extent to which the clearance pattern shall follow the findings of the building survey that has categorized the condition of the area's residential structures.

The two limiting cases in this bargaining process are represented by a local team fighting tooth and nail to save every home in its neighborhood, with the result that little if any clearance will be politically feasible, and a local team urging clearance and insisting that the LPA demolish all the residential structures labeled deteriorated or dilapidated by the building survey. If one locates the three projects under study along the spectrum between these two extremes, Charlestown can be found closer to no clearance, Washington Park to maximum clearance, and the South End somewhere between the two.

As has been pointed out, during the survey and planning stage each BRA project team rated the buildings in its area[2] in one of four categories ranging from "A" (buildings in satisfactory condition) to "D" (buildings in need of major repair), with "B" and "C" representing minor and extensive repair, respectively. Buildings in condition "D" would automatically justify clearance on the basis of structural deficiencies. Those in "C" could also be considered sufficiently substandard to warrant demolition, though of course not as clearly as those in condition "D." What is important at this point is not the criteria that establish into which category a building is to fall but rather the percentage distribution between the four categories as indicated by Table 6.1.[3]

TABLE 6.1 RELATIONSHIP BETWEEN STRUCTURAL CONDITION OF NEIGHBORHOOD BUILDINGS AND RESIDENTIAL CLEARANCE

PROJECT	Building Condition					Residential Buildings in Project Area*	% and Number of Residential Buildings to Be Cleared
	A	B	C	D	Total		
Charlestown	23	27	39	11	100%	2,540	11% (270)
South End	5	30	47	18	100%	4,075	25% (1,089)
Washington Park	23	40	20	17	100%	2,813	35% (1,083)

* This figure includes vacant structures and must be treated as a rough estimate.
Source: Statistics compiled from BRA, "Application for Loan and Grant Part I: Final Project Report," Section 221, South End. Ibid., Charlestown. Ibid., Washington Park.

If demolition were based on the condition of buildings alone, one would estimate that the South End would have the greatest percentage of clearance. Assuming that most "D" and some "C" buildings would be demolished,

2 These figures constitute all the buildings in the area, but the overwhelming percentage are residential.
3 While the Urban Renewal Manual goes into some detail in citing the characteristics of building defects that determine into which category a structure should fall, enough leeway is allowed to indicate that the individual BRA project staffs may have used somewhat different criteria for evaluating buildings. Despite the probability of differing interpretations in the three districts under study, the categories do provide a significant basis upon which to compare the condition of the residential properties in each project area.

Charlestown, given its enormous amount of housing in the "C" category, might be expected to have demolition equal to if not greater than Washington Park. It is, of course, unrealistic to anticipate the exact amount of clearance on the basis of building conditions; yet there clearly is a profound absence of correlation between the amount of clearance decreed by the final plans in each area and the findings of the building condition survey, a point that Table 6.1 vividly demonstrates.

There may not be a statistically significant inverse relationship between building conditions and percentage of clearance, but the lack of direct correlation between conditions and demolition is apparent. Washington Park has 6 percent more "D" condition housing than Charlestown and more than three times as much residential clearance. If one includes the "C" category as a basis for some clearance, the disparity becomes even greater, for Charlestown has twice as much housing in this condition as has Washington Park.

While it is impossible to understand the amount of clearance in each project on the basis of "objective" physical criteria, our analysis of the local teams and their view of a favorable outcome for the renewal game provides the rationale behind the percentage of clearance in each area and the lack of relationship between that figure and the findings of the building survey.

RELOCATION

Since some housing has to be cleared and thus some households relocated, to what extent are new housing opportunities provided for those relocatees within the renewal project area? Each of the three plans under consideration includes hundreds of 221 d3 rental housing units. On the optimistic assumption that construction and relocation are phased together, this housing provides neighborhood relocation for those able to pay $75 a month for a one-bedroom apartment and $10 more for each additional room. The critical group within the relocation camp, however, is composed of those whose incomes are so low as to prohibit carrying the rent of 221 d3 housing. If we assume that the housing needs of these low-income households are to be met to some degree within the renewal project area, what is the extent to which the local team has negotiated a plan that takes into consideration such needs?

One rough way of estimating the degree to which lower-income individuals and families have been planned for as part of the postrenewal neighborhood is to examine the number of relocatees from each project area who are eligible for public housing and match that figure against existing and proposed public housing facilities in the project area. Table 6.2 gives those figures for the areas under study.

Obviously, it is unrealistic to assume that all project relocatees who are eligible will either want or be able to move into those public housing units located in their district. Not only are most existing quarters filled, but any turnover is competed for by low-income families displaced by public action from other parts of Boston. Moreover, federal regulations prohibit reserving new units exclusively for relocatees from the project area in which they are located.

TABLE 6.2 PROVISIONS FOR RELOCATEES

| | Project Areas | | |
	Charlestown	South End	Washington Park
Number of families displaced eligible for public housing and as % of total relocatees	326 (62%)*	1,112 (65%)	1,275 (75%)
Individuals displaced eligible for public housing and as a % of total relocatees	—*	540 (30%)	307 (54%)
Existing number of public housing units in the area	1,149	886	0
Proposed public housing	0	300	0
Proposed housing for the elderly	200	500	200
Total publicly aided housing; postrenewal	1,349	1,686	200

* Charlestown individuals and families eligible for public housing are described in one category.
Source: Statistics compiled from BRA, "Application for Loan and Grant Part I: Final Project Report," Section 223, South End. Ibid., Charlestown. Ibid., Washington Park.

On the other hand, the disparities among the three projects are so great in terms both of pre- and postrenewal public housing that one can clearly say something about the local team's sense of responsibility for low-income relocatees. Washington Park, with a relocation load of 1,275 families eligible for public housing, neither has nor contemplates building units to serve anyone in that category who is not a member of the elderly population. Charlestown, already supporting a public housing project which constitutes over 16 percent of the residential units in the Town, is building an additional 200 units of housing for the elderly which may serve many of the 122 elderly families and individuals to be relocated under the Charlestown plan. The South End, while far from absorbing all of its relocation load eligible for public housing, has added considerably to its existing stock of publicly subsidized units.[4]

[4] The South End, as was pointed out earlier, is also making an effort to handle its low-income relocatees through a number of other programs—nonprofit rehabilitation housing and the Rent Supplement Program.

REHABILITATION

For those residents of the three areas unaffected by demolition, the cost of rehabilitation emerges as the most significant element of the renewal plan. As has been pointed out, if the expenditures necessary to bring residential structures up to building code standards are prohibitively high, such costs can drive owners and renters from a neighborhood just as surely as demolition.

The 1960 census reported the expenditure of family income on gross rent in the three project areas as shown in Table 6.3. While a rough approximation, the ranking of expenditure and the relationship between income and rent levels among the three areas is certainly valid.

TABLE 6.3 RENTAL EXPENSE

Project	Median Income	Median Gross Monthly Rent	Annual Rent as a Percentage of Annual Income
Charlestown	$5,350	$58.50	13%
South End	3,650	51.00	17%
Washington Park	5,023	80.00	19%

Source: "Social Facts by Census Tract 1960," United Community Service.

If one makes the very simple assumption that equal amounts of investment were required to bring houses up to code standard in each area and that the increase in monthly debt service incurred would thus be the same in all projects, the residents of Washington Park would be the hardest hit, as they are already paying not only the highest absolute amount but also the highest percentage of income for rent.

Table 6.4[5] is a summary of BRA estimates of investment necessary to bring residential structures up to code standard. While the figures are not radically different in all cases, it is interesting to note that in seven out of nine categories in which the comparison can be made, the estimates for rehabilitation in Washington Park are the highest of the three project areas.

Of the three areas under study, Washington Park emerges as the project in which the style and structure of the residential rehabilitation game dictated a planning solution that had the harshest impact in demolition, relocation of low-income residents, and rehabilitation costs. These statistical findings should not come as a surprise. Analysis of the community prior to renewal's entry into the area, as well as of the character of the neighborhood

5 The figures in Table 6.4 should be taken as rough estimates. Their significance lies in the cost spread among similar types of units in the different projects rather than in the absolute value of the estimates themselves. All the estimates are, without question, optimistically low.

TABLE 6.4 DOLLAR COSTS NECESSARY TO BRING PROPERTY TO CODE STANDARD

| | Number of Units in Each Residential Structure | | | | | |
	1	2	3	4	5	Lodging House
CONDITION "A":						
Charlestown	$350	$450	$550	NA	NA	NA
South End	450	625	500	$3,000	$2,225	$825
Washington Pk.	272	462	690*	270	NA	NA
CONDITION "B":						
Charlestown	700	1,300	1,650	NA	NA	NA
South End	900	975	800	3,700	2,800	1,500
Washington Pk.	1,200*	1,330*	2,640*	890	NA	NA
CONDITION "C":						
Charlestown	1,700	2,150	3.050	NA	NA	NA
South End	1,535	1,610	1,428	6,085	3,525	2,370
Washington Pk.	2,460*	3,407*	5,142*	2,000	NA	NA

* Washington Park estimate highest of the three.
NA = not applicable.
Source: Statistics compiled from BRA, "Application for Loan and Grant Part I: Final Project Report," Section 221, South End. *Ibid.*, Charlestown. *Ibid.*, Washington Park.

team, make such a solution understandable. Charlestown, the community in which Logue's renewal system was shattered to pieces, emerges from the process with the largest percentage of its residential structures left standing, and its relocatees, homeowners, and renters least affected by the social and economic costs of demolition, relocation, and rehabilitation.

In the objective characteristics of the renewal plan, as in the style and structure of the planning game, the critical distinction between Charlestown and Washington Park is essentially the difference between a local team that views the entire population of its district as a constituency to be defended and a team that sees only a part, although perhaps a major part, of its district as the group to whom it feels responsible.

7

Planning Game Issues and Assumptions

The previous chapter focused on a specific comparison of the three Boston case studies in order to examine the extent to which the diversity of neighborhood shaped the style and form of the planning game, the role and character of the participants, and the content of the plan emerging from the negotiating process. There are, however, other issues raised by a study of rehabilitation planning games which lend themselves to more general discussion. We have now to consider what an analysis of the Boston experience can tell us about the dynamics of the neighborhood rehabilitation planning game, the relevance of previous interpretations of the character of the rehabilitation game and its participants, and the implication of our conclusions for future neighborhood planning efforts.

PARTICIPATION IN THE PLANNING GAME

The basic question in Chapter 1 was: To what extent are there social groups in American society that cannot or will not subscribe to the values and costs built into the rehabilitation process? In his answer to the question Wilson cut the class spectrum into two parts, arguing that "middle class persons who are beneficiaries of rehabilitation will be planned with; lower class persons who are disadvantaged by rehabilitation will be planned without."[1]

Herbert Gans took a closer look at the dichotomy and concluded that "lower-class persons" could be more usefully subdivided into "working class" and "lower class," but that the cultural gap between middle-class planners and either of these groups precluded meaningful renewal negotiations.

On the basis of experience in the three Boston renewal games, it is clear that the rehabilitation planning game can include members of the working class as well as of the middle class. The distinction Gans makes between working and lower class constitutes the dividing line between those capable of direct participation and those whose interests are dependent on the good will of a spokesman. If one sorts the interest groups in the Boston study cases into middle-, working-, and lower-class categories, the results clearly indicate that the residential rehabilitation game is not one in which the lower class can directly participate in a meaningful way. The problem is not simply mobilization but conflicting life styles that produce situations such as that in Washington Park where the force uniting the middle and working classes was the presence of lower-class Negroes.

"PUBLIC REGARDING" AND "PRIVATE REGARDING"—A REINTERPRETATION

While the concept of "public regarding" middle class and "private regarding" lower class leads Wilson astray in his analysis of the Charlestown and Washington Park planning games, his terminology can be put to good use when freed from its correlation with social class. In reviewing the Boston experience, it is analytically helpful to think of the "public regarding"–"private regarding" dichotomy as a way of describing the attitudes of those in the local project area engaged in the renewal planning game. Thus, a "public regarding" member of the team is one who thinks of the impact of residential renewal on the entire spectrum of interest groups present in the project area, while a "private regarding" member is one concerned with promoting the cause of only some of the interest groups in the area at the time of renewal planning. For example, USES was a "public regarding" actor in the South End renewal game. Committed to a unitary view of the neighborhood, USES was prepared to promote and defend the right of all interest groups, with the exception of the Night People, to a place in the postrenewal South End. On the other hand, Washington Park's Freedom House must be considered a "private regarding" interest responding, in Wilson's words, "in terms of

1 James Q. Wilson, "Planning and Politics: Citizen Participation in Urban Renewal," *Journal of the American Institute of Planners*, Vol. XXIX, No. 4 (November 1963), p. 247.

specific threats"[2]—in this case, to invasion by the Black Proletariat. Unlike USES, Freedom House had very specific limits on the range of groups it would support for a place in the renewed Washington Park.

If by "public regarding" we mean a team that thinks "in terms of general plans, the neighborhood or community as a whole, and long-term benefits,"[3] I would argue that of the three studies the neighborhood situation best described as "public regarding" is Charlestown. There, despite all the conflict and in large measure because of it, there was detailed analysis of the implications of the plan for local residents, the most significant effort to determine rehabilitation costs, and adamant concern that all the people of Charlestown, including relocatees, be able to remain in the area to savor the blessings of a physically renewed community.

It is, however, important to point out that "public regarding" is not a measure of a group's effectiveness in the planning game. In fact, one can well argue that organizations like USES with a broad ideological commitment to all residents spread their effort so thin as to be unable to adequately pursue any specific goal. The Snowdens were successful in carrying out their goals for renewal planning in large part because they knew exactly whom they represented and what renewal should do for Washington Park. In the South End an organization committed solely to the well-being of the elderly poor or of the Skid Row population, and willing and able to enter the lists of the planning game, would have been far more effective than USES in ensuring a larger place for those groups in the renewed South End.

THE ECONOMICS AND POLITICS OF EXCLUSION
FROM THE RENEWED COMMUNITY

The Boston experience makes clear the importance of distinguishing between exclusion of interest groups from the plan for a renewed community because of life-style conflicts and exclusion because of economic reasons.

As we have noted, there may be people in a project area who are aware of a renewal plan, who are given an opportunity to participate in the formulation of that plan, who vote for it at a public hearing, and yet who are uprooted by the renewal process. This uprooting can happen in two ways—by demolition or by the costs of rehabilitation. To have one's house taken by eminent domain is not, per se, an event that all owners find repugnant. As was seen in Washington Park, some homeowners viewed renewal as a means of getting out from under an intolerable housing situation in which one wants to sell but can find no buyer. In such a case residential renewal performs a service that the market is unable to carry out. For most people,

2 *Ibid.*, p. 245.
3 *Ibid.*

however, be they homeowners or renters, relocation can only be viewed as a burden. Forced to enter the housing market not at a time of their own choosing, they may look long and hard before finding a home which they like and can afford.

While communication gaps may leave residents unaware that their homes are slated for demolition, the designation of who is to be displaced by clearance is public information at the moment of plan approval. What is less clear at the moment the community is asked to pass judgment on the renewal plan is the impact that rehabilitation costs will have on the local population. While the Charlestown project saw serious and extensive efforts to establish the feasibility of rehabilitation for local property owners, the other two areas had had only marginal experience with rehabilitation in any district-wide sense at the time of plan approval.[4]

The full impact of the rehabilitation process is impossible to anticipate, the detailed BRA studies of rehabilitation feasibility notwithstanding. It is perfectly possible, for example, that individuals who have participated in the renewal planning game with every expectation of being part of the renewed community, and whom there was every intention of including, will be uprooted by the costs of rehabilitation. Into this category fall many of the elderly lodging house owners in the South End, some Blue-Collar Negroes in Washington Park and some Townies.

For these interests the possibility of participation in the renewed community hinges on the economic issue. To benefit from renewal, they need flexible, long-term financial assistance. There would be no complaint in the South End if "good" tenants were given rental supplements to enable them to cope with the increased rooming costs brought about by the rehabilitation process. In Charlestown any program to help residents, especially the elderly, to carry rents and mortgage payments would be viewed with approbation. In Washington Park economic help for elderly white tenants and Blue-Collar Negroes would be politically acceptable. There exists, however, a gap between the political acceptability of interest groups and the public financial mechanisms available to enable the lower-income elements of such groups to carry the increased rents and mortgages demanded by the rehabilitation process. In the past few years the federal establishment has responded to the need for public mechanisms to ease the economics of rehabilitation for peo-

---

[4] In Washington Park, Chester Rapkin conducted a detailed and extremely sophisticated analysis of the social and economic factors influencing the feasibility of massive residential rehabilitation. His findings for the original 186-acre project were not optimistic, and his report was not widely circulated. One of the arguments of those in opposition to the style and product of the Washington Park rehabilitation planning game was the fact that very few people were made aware of Rapkin's findings and that his suggestions for easing the financial hurdles of rehabilitation were not acted upon by the BRA.

ple of low income by the provision of direct loans and grants for rehabilitation and of rent supplements for needy families. These programs, however, serve a small and highly circumscribed market and require cutting through massive red tape.[5] The solution to the economic problems of rehabilitation is theoretically quite simple. The federal government has only to make more money available to more people, for exclusion from the rehabilitated neighborhood for economic reasons is, at least at the local level, a question of resource allocation, not political negotiation.

Exclusion from the renewed community because of life style poses far more complex problems—problems that cannot be solved, at least in the short run, solely by a greater allocation of public resources. In Washington Park acceptance of renewal by the Blue-Collar Negroes and the Negro Elite was predicated on the removal of "blighted housing"—housing that belonged mostly to members of the Black Proletariat. In the South End, despite some limited compromises, the Skid Row community's dispersal was demanded by participants in the planning game. It was the BRA's judgment that, had it wished to champion the rights of the Skid Row community or the Black Proletariat, the organization's relationship with the neighborhood groups upon whom it depended for political sanction would have been jeopardized. Groups whose continued presence is antithetical to the goals of the vocal majority in a neighborhood stand little chance of being brought into the planning process. Since approval is needed from articulate interests for both the public hearing and the execution period, political acumen warns the LPA operating in a hostile political environment not to push for the welfare of a group alien to the neighborhood's vocal interests.

While financial resources alone cannot generate instant solutions to the problems of life-style conflict, money can become a key mechanism for including "undesirable" interests in the renewed community. A massive grant for a problem group can help to buffer that interest from the rest of the community. For example, a drying-out center can be a store-front operation existing on a shoestring in the middle of a residential block, or it can be a new, well-designed, well-endowed facility set off from the residential area, drawing upon the best resources of the medical community. Local interest groups will be unhappy about the center in either case, but the second setup will generate far less cause for protest than the first and may, over time, neutralize community hostility to the problem group.

Money is also a means of getting around local opposition if the LPA is

---

[5] See "Report on South End Urban Renewal Plan for Boston City Council Hearing" (Urban Field Service, March 25, 1968), and Jay Nathan, "Rehabilitation Is Not Working as a Resource for Community Development," *The Journal of Housing*, No. 22 (1967), pp. 619–621, for a report of local problems with these programs.

willing and skillful enough to use the leverage of other possible public grants in the renewal area to force the inclusion of unwanted institutions and interest groups. Such pressure can be successful only if two conditions are fulfilled: the level of resource allocation that the public agency is able to withhold or grant must be so tempting as to ensure that no community group could afford to turn it down, and the LPA must have sufficient political clout to be able to meet "private regarding" interests head on. If the LPA is unsure of its political viability, it will respond to the strongest community voices rather than initiate action on behalf of those interests that may be isolated or excluded from the planning game. And gaining sufficient political stature is a function of the LPA's continued access to money and of the LPA's capacity to institutionalize that power over local decision making which is provided on an *ad hoc* basis by access to federal funds.

Some have argued that Logue and Collins were in a position to exert this kind of pressure had they desired to do so. But the exact relationship between Logue's perception of his political latitude and his view of the degree to which problem groups should be included in the renewed community is a difficult one to determine. It is fair to say however, that with regard to problem interests, Logue was conservative in his appraisal of the leverage afforded him by renewal funds. The political climate of Boston, the uncertainties and vagaries of the renewal funding process, and the absence of significant public programs to handle the social side of urban renewal perhaps gave him little option but to play a cautious hand.

RESIDENTIAL ENCLAVES AND THE FRAGMENTATION OF DECISION MAKING

The quasi-legal decision making conferred upon neighborhood groups by the rehabilitation planning game tends to blur a major distinction between urban neighborhoods and suburbs. A cogent statement of that distinction was made by Robert Wood several years before he became Undersecretary of the Department of Housing and Urban Development:

What distinguishes suburb and neighborhood . . . are the added dimensions of community which separate political boundary lines contribute. . . . Superimposed on group values and land values and economic values is a cultural component provided by the simple fact that a political entity is in existence. . . .

Above all, there are political institutions established and in being by legislative fiat, public officials to be chosen, and an electoral process to be gone through in every suburban town and belonging to that town alone. In short, the suburb has one vital advantage over any city neighborhood in its struggle to preserve itself against metropolitan dominance and to build a small community again. It has power to pit against power, and, in and of itself, that power strengthens the community.[6]

Much of this structural distinction between neighborhood and suburb is

[6] Robert C. Wood, *Suburbia: Its People and Their Politics* (Boston: Houghton Mifflin, 1958), pp. 126–127.

lost when one considers the impact of the rehabilitation game on the decision-making capability of the central city's residential areas. The logical result of a city-wide rehabilitation program like Boston's is a series of semi-autonomous neighborhoods, each with an extra-legal legislative body capable of influencing renewal decisions, which are then binding on the municipality as a whole. Rehabilitation area teams are able to enjoin city agencies to build a protective wall around their district in exchange for local cooperation in plan approval and investment in rehabilitation.

In a city blanketed by neighborhood organizations it is difficult to find locations for "undesirable" groups and institutions, and when forced to clear each location decision with the neighborhood residents, the city may become immobilized by the political independence of the individual neighborhoods.

A classic example of the problems caused for the formal city political processes by disaggregating decision making to the political market place of the neighborhood is illustrated by a bitter exchange between City Councilor William Foley and Logue during the City Council hearings on the South End plan when the issue of the amount and type of housing that renewal would put into the neighborhood was under discussion. Reacting to Logue's description of planning in that district and to his statement that local residents did not want more public housing than was proposed, Foley shouted:

This way of working out a plan as you represent it, I doubt it happened that way. . . . We [the City Council] are not supposed to decide whether the people want this particular plan in the South End. We are supposed to decide whether this plan is the best plan for the South End, whether it needs a public subsidy to accomplish it; and I think there is a fourth issue, basically we are supposed to decide whether this is good for Boston.[7]

From Logue's point of view, a plan that had political support of residents of a neighborhood was by definition the right plan for that area and a sum of what the individual neighborhoods want is the proper plan for the city as a whole.

Foley, in taking Logue to task for the character of the South End planning game and its failure to provide more public housing, put his finger on a complex problem inherent in the neighborhood rehabilitation game: in the political market place in which a neighborhood plan is hammered out, there is no way to guarantee that all the groups in the neighborhood benefit from the plan or that the plan is good for the larger community outside the artificial walls created by the project boundaries.

The rehabilitation game is structured to deal with a residential district as the appropriate-sized unit over which to bargain. In the process of planning

---

[7] City of Boston, City Council, "South End Urban Renewal Project: Before Committee on Urban Renewal," Stenographic Transcript, November 10, 1965, p. 741.

that district becomes an end in itself, a circumscribed community. Nothing symbolizes this separate community concept more clearly than the Charlestown and South End illustrative site plans that were produced for distribution to local residents before the BRA hearings in each of the areas. These maps delineate in detail future land use within the project area, yet there is no sense of the city outside the boundaries, no way of telling how the plan relates to the rest of Boston. Lifted out of their urban setting, the districts appear as independent communities, self-sufficient and set apart from the complex world around them.

THE PLANNER AND THE RESIDENT ENCLAVE

Many observers of the urban renewal process view plan making at the neighborhood level as more democratic than objective planning. Yet, disaggregative decision making may pose extreme difficulties for local residents and institutions that are politically unacceptable to those with greater chance of making their presence felt in the renewal planning game. The concept of local participation in plan design does not, then, *necessarily* ensure the most favorable outcome to that process for all groups in the neighborhood. For example, without consulting anyone in the neighborhood, a move on the part of officials in the Boston Housing Authority to build well-designed low-rise units of public housing in Washington Park would have done more to benefit the low-income Negroes in the area than any plan that could possibly have emerged from negotiations with the "original" Washington Park Steering Committee.

In further criticism of the neighborhood approach, one might well argue that disaggregating decision making to the level of the residential district and allowing "the powerful" to sanction changes for that area ignores the fact that a plan that has met political approval in the community may not necessarily be one that is geared to look to the future of the area or the city. The renewal plan is to remain in operation for forty years; thus, the planner is in a sense devising a proposal not merely to benefit present residents but also to serve a multitude of people who may not even be living in the area at the time of renewal negotiations. And because of the dynamic flow of urban residents, undoubtedly a number of the people involved in negotiations during the planning period will move out of the area before the renewal program is actually executed.

When the LPA planner becomes involved in the politically charged renewal game, he makes compromises that, while responsive to the demands of the neighborhood, may not over the long run be economically, technically, or even socially sound. For example, it can be argued that the amount of housing in Charlestown which from an economic and structural point of view it makes sense to rehabilitate is far less than the 90 percent that is currently programmed. While representing a triumph for the Town's bargaining capacity, the reduction of demolition does not consider the enormous cost that rehabilitation may entail and the fact that many of the houses may not survive despite extended repairs. Yet, geared to achieving political approval, the LPA planner may tend to submerge entirely his *expertise,* derived from knowledge of objective standards of building conditions, open space needs, and separation of land uses, in his quest to survive the rehabilitation planning game.

In the rehabilitation planning game, the successful planner is one who can ride out the political cross currents generated in the local project area. Planning becomes a question of political feasibility—of the here and now at the project level. The neighborhood becomes the city. The time dimension becomes the present.

THE NEIGHBORHOOD AND CITY HALL

The Boston experience with neighborhood involvement in decision making regarding the allocation of public resources was an early essay into what became a far more radical innovation in the War on Poverty's "maximum feasible participation of the poor." While Logue's system was concerned with ensuring the involvement of the powerful, whatever their economic status, community action programs have since emphasized that poor people constitute the critical group to be included in the decision-making process. Where Logue was able to delegate authority to the mandated neighborhood group because of his assemblage of power in City Hall, the original community action program bypassed city government entirely and set up a power base dependent for financial backing on a direct linkage with the federal government.

Where the Office of Economic Opportunity approach signified a clear rejection of the cities' formal decision-making role, Logue's neighborhood negotiations represent a curious mixture of bypassing the system and working within it. From Councilor Foley's point of view, Logue's justification for certain planning decisions because "that's what the neighborhood wants" was a clear transfer of authority from elected to appointed officials and citizens, a process that left only a small role for the elected City Councilor whose job it was to consider the impact of renewal decisions on Boston as a whole. From the vantage point of OEO, Logue's approach represented a highly structured bargaining process between the LPA and those who had power in the local neighborhoods, a process in which plan approval rather than maximum neighborhood participation constituted the primary goal toward which citizen involvement was directed. Whether one agrees with him or not, it must be said that Logue's rationale for involving local people has a clarity of purpose that has eluded OEO organizers, who have often been at odds over the primary reason for and goal of "maximum feasible participation."[8]

The Logue and the OEO strategies represent two fundamentally different approaches to the problem of relegating decision making to the neighborhood level. Logue's system works within the established institutional framework while making that framework more responsive to local needs. Yet, only with greater centralization and control by the Mayor's office over the institutions of city government will the necessary responsiveness be forthcoming.

The logical extension of Logue's approach is, then, far greater control within the Mayor's office of all public programs necessary to revitalize the city, followed by a redelegation of those powers to the local level to serve neighborhood demands. The neighborhood city hall concept is an example of decentralized decision making working within the framework of existing institutions. The mayor can respond to local needs because he has the power to be responsive. While local residents working through neighborhood city halls may make decisions that become binding upon the city as a whole, those decisions are made as a result of negotiation with the established institutions of government.

The logical outcome of the OEO approach to decentralized decision making is to bypass the political and administrative institutions of the city and to look to the neighborhood itself as the framework within which to ratify all decisions bearing upon community development. This position takes on operationality in the form of the neighborhood corporation, a combined governing body and development foundation to which all neighborhood residents would belong. Under this concept the neighborhood becomes a ward republic, managing its own affairs and directly soliciting and receiving federal and state funds. In its application to all the residential districts of a city, the neighborhood corporation concept produces a series of independent social systems turned inward on themselves.[9]

The operational viability of a city broken into a number of self-sufficient communities is open to question, as is the willingness of central city mayors to preside over the demise of what limited authority they currently hold. While the neighborhood as a self-sufficient economic, social, and political unit has an appealing ring in this age of megalopolis, the complex interrela-

---

[8] See Peter Marris and Martin Rein, *Dilemmas of Social Reform* (New York: Atherton Press, 1967), and Edmund Burke, "Citizen Participation as Strategies," unpublished paper (Boston College, School of Social Work, 1967), for discussion of goal conflicts surrounding citizen participation in neighborhood decisions.
[9] For a fuller discussion of the neighborhood corporation in theory and practice see Milton Kotler, "Two Essays on the Neighborhood Corporation," *Urban America: Goals and Problems* (Congress of the United States, Joint Economic Committee, August 1967), pp. 170–191.

tionships of urban industrial life make it a solution that seems ultimately to avoid rather than to face the problem of governing the cities of the 1960's.

It can, however, be argued that a modified neighborhood concept is not necessarily incompatible with increasing establishment power represented by the neighborhood city hall concept. Neighborhood corporations' involvement in the delivery of social services, in the construction and maintenance of housing, and in the provision of economic and educational programs and opportunities for local residents is feasible within a neighborhood that has not formally cut itself off from the city around it and that recognizes the necessity of maintaining a close working relationship with City Hall.

There is obviously a delicate equilibrium to be maintained between local involvement in determination of issues affecting the neighborhood and the requirements of a complex and highly interrelated urban system. Those who, in William Foley's words, have to consider "whether this is good for Boston" must still have sufficient independence and power to respond to the needs of those groups that are a product of urban industrialized society which no neighborhood wants to shelter. The Skid Row people, the multiproblem families, the mentally ill, the paroled convicts must be accommodated somewhere. And it is most unlikely that any neighborhood, no matter how enlightened, is going to feel any more responsible to do so than the independent community of Wood's Suburbia feels it necessary to harbor low-income groups. But a strong central government, which through its neighborhood city halls has been responsive to local needs and demands, will be in a good bargaining position when it becomes necessary to decide where to house the problem people of the modern city.

THE TRIUMPH OF COMPREHENSIVE PLANNING

"Make no little plans, for they have no power to stir men's minds,"[10] has served as the city planners' rallying cry for well over half a century. Yet, with few if any exceptions, the kind of plans Daniel Burnham was thinking of have rarely gotten beyond the shelves of the nation's city halls, a point that Edward Banfield and others have made on more than one occasion.[11] In fact, studying the irrelevancy of comprehensive planning for structuring the development dynamics of the city has become a stock item of business for urbanologists.

Some academic observers make a clear distinction between old-line planners incapable of implementing their politically naïve comprehensive plans

[10] Lewis Mumford, *The City in History* (New York: Harcourt, Brace & World, 1961), p. 402.
[11] See Edward C. Banfield and James Q. Wilson, *City Politics* (Cambridge: Harvard University Press and the M.I.T. Press, 1963) and Alan Altschuler, *The City Planning Process* (Ithaca: Cornell University Press, 1965).

and the "new men of power,"[12] the entrepreneurs of urban renewal who bend city politics to their own ends. From this point of view, the successful renewal chieftains represent a new breed of planner—one geared to action, to implementation, and to political realities.

However, this dichotomy is an oversimplification: it must be forcefully emphasized that one of the great ironies of the rehabilitation planning game is that the process, for all Ed Logue's scorn of master plans and master planners, is oriented around as comprehensive a land-use design as Daniel Burnham could have hoped to behold. In fact, the current structure for planning and executing renewal projects represents the triumph of the comprehensive ideal, for behind both the renewal plan and the traditional master plan lies this similar assumption: the efficient and economic allocation of public and private development funds dictates that the developmental response to urban growth be based upon detailed consideration of *all* the interrelationships affecting land use *before* proceeding to implement any one development decision.[13]

Theoretically, the renewal planner is justified in thinking there is in his approach a closer link between planning and implementation than in the typical master plan situation. In fact, however, many of the criticisms leveled at master planning can be directed to the urban renewal approach. Both presuppose, quite unrealistically, a firm control of a large number of the complex realities of urban life. While the LPA obviously has far greater power to implement its plan than the traditional city planning commission had, it cannot control all public, let alone private, inputs necessary to realize its proposals.

Thus while the renewal program is being put into execution over a five-, six-, or seven-year period, the district to be transformed into the community shown on the illustrative site plan will inevitably change in ways impossible to forecast and quite unrelated to the assumptions of the renewal proposal. Homeowners who may well have supported the plan at the public hearing may feel overwhelmed by the prospect of investing in rehabilitation and consequently move elsewhere. People with little awareness that there is a renewal plan afoot may move into the district. Facts on family relocation,

---

12 Jewel Bellush and Murray Hausknecht, *Journal of the American Institute of Planners*, Vol. 32, No. 5 (September 1966), pp. 289–297.

13 The assumption behind the present renewal process—that to ensure efficient use of public and private resources over-all planning must precede any investment in actual project development—is very much like the argument advanced by those in the area of economic development who advocate "balanced" growth on the grounds that "to make development possible it is necessary to start, *at one and the same time,* a large number of new industries which will be each others' clients through the purchases of their workers, employees, and owners." (Albert O. Hirshman, *Journeys Toward Progress* (New York: Anchor, 1965), p. 51.)

gathered with meticulous care by the local staff, and detailed rehabilitation schedules become obsolete rapidly. The dynamic quality of urban life will not halt at the boundaries of the project area just because a renewal proposal has been passed. Activity in the city swirls on, beating at the district with new forces that are bound to influence the outcome of renewal execution.[14]

While the local neighborhood may fail to hold still for the renewal process, the public agencies upon whom the LPA relies for community facilities and services may fail to move at all. In Boston the construction of schools, for example, is a function entirely outside the BRA's control, yet schools are probably the single most significant input on the public side of the rehabilitation equation. The BRA can clear the sites for the proposed schools and advise on architectural renderings, but here its power ends. Waiting for the schools to be built can be a long and disheartening experience, complicated by a host of factors unrelated to problems of physical construction.[15] Thus, while the BRA has access to some of the levers of project execution—thereby putting it light years ahead of the traditional planning board—it does not control them all and perhaps does not even control the most significant of them.

Even if one minimizes the neighborhood changes unanticipated by the renewal plan and the difficulties in fulfilling the public and private terms of the rehabilitation planning game, the gap between political affirmation and actual execution of the plan is a frustrating experience for the LPA and the local neighborhood teams. Conditioned to thinking of the plan as a total concept, people find it difficult to accept the fact that its elements will come into being only one building, one park, and one street at a time. Thus the emotional letdown after the public hearing is profound. The drive to get through the hearing, the "eye of the needle," as one BRA planner calls the event, leaves both the renewal staff and local neighborhood team exhausted. Never again will the proponents be as united as when they marched to the public hearing to vote for rehabilitation of their neighborhood. The process

14 For example, two years after the South End plan was approved the project was in deep trouble. Construction of schools and new 221 d3 housing was falling behind schedule. The relocation time table had been shifted with the result that far greater numbers of families were being moved during the early stages of the plan than had been anticipated. Most significantly of all, rehabilitating the South End for low-income families was proving to be an almost hopeless task. Neighborhood groups that had come into existence since the plan's approval were calling for a revision of the plan to include a massive new low-income rehabilitation program. A series of City Council hearings were considering the possibility of changing the plan to include more units of leased public housing in the 221 d3 projects. The worst predictions of the area's Cassandras were coming true, and the coalition that Dick Green had laboriously pieced together for the public hearing had fallen into disarray. The most vivid way in which the plan had failed, however, was in its inability to produce residential rehabilitation for low-income families.

15 For example, the issue of de facto segregation has almost brought school construction in Washington Park to a halt.

of myriad decisions, compromises, and negotiations will be repeated over and over as the long, "achingly slow, and essentially undramatic"[16] process of rehabilitation goes on.

From our discussion it seems clear that one of the most significant flaws in the structure of the renewal process is the sharp line drawn between project planning and project execution.[17] On the basis of the Boston experience one can argue that this rigorous dichotomy makes it impossible for the LPA to act quickly and effectively on clearly perceived problems. For example, five years went by in Charlestown between Leo Baldwin's first rallying cry and the day the Boston City Council approved a plan for the area. Many aspects of the final plan were almost unanimously supported from the beginning. All Townies believed that taking down the "El," making rehabilitation funds more readily available, and building new schools were necessary if Charlestown were to survive as a residential community. Yet, given the comprehensive character of the renewal process, no federal assistance in any one of these areas could be forthcoming until all planning issues had been resolved.

Clearly, there is a lack of flexibility, sensitivity, and realism in such an approach to the renewal of urban residential areas. Rather than being provided the latitude to zero in on specific neighborhood needs—a new school, a residential block whose owners are crying for rehabilitation funds—or problems—an "El," a junk yard—the LPA must spend its energy mounting massive rehabilitation planning games, such as those described in this study, in order to arrive at the moment when the first dollar of project execution money can be spent.

The maze of red tape and expended time that results from separating planning from execution has produced a climate that alienates many from involvement in the renewal program. Ironically, while one of the original purposes of comprehensive planning was to provide a framework for efficiently coordinating public and private action, the emerging character of the renewal process has in some cases driven off the very inputs that a comprehensive planning approach was supposed to assure. The following explanation by a high FHA official as to why he would rather promote innovative rehabilitation efforts outside urban renewal areas points up the degree to which the renewal process—originally conceived of as a solution to the

---

[16] Walter P. McQuade, "Boston: What Can a Sick City Do?" *Fortune*, Vol. LXIX, No. 6 (June 1964), p. 166.
[17] The one exception to this split is the early land mechanism that Logue took advantage of in Castle Square in the South End and in several parcels in Washington Park. Early land acquisition is difficult to maneuver, as it produces a turbulent flow of red tape, but it offers the one existing means of getting some form of action *before* the renewal planning proposal has been formally approved in its totality.

problem of declining neighborhoods—is now in certain ways itself a barrier to solutions:

It is worth noting, also, why FHA's recent actions in rehabilitation have invariably been outside of urban renewal areas. [First,] . . . we were trying to produce tangible results fast. We could proceed with more speed and flexibility without becoming involved in the extensive series of national and local actions and reviews which are required to bring an urban renewal project into being. [Second] . . . non-profit groups and foundations, and even branches of the city government . . . frequently sought to avoid what they thought to be the time-consuming process of the urban renewal program.[18]

A solution for many of the problems posed by the separation of planning and execution has finally found its way into national legislation. As this is written, the Housing and Urban Development Act of 1968 has just been passed by the United States Congress. The bill itself is a broad and far-reaching one that, if funded even in modified form, would constitute a major advance in national housing legislation. The administration's solution to the dichotomy of planning and execution comes in the form of an amendment to the urban renewal law which would permit the funding of Neighborhood Development Programs. As HUD Secretary Weaver testified before the Senate Subcommittee on Housing and Urban Affairs,

Under a Neighborhood Development Program, a community could receive assistance to carry out urban renewal activities . . . through annual grants for two-thirds . . . of the net costs of the year's activities undertaken under their Neighborhood Development Program.

The activities assisted would be those now eligible for assistance in urban renewal projects. The principal difference would be that each year the community would request assistance for specific activities it proposed to carry out that year. These activities could include continuation of detailed planning as well as actual physical work.

Under this system there need be no lag between the decision that an area is in serious physical condition and the beginning of the actual activities to correct these conditions. Plans governing the physical activities of the local public agency would be flexible. Changed circumstances and changed needs would not require the scrapping of prematurely prepared detailed plans.[19]

The Neighborhood Development Program concept checks one of the major flaws in the system with which Ed Logue had to deal. By blending planning and development activity the renewal game takes on a new character, one offering a greater number of options and eliminating the "all or nothing" pressure of the current planning system.

BEYOND THE PLANNING GAME

Though the proof of the pudding is in the eating, the investigations of this study terminate at the first bite. Our entire discussion of the residential rehabilitation planning game in three of Boston's oldest neighborhoods is but a

[18] Carter McFarland, "Residential Rehabilitation: The State of the Art and its Potential," Mimeograph, Washington, D.C., April 1966, p. 34.
[19] Robert Weaver, Statement before the Subcommittee on Housing and Urban Affairs of the Committee on Banking and Currency, U.S. Senate, March 5, 1968.

prologue to the main event; our job ends before the enormous amount of time, money, and energy expended by the BRA and the local neighborhood teams turns over a spade of earth or tears down a single building. The final product of the complex and time-consuming *planning* game is a comprehensive proposal for the physical revitalization of an urban residential district. With political sanctions for that proposal in hand, the process of *project execution* can begin.

The local team that has negotiated the plan with the renewal authority can be expected to lead the drive for rehabilitation's successful execution. During the period in which the plan is being carried out there is clearly a need for an articulate citizens' organization to keep attention focused on the goal of revitalizing the neighborhood. As a BRA paper on rehabilitation states, local "leaders have the capacity to use their muscle in support of such a program [rehabilitation]. . . . If a family is reluctant [to rehabilitate] then the process of group meetings and personal conferences brings individual attention and implied social pressure to bear and swings the family into line."[20] Thus the BRA continues to be dependent on the good will of the project "powerful," even after the public hearing.

Given the changing nature of the area's needs and demands, friction may arise during project execution over the right of the residential team to make binding decisions for the neighborhood as a whole. The following example from the Washington Park experience illustrates the kind of issue that can arise.

A little more than three years after final plan approval in the district it was obvious that the fears of the ministers and other doubters during the planning period were being fulfilled. The renewed Washington Park was simply not producing rentals that could be afforded by low-income people of any kind—Black Proletariat, Blue-Collar Negro, or elderly white. A survey by one Boston paper reported that "Many people in the community are concerned about the lack of low income housing. Almost all organization leaders referred to this problem. A surprisingly large number of residents, especially homeowners, also mentioned it."[21]

As a result of pressure from increasingly articulate and organized civil rights groups as well as his own recognition that a large segment of the Washington Park relocation load had little or no opportunity to live in the project area, Logue proposed to build thirty units of large-family public housing on a site in the Upper Roxbury section of the renewal district. He brought this suggestion to the same Freedom House—CURAC leadership that had produced a positive turnout at five public hearings. After several

20 BRA, "A Working Paper on Rehabilitation," Mimeograph, Winter 1964–1965, p. 41.
21 *The Christian Science Monitor*, March 24, 1966.

resounding battles, the noise and conflict of which were reminiscent of Charlestown, the proposal was voted down 45 to 29. Otto Snowden led those opposed to the thirty units. In reporting the meeting to the BRA Board and recommending that the proposal for public housing be dropped, Logue said, "While I think the community decision was a mistake, I think it is a decision which should be respected in accordance with our philosophy of planning and executing neighborhood renewal projects with people."[22] From Logue's point of view, the community had spoken. The people who had put renewal over the top in Washington Park during the planning game—the Negro Elite and Blue-Collar Workers—had predicated that support on the emergence of a middle-class life-style community in Washington Park as a result of their efforts. Public housing, especially for large families, was not a part of their vision. To those who criticized him for paying heed to a hand vote of 74 in an area of 20,000 people, Logue replied simply, "You don't change the rules of the game just because you don't like the results."[23]

Therein lies the essence of the rehabilitation planning game. Unless new interests mobilize in the community during project execution, the LPA will, of political necessity, stand with those interests that supported the renewal plan at the public hearing because they continue to represent the community powerful.[24]

[22] *The Boston Globe*, May 5, 1966.
[23] Edward Logue, Statement before the Mayor's Citizens Advisory Committee, May 5, 1966.
[24] In contrast to the Washington Park situation, the emergence in the South End of a vocal organization representing low-income interests has produced the political clout to "change the rules of the game."

8
The Model
Cities Program:
Lessons
Worth
Learning
from the
Rehabilitation
Planning
Game

One of the last acts of the Eighty-Ninth Congress was to pass the Demonstration Cities and Metropolitan Development Act in the fall of 1966. The key feature of that act, the Model Cities Program, formally recognizes that revitalization of the physical contours of a residential district is not a sufficient mechanism for bettering the lives of all groups living in that area. The goal of Model Cities is to improve the total quality of life within a specific target neighborhood by putting heavy emphasis on innovation and flexibility and by comprehensiveness and coordination in attacking both the social and physical problems of old urban neighborhoods. Thus, Model Cities provides in formal comprehensive legislation a federal version of the program that Logue strove but ultimately failed to create for the Boston neighborhoods.

At this moment the 75 communities awarded Model Cities planning money are formulating comprehensive programs for their Model Neighborhoods. While it is too early to pass judgment on the Model Cities planning process, let alone on the final product, it is not too early to judge the extent to which the assumptions underlying that planning approach have been guided by the urban renewal experience, and one way to determine the degree to which the new program has side-stepped the pitfalls of the old is to examine how it has dealt with the problems discussed in Chapter 7.

PARTICIPATION IN THE PLANNING GAME: THE ECONOMICS AND POLITICS OF EXCLUSION FROM THE MODEL NEIGHBORHOOD

Model Cities puts greater formal emphasis on local participation in the planning process than urban renewal does. And, like the Poverty Program, citizen involvement is viewed as a key element in the evolution of a Model Cities plan. In fact, citizen participation language has been made stronger since the first "Program Guide" was written in December 1966. That initial Model Cities guide calls for "widespread citizen participation"[1] but never defines what is mean by "widespread" and never gets beyond the level of exhortation. However, an October 1967 policy letter to the City Demonstration Agency (CDA), the local agency responsible for the development of a city's Model Cities Program, is far more specific and states that

The neighborhood participation structure must have clear and direct access to the decision-making process. . . . In order to initiate and react intelligently in program matters, the participation structure must have the technical capacity for making knowledgeable decisions . . . [which entails] some form of professional technical assistance in a manner agreed to by the neighborhood residents.[2]

Without much reading between the lines one can see that the Model Cities Administration advocates staff assistance directly responsible to residents of the Model Cities area.

For all its careful concern for meaningful citizen involvement, there is little recognition in the "Program Guide" of the diversity that this involvement might have to reflect to include "all elements of the local population from all parts of the area."[3] As the three Boston studies indicate, the interest groups in an urban area can constitute a complex mixture of attitude, ethnic diversity, income, and motivation. Moreover, the social and political dynamics of the groups living in a target district may make it extremely difficult to secure full participation of all neighborhood interests.

The politics of exclusion discussed at length in Chapter 7 are as applicable to Model Cities as to urban renewal. Reconciling diverse interests and balancing their needs and demands is a time-consuming and sometimes impossible business, as Dick Green's experience in the South End makes clear.

---

1 Department of Housing and Urban Development, "Improving the Quality of Urban Life: A Program Guide to Model Cities," December 1966, p. 14.
2 Department of Housing and Urban Development, Model Cities Administration, "CDA [City Demonstration Agency] Letter Number Three," November 1967.
3 Department of Housing and Urban Development, "Improving the Quality . . . ," op. cit., p. 14.

While renewal planning had no prescribed time limit, the planning phase for Model Cities is set at nine to twelve months. Because of the organizational and planning complexities of developing a comprehensive social and physical program, it is doubtful whether meaningful involvement of a majority of the area's interest groups can be achieved in a year's time.

If the Model Cities planning period is to be successful in considering the needs and desires of all local groups, the CDA must find a means of responding to more than just the articulate voices in the community. Political pressure from the neighborhood articulate may, as in urban renewal planning, dictate the exclusion of certain interests for life-style reasons.

RESIDENTIAL ENCLAVES AND THE
FRAGMENTATION OF DECISION MAKING

Like the rehabilitation planning game, Model Cities is district-oriented. "It calls for a comprehensive attack on social, economic, and physical problems in selected slum and blighted areas . . . to develop 'model' neighborhoods."[4] Once again a line is to be drawn around a segment of a city's housing stock into which will be poured public programs to elevate the quality of neighborhood life. Once again the LPA, or in this case the CDA, will look to local residents for political sanction. Because of the increasingly stringent guidelines for citizen involvement, political sanction from local residents will be far more formalized under Model Cities than in urban renewal. One major issue, then, is to what extent decisions affecting the Model Neighborhood will be determined solely by people living in that residential enclave and to what extent the program will seek to link the neighborhood to the urban system of which it is a part.

The Model Cities guide does recognize the impact of its program on the larger urban community when it states:

Opportunities should also be afforded to city-wide and metropolitan groups to discuss the impact of the demonstration program on their particular areas and interests and to bring to bear their points of view in the planning and execution of the demonstration program.[5]

Yet recognition of the larger social system does not thereby give that system a role in decision making, nor does it mitigate the local Model Cities team's ability to use the program as a means of walling themselves off from the city around them. Model Neighborhoods remain free to emphasize their uniqueness and their detachment from the city at large, or to recognize the degree to which their well-being depends upon the strength and adaptability of city-wide institutions.

The issue of the neighborhood's relationship to its environment is directly

4 *Ibid.*, p. 1.
5 *Ibid.*, p. 14.

related to the issue of leverage over public programs. Model Cities tries to co-ordinate the many public and private programs and organizations directed at the total spectrum of social and physical needs in the target area. Some-how the agencies and organizations concerned with health, welfare, social services, education, crime, housing, training, community facilities and ser-vices and recreation must be blended into a five-year program which will improve the quality of life in the Model Neighborhood. Yet allocating deci-sion making to the neighborhood level dilutes to some degree whatever power the CDA may have over those programs and organizations. Urban renewal teaches that without centralized control over the public agencies responsible for the inputs needed for promoting social and physical change, there is little likelihood that negotiation within the boundaries of the neigh-borhood will bring about the necessary agency performance. As has been pointed out, Logue could not control the School Board or the Boston Hous-ing Authority, and the results of that absence of leverage posed an enormous problem for the credibility and feasibility of the renewal program. Yet the problems of coordination and power inherent in the Model Cities approach makes Logue's problem look like child's play by comparison. One can argue here, as was done in Chapter 7, that only by *first* centralizing power in City Hall and *then* throwing it out to the neighborhoods on a line closely linked to City Hall will the necessary coordination be brought about. But the rapid pace with which Model Cities planning must be carried out may prohibit or severely curtail this two-step process.

The Triumph of Comprehensive Planning

In describing the approach to be taken to "problem analysis, goals, and pro-gram strategy,"[6] the Model Cities administration puts great emphasis on flexibility and open-ended planning. A CDA letter states,

All elements of the Five Year Plan need not be established in detail during the initial planning period. . . . Subsequent program refinement and program changes are, therefore, anticipated. . . .

The Model Cities planning documents developed during the initial planning period should not be considered final statements but only the first steps in a process of dynamic planning and programming.[7]

If the Washington administrators of the program actually practice what they preach, Model Cities will avoid the disfunctional aspects of urban re-newal's rigid separation of planning and execution. Model Cities has learned from the renewal experience that plans must constantly be revised and ex-tended if they are to keep pace with the dynamic and ever-changing life of

6 Department of Housing and Urban Development, Model Cities Administration, "CDA Letter Number One," November 1967.
7 *Ibid.*, p. 15.

the cities.[8] Yet while the new program has wisely included planning as an integral part of the execution period, it has not done the converse—it has not made execution part of the initial planning period. In other words, there is little effort being made by the Model Cities Administration to promote the execution of program elements during the initial planning period. No supplemental funds, the Model Cities money for program execution, are to be allocated to the 75 cities until the end of the planning period. Moreover, the 312 loan and 115 grant programs for residential rehabilitation will not be available in any Model Cities area until that neighborhood has an approved renewal plan. Such approval will clearly take at least a year, and probably much longer. Thus, the only existing fund programs for dealing with low-income housing rehabilitation will not be available to Model Neighborhoods until some uncertain future date.

To make the new program a reality to the people of the Model Cities areas, there must be action during the planning period. Because of the increasing skepticism bred in no small part by experience with urban renewal, action during the planning period may be the only way to arouse local involvement in the Model Cities Program.

A SUMMING UP

Model Cities has learned some lessons from the urban renewal experience. But whether or not the new program has learned enough to be able to carry out its ambitious task of coordinating the social and physical attack on the ills of old neighborhoods remains to be seen. However, owing to the tenor of the times, past experience may not provide sufficient direction to carry the fledgling program over the top. Long hot summers and cries of Black Power may put intolerable strains upon Model Cities—strains that may ultimately snap the tenuous lines of communication being developed during the planning period.

In the wake of the report of the President's Commission on Civil Disorders and the death of Martin Luther King, it would be difficult even for a determined optimist to be sanguine about the future of old urban neighborhoods. Yet, within a general atmosphere of uncertainty, it must be assumed that any large central city desiring to rehabilitate its aging residential areas through the Model Cities Program cannot help finding itself in somewhat the same situation that the BRA did in 1960 when that organization first began to mobilize support for the rehabilitation planning game. No matter

---

8 The specter of riots in the Black Ghettos of the central cities makes the relevance of planning at all, let alone for a five-year program, problematic. Urban life under any circumstances is a maze of uncertainties. Planning for the American city in 1968 represents the quintessence of those uncertainties.

how differently the game may be structured in other cities, the unique socio-economic characteristics of the neighborhood in which the planning is being promoted cannot help significantly affecting the outcome of the process and the manner in which the planners go about their task of steering a proposal through the complexity of interest groups and the diversity of neighborhood.

Appendix A
Methodology

My interest in Boston's rehabilitation planning game began during the year in which I was employed by United South End Settlements as a community organizer. In 1962–1963 I worked with South End neighborhood associations and participated in countless meetings among various combinations of citizens, ABCD, BRA, and USES officials, and thereby had a minor part in some of the more turbulent events of the planning game's history. I also attended a number of meetings in Washington Park and Charlestown in order to see what the South End could learn from renewal events elsewhere in the city. As a result of these visits, I observed the now legendary Charlestown January 7, 1963, hearing, as well as the less spectacular but nonetheless revealing Washington Park hearing of the same month and year.

While working in the South End, I came to feel that the players in that area's planning game were divided into those who genuinely cared about the district and its people and those for whom renewal was simply a means of earning a living or a mechanism for radically changing the composition of the South End's population. While by no means always the case, it often seemed that this dichotomy found the social workers and community leaders on one side and the BRA and City Hall on the other. I soon became co-opted by the Boston attitude that views everything emerging from City Hall with suspicion and each change and delay in the BRA operation as either bureaucratic bungling or part of a carefully plotted scheme to "con" the neighborhood. I fell into the local pattern of talking about "them." "Them" referred to City Hall and the forces "out there" that would hurt the neighborhood if the residents didn't maintain eternal vigilance. Some of "them" were good people, some were bad, but all had to be watched. On the other hand, there were times when the rambling concern of the social workers for "role-function and responsibility" and "articulating the needs of the community" became equally intolerable, at which point the BRA staff seemed hardheaded but sincere and articulate agents for constructive change.

In the last analysis, one could not help feeling frustrated by the confusion and misunderstanding among the BRA, USES, ABCD, and the local community, the delays caused by brush fires elsewhere in the BRA system, and the lack of any kind of communication with vast segments of the area's population. At the same time, one had to admire a situation in which a public agency and a local citizens' organization were dramatically engaged in the process of hammering out a physical plan for an enormously complex piece of urban real estate.

I emerged from my year in the South End holding an ambivalent attitude toward the renewal planning game. On the one hand, I felt that more people than realized the fact were going to be disadvantaged by the process. On the other hand, I often felt that residential rehabilitation was the only way that much of the South End as an urban neighborhood could be preserved and that, with luck and an enormous input of public resources in social renewal, the exercise might turn out dramatically for the good. In any event, I entered upon my study neither with illusion about the powers of renewal to serve as a universal panacea to urban ills nor with a categorical feeling that renewal as such was a bad thing.

Long after I began my investigation of the residential planning game, I read a comment by R. M. MacIver describing the framework within which I wanted to examine the residential planning game:

The verification of a hypothesis of social causation is consequently conducted on two levels. We employ statistical analysis and other methods common to all the sciences in order to learn whether and to what extent and in what areas and over what length of time the phenomenon under consideration is associated with certain other phenomena. These methods furnish a test that any hypothesis must first pass before it can be accepted as a legitimate claimant for further investigation. If it meets this requirement we continue the search on another level. We seek to discover whether the association or correlation of phenomena is meaningful, whether it depends on the dynamic response of social beings to changed situations.

. . . Every act is the act of a personality, and every personality is bred within a social system and every social system exhibits its cultural complex. . . . Every social phenomenon is the expression of *some* meaningful system.[1]

A major concern of this study has been to relate the course of unique events to a social setting. Thus, research methods have been aimed at investigating both the aggregate characteristics of three social situations and, in MacIver's words, the "dynamic response" of the individuals and organizations within those settings. Research can therefore be divided into two major categories: one aimed at identifying aspects of the social system, the other directed at the particular response within the social system. Aggregate data for the former category were derived from four major sources: (1) census tract material for 1950 and 1960; (2) research compiled by the BRA; (3) data collected by ABCD; (4) the files of Boston's Election Board. Added to these sources are miscellaneous surveys and polls conducted by settlement houses and organizations in one or another of the communities. The dynamic response category is also based on four major sources: (1) the files of the BRA; (2) the files of organizations and individuals in the project areas; (3) newspapers; (4) interviews in each community.

Interviewing is the only category requiring further elucidation. In each community I talked at length with approximately 25 people: community leaders for and against renewal, present BRA staff who participated in the planning game, and, wherever possible, past members of the BRA team who had been part of the earlier planning negotiations. In all, a total of 70 people were interviewed, in sessions which ranged from a single half-hour interview to several meetings with one individual adding up to ten hours. The average interview lasted two hours. Throughout the period I was researching the three areas there were several BRA employees to whom I returned with some regularity. These were individuals who, having worked in more than one of the districts under study, served as good sounding boards for comparing the planning games in the three renewal areas.

My method for selecting whom I wanted to interview among community spokesmen was easy in the South End. I knew who the leaders were and had kept up sufficiently with events after leaving the area to know who was still involved and to what degree. In the other two areas, I had to feel my way along. Transcripts of hearings before the BRA and the City Council as well as minutes of meetings and newspaper articles provided names. The BRA was able to categorize different individuals in Washington Park and Charlestown as being important in one or another community group. In Washington Park Mrs. Snowden was of great help in identifying leaders with different points of view toward the renewal game. While I may not have a quantifiable way of measuring my interviewees' power and influence on

[1] E. M. MacIver, *Social Causation* (New York: Harper and Row, 1964), pp. 390–392.

decision making, I can document the fact that they were actively involved in the working out of or opposition to the rehabilitation plan for their neighborhoods.

When initially setting out to interview both local and BRA teams, I was undecided about whether to employ an open-ended interview or to quantify my results more rigorously around specific questions which could be used comparatively across all three project areas. My approach in the South End began as an effort to arrive at quantifiable data. I had prepared a long interview schedule that was broken down into areas such as attitudes toward the BRA and socioeconomic characteristics of the community. Sometimes this approach was successful, and a great deal of data were forthcoming. On the other hand, I soon realized that the highly structured nature of the schedule tended to shorten people's comments. As soon as respondents saw that they were answering a battery of questions, they regimented and clipped their answers to meet the test. Therefore, in situations where I found the structured approach was obviously destroying spontaneity, I slid out of the schedule and talked in terms of general categories.

In the South End, Dick Green, with whom I had worked when employed by USES, was very helpful, and other people were equally generous with their time. After five weeks of talking and observing in the community, I moved on to Charlestown with a somewhat heavy heart, feeling that the accessibility of the South End would not be repeated there.

The warm receptiveness of the Charlestown Project Director Frank Del Vecchio and his staff was unexpected. Because of the besieged fortress mentality that often surrounds public agencies, especially those under fire, the attitude of the most fired-upon staff in the city of Boston, the BRA Charlestown team, came as a welcome surprise. Del Vecchio introduced me to community leaders, took me to meetings of local organizations, encouraged me to seek out spokesmen for the opposition, and made his files available to me. Thus, although denied the opportunity to participate in the Second Battle for Charlestown, for over a month I was very much an observer of the affairs of that community. This involvement came in the winter of 1966, after the plan had been approved, but the time was close enough to the planning phase to afford a vivid sense of the emotions and conflicts that had gone on during the earlier period.

As things turned out, my interview approach in Charlestown differed from that in the South End. The welcome offered by the BRA staff helped immensely to get me into the community, yet I quickly realized that simply understanding the logic, weight, and course of events would be in and of itself a monumental task. Where I had tried to follow a quantifiable interview schedule in the South End, the Town required a more reportorial job of eliciting the structure of history rather than the structure of attitudes and opinions. In a complex political maze like Charlestown, the researcher, if not careful, soon finds himself bogged down in endless detail that, while fascinating in and of itself, does not add much to an understanding of events at the level of the community social system.

My final area for field research was Washington Park. While the BRA and Freedom House were most cooperative, especially Freedom House, where Mrs. Snowden made all her files available to me, Washington Park poses some serious problems for the researcher. First, renewal planning for that community took place prior to 1963. While in the other two areas citizens' reactions can be only to the stages before approval, in Washington Park three years have passed since the planning game ended and attitudes toward the BRA, Freedom House, and all the other events and organizations of that period are now toned by experience in the execution phase. Second, conflict over civil rights and the Poverty Program has manifested itself in Washington Park, and what people now say they thought or did in 1960 and 1961 may reflect their current thinking on these two subjects. In the third place, one faces in Washington Park the problem of being a white researcher in a Negro community that has been bombarded with questionnaires and interviewers and is frankly tired of both. A fourth problem is that the BRA staff currently operating in Washington Park is not the one involved in the planning game, and only two major figures from that period remain. Thus, it is hard to be sure that what people are saying today about the staff of the planning game period is not really a backward projection of their attitude toward the present project team, an attitude that, according to a recent article in a Boston paper, reflects less than total approval.[2]

There are certain aspects of the Washington Park situation, however, that mitigate the problem of time and distance. The project was the smoothest running of the three, and thus the internal weavings of plot, character, and action which dominate especially the Charlestown picture are less relevant to the Washington Park scene. Moreover, Freedom House has the most complete set of public meeting records of any agency or individual in any of the project areas. Where it was good fortune in Charlestown and the South End to come upon people who had kept minutes of various committees, it was not luck in Washington Park, where many formal documents exist to augment faded or restructured memories.

During the interviewing period, I spent a good deal of time simply walking about the three project areas, eating in local restaurants, and attending public meetings whenever possible. In a very real way my previous knowl-

2 *The Christian Science Monitor,* March 24, 1966.

edge of the social and physical patterns of the South End was a spur and a standard to be aimed at in the other areas. Obviously, I was unable to become as knowledgeable as Gans was when he immersed himself in Boston's West End. While I did use five of the six approaches mentioned in *The Urban Villagers*, in Gans's description of his participant-observer role,[3] the difference in degree is, of course, extensive. However, I did not set out to write a book about any one of the districts under examination. My prime concern in each of these communities was to get a sense of the socioeconomic dynamics of the district and the way in which the rehabilitation planning game reflected those dynamics.

[3] In discussing his field work, Gans mentions the following approaches: (1) use of the West End's facilities; (2) attendance at meetings, gatherings, and public places; (3) informal visiting with neighbors and friends; (4) formal and informal interviewing of community functionaries; (5) use of informants; (6) observation. See Herbert Gans, *The Urban Villagers* (New York: The Free Press of Glencoe, 1962), p. 337. Of these six, only (5) does not apply to my own experience.

SELECTED BIBLIOGRAPHY

BOOKS

Abrams, Charles. *The City is the Frontier.* New York: Harper and Row, 1965.

Altshuler, Alan. *The City Planning Process.* Ithaca: Cornell University Press, 1965.

Anderson, Martin. *The Federal Bulldozer.* Cambridge: The M.I.T. Press, 1964.

Banfield, Edward C. *Political Influence.* New York: The Fress Press of Glencoe, 1965.

———— (ed.). *Urban Government.* New York: The Free Press of Glencoe, 1961.

Banfield, Edward C., and James Q. Wilson. *City Politics.* Cambridge: Harvard University Press and The M.I.T. Press, 1963.

Dahl, Robert A. *Who Governs?* New Haven: Yale University Press, 1961.

Davies, J. Clarence, III. *Neighborhood Groups and Urban Renewal.* New York: Columbia University Press, 1966.

Firey, Walter. *Land Use in Central Boston.* Cambridge: Harvard University Press, 1947.

Gans, Herbert. *The Urban Villagers.* New York: The Free Press of Glencoe, 1962.

Glazer, Nathan, and Patrick Moynihan. *Beyond the Melting Pot.* Cambridge: The M.I.T. Press, 1964.

Greer, Scott. *Urban Renewal and American Cities.* New York: Bobbs-Merrill, 1965.

Grigsby, William G. *Housing Markets and Public Policy.* Philadelphia: University of Pennsylvania Press, 1963.

Gruen, Victor. *The Heart of Our Cities.* New York: Simon and Schuster, 1964.

Handlin, Oscar. *Boston's Immigrants.* Revised edition. Cambridge: Harvard University Press, 1959.

Harrington, Michael. *The Other America.* Baltimore: Penguin Books, 1963.

Hoffer, Eric. *The True Believer.* New York: Mentor Books, 1958.

Jacobs, Jane. *The Death and Life of Great American Cities.* New York: Random House, 1961.

Kaplan, Harold. *Urban Renewal Politics.* New York: Columbia University Press, 1963.

Levin, Murray B. *The Alienated Voter: Politics in Boston.* New York: Holt, Rinehart and Winston, 1962.

Long, Norton E. *The Polity.* Chicago: Rand McNally, 1962.

Loring, William, Frank Sweetser, and Frank Ernst. *Community Organization for Citizen Participation in Urban Renewal.* Prepared by the Housing Association of Metropolitan Boston for the Massachusetts Department of Commerce; Cambridge: Cambridge Press, 1957.

MacIver, E. M. *Social Causation.* Revised edition. New York: Harper and Row, 1964.

Marris, Peter, and Martin Rein. *Dilemmas of Social Reform.* New York: Atherton Press, 1967.

Merton, Robert K. *Social Theory and Social Structure.* Revised and enlarged edition. New York: The Free Press of Glencoe, 1957.

Meyerson, Martin, and Edward C. Banfield. *Boston: The Job Ahead.* Cambridge: Harvard University Press, 1966.

————. *Politics, Planning and the Public Interest.* New York: The Free Press of Glencoe, 1955.

Rossi, Peter H., and Robert A. Dentler. *The Politics of Urban Renewal.* New York: The Free Press of Glencoe, 1961.

Shostak, Arthur, and William Gomberg (eds.). *Blue Collar World.* Englewood Cliffs, N.J.: Prentice-Hall, 1964.

————. *New Perspectives on Poverty.* Englewood Cliffs, N.J.: Prentice-Hall, 1965.

Stein, Maurice R. *The Eclipse of Community.* New York: Harper and Row, 1964.

Warner, Sam B., Jr. *Streetcar Suburbs.* Cambridge: Harvard University Press and The M.I.T. Press, 1962.

Warren, Roland L. *The Community in America.* Chicago: Rand McNally, 1963.

Watts, Lewis, Howard Freeman [*et al.*] *The Middle Income Negro Family Faces Urban Renewal.* Massachusetts Department of Commerce and Development, 1964.

Whitehill, Walter M. *Boston: A Topographical History.* Cambridge: Harvard University Press, 1959.

Whyte, William F. *Street Corner Society.* 2nd edition. Chicago: University of Chicago Press, 1955.
Wilson, James Q. *Negro Politics.* New York: The Free Press of Glencoe, 1965.
———— (ed.). *Urban Renewal: The Record and the Controversy.* Cambridge: The M.I.T. Press, 1966.
Wolfe, Albert Benedict. *The Lodging House Problem in the City of Boston.* Cambridge: Harvard University Press, 1913.
Wood, Robert C. *Suburbia: Its People and Their Politics.* Boston: Houghton Mifflin, 1958.
Woods, Robert A. (ed.). *The City Wilderness.* Cambridge: Houghton Mifflin, 1898.
Woods, Robert A., and Albert J. Kennedy. *The Zone of Emergence.* Abridged and edited with a preface by Samuel B. Warner, Jr. Cambridge: Harvard University Press, 1962.

ARTICLES AND PERIODICALS
Architectural Forum. Special Issue: "Boston." Vol. 120, No. 6 (June 1964).
Axelrod, Morris. "Urban Structure and Social Participation," *American Sociological Review,* Vol. XXI (February 1956), pp. 13–18.
Banfield, Edward C., and James Q. Wilson. "Public-Regardingness as a Value Premise in Voting Behavior," *The American Political Science Review,* Vol. LVIII, No. 4 (December 1964), pp. 876–887.
Barth, Ernest A. T. "Community Influence Systems: Structure and Change," *Social Forces,* Vol. 40, No. 1 (October 1961), pp. 58–63.
Bell, Wendell, and Maryanne Force. "Urban Neighborhood Types and Participation in Formal Associations," *American Sociological Review,* Vol. XXI, No. 1 (February 1956), pp. 25–34.
"Citizen Participation in Urban Renewal," *Columbia Law Review,* Vol. 66 (March 1966), pp. 485–607.
Colebrook, Joan. "Boston's South End: Land of the White Hunter," *The New Republic,* March 6, 1965, pp. 8–12.
Davidoff, Paul. "Advocacy and Pluralism in Planning," *Journal of the American Institute of Planners,* Vol. XXXI, No. 4 (November 1965), pp. 331–338.
Drake, St. Clair. "The Social and Economic Status of the Negro in the United States," *Daedalus,* Vol. 94, No. 4 (Fall 1965), pp. 771–814.
Duggar, George S. "The Relation of Local Government Structure to Urban Renewal," *Law and Contemporary Problems,* Vol. XXVI (Winter 1961), pp. 49–69.
Form, William H. "The Place of Social Structure in the Determination of Land Use," *Social Forces,* Vol. 32, No. 4 (May 1954), pp. 317–323.
Fried, Marc, and Peggy Gleicher. "Some Sources of Residential Satisfaction in an Urban Slum," *Journal of the American Institute of Planners,* Vol. XXVII, No. 4 (November 1961), pp. 305–315.
Frieden, Bernard J. "Towards Equality of Urban Opportunity," *Journal of the American Institute of Planners,* Vol. XXI, No. 4 (November 1965), pp. 320–330.
Gans, Herbert. "The Balanced Community: Homogeneity or Heterogeneity in Residential Areas," *Journal of the American Institute of Planners,* Vol. XXVII, No. 3 (August 1961), pp. 176–184.
————. "The Failure of Urban Renewal," *Commentary,* Vol. 39, No. 4 (April 1965).
————. "Social and Physical Planning for the Elimination of Urban Poverty," *The Washington University Law Quarterly,* February 1963.
Glazer, Nathan. "The Renewal of Cities," *Scientific American,* Vol. 213, No. 3 (September 1965), pp. 195–204.
Greer, Scott. "Urbanism Reconsidered: A Comparative Study of Local Areas in a Metropolis," *American Sociological Review,* Vol. XXI, No. 1 (February 1956), pp. 19–25.
Hawley, Amos. "Community Power and Urban Renewal Success," *American Journal of Sociology,* Vol. LXVIII (January 1963), pp. 442–431.
Kotler, Milton. "Two Essays on the Neighborhood Corporation," *Urban America: Goals and Problems,* Joint Economic Committee, Congress of the United States, August 1967, pp. 170–191.

Mann, Lawrence D. "Studies in Community Decision Making," *Journal of the American Institute of Planners,* Vol. XXX, No. 1 (February 1964), pp. 58–65.

McQuade, Walter. "Boston: What Can a Sick City Do?" *Fortune,* Vol. LXIX, No. 6 (June 1964).

Miller, S. M., and Frank Riessman. "The Working Class Subculture: A New View," *Social Problems,* Vol. 9 (1961), pp. 86–97.

Nathan, Jay. "Rehabilitation Is Not Working as a Resource for Community Development," *The Journal of Housing,* No. 11 (1967), pp. 619–621.

Rodman, Hyman. "On Understanding Lower-Class Behavior," *Social and Economic Studies,* 8 (December 1959), pp. 441–450.

Snowden, Otto and Muriel. "Citizen Participation," *Journal of Housing,* No. 8 (September 1963).

"The South End Today," *Boston* (October 1965), pp. 34–41 and 54–59.

Wilson, James Q. "Planning and Politics: Citizen Participation in Urban Renewal," *Journal of the American Institute of Planners,* Vol. XXIX, No. 4 (November 1963), pp. 242–249.

———. "The Citizen in the Renewal Process," *Journal of Housing,* No. 11 (1963), pp. 622–627.

———. "Urban Renewal Does Not Always Renew," *Harvard Today* (January 1965), pp. 2–8.

Wingfield, Clyde J. "Power Structure and Decision Making in City Planning," *Public Administration Review,* Vol. XXIII, No. 1 (June 1963), pp. 74–80.

Wingo, Lowdon, Jr. "Urban Renewal: A Strategy for Information and Analysis," *Journal of the American Institute of Planners,* Vol. XXXII, No. 3 (May 1966), pp. 143–154.

Zimmerman, Carle. "The Evolution of the American Community," *American Journal of Sociology,* Vol. XLVI (May 1941), pp. 809–817.

DOCUMENTS AND REPORTS

Action for Boston Community Development.
Demone, Harold, and Edward Blacker. "The Unattached and Socially Isolated Residents of Skid Row." Boston, July 1961.
Edwards, Rheable, Laura Morris, and Robert Coard. "The Negro in Boston." Boston, 1961.
Mitchell, Albert, Dorothy Abramson, and Joseph Dee. "A Plan for Citizen Involvement in Community Development." Boston, February 1962.

Banfield, Edward, and Martha Derthick (eds.). "A Report on the Politics of Boston." Cambridge: Harvard University Press and The M.I.T. Press, 1960.

Boston Redevelopment Authority.
General:
"1965–1975 General Plan for the City of Boston and the Regional Core." November 1964.
Charlestown:
"Proposed Charlestown Renewal Project: Before B.R.A. Board." Stenographic Transcript. January 7, 1963.
"B.R.A. Urban Renewal Plan: Charlestown Urban Renewal Area." February 15, 1963.
"Report on the Removal and Relocation of the Charlestown Elevated Rapid Transit Structure." August 1964.
"Application for Loan and Grant Part I: Final Project Report Charlestown Urban Renewal Area." February 25, 1965.
"Charlestown Renewal Area: Public Hearing Held by B.R.A." 3 volumes. Stenographic Transcript. March 14, 1965.
South End:
"Specifications for the South End Urban Renewal Plan as Presented to the South End Urban Renewal Committee on October 5, 1964." (With Amendments, May 17, 1965.)
"South End Urban Renewal Area Before the Boston Redevelopment Authority." Stenographic Transcript. August 23, 1965.

"Project Area Report: Application for Loan and Grant Part I: Final Project Report." Fall 1965.
Washington Park:
Rapkin, Chester. "The Washington Park Urban Renewal Area." December 1961.
————. "The Seaver-Townsend Urban Renewal Area." January 1962.
"Survey and Planning Application Washington Park Urban Renewal Area." Winter 1962.
"Before B.R.A. June 25, 1962 on Early Land Acquisition." Stenographic Transcript.
"Washington Park Urban Renewal Area: Application for Loan and Grant Part I: Final Project Report." January 25, 1963.
"Washington Park Urban Renewal Area: Public Hearing Held by Boston Redevelopment Authority January 14, 1963." Taped Transcript.
City of Boston, City Council
"South End Renewal Area—Before Committee on Urban Redevelopment, Rehabilitation, and Renewal." (Early Land Acquisition.) Stenographic Transcript. July 12, 1962.
"Early Land Acquisition: Washington Park—Before Committee on Urban Redevelopment, Rehabilitation, and Renewal." Stenographic Transcript. August 9, 1962.
"Washington Park Urban Renewal Project: Before the Committee on Urban Redevelopment, Rehabilitation, and Renewal." 2 volumes. February 7 and 13, 1963.
"Exposition of Urban Renewal Project in Charlestown: Before Committee on Urban Renewal." Stenographic Transcript. April 7, 1965.
"Charlestown Urban Renewal Project: Before Committee on Urban Renewal." 12 volumes. Stenographic Transcript. April 27, 28, and 29 and May 11, 12, 13, 18, 19, and 20, 1965.
"South End Urban Renewal Area: Before Committee on Urban Renewal." 4 volumes. November 9, 10, and 12, 1965.
City of Boston. "The 90 Million Dollar Development Program for Boston." *City Record*, September 24, 1960.
Department of Housing and Urban Development. "Improving the Quality of Urban Life: A Program Guide to Model Cities," December 1966.
Model Cities Administration, "CDA Letters: 1,2,3," November 1967.
United South End Settlements, "United South End Settlements: The Story and the Scope." Spring 1965.
Urban Field Service, "Report on South End Urban Renewal Plan for Boston City Council Hearing," March 1968.

NEWSPAPERS
The Boston Globe. January 1961–May 1966, intermittently.
The Boston Herald. January 1961–May 1966, intermittently.
The Boston Traveler. January 1961–May 1966, intermittently.
Charlestown Patriot. April 1960–June 1965, intermittently.
The Christian Science Monitor (Boston edition). January 1961–March 1966, intermittently.
The Record American. January 1960–January 1963, intermittently.
Roxbury Citizen. January 1960–January 1963, intermittently.

UNPUBLISHED MATERIAL
Arnone, Nancy R. "Redevelopment in Boston: A Study of the Politics and Administration of Social Change." Unpublished Ph.D. thesis, Department of Political Science, M.I.T., February 1965.
Baldwin, Leo. "The C.U.R.E.: The Charlestown Renewal Effort 1960–1965." Manuscript, March 1966.
Burke, Edmund. "Citizen Participation as Strategies." Manuscript, Boston College School of Social Work, 1967.
Cole, William. "Charlestown." Unpublished section of *Zone of Emergence*, by

Robert A. Woods, and Albert J. Kennedy, 1910. Manuscript on file at United South End Settlements.

Fraggos, Charles. "A Settlement's Role in Community Development: A Decade of Experience." Paper presented at National Conference on Social Welfare, Atlantic City, May 26, 1965.

Rabinovitz, Francine. "Politics and Planning: On the Role of the Expert in Urban Development." Unpublished Ph.D. thesis, Department of Political Science, M.I.T., February 1965.

Stern, David. "Citizen Planners for Urban Renewal." Unpublished Honors thesis, Department of Social Relations, Harvard College, April 1966.

Thompson, Samuel. "An Analysis of the Origins and Development of Citizen Participation in City Planning." Unpublished Ph.D. thesis, City and Regional Planning Department, Graduate School of Design, Harvard University, June 1966.

Williams, Constance. "Citizen Participation in Urban Renewal—The Role of the Resident." Unpublished M.C.P. thesis, Department of City Planning, M.I.T., May 1964.

Index